Fern

My Story

FERN BRITTON

MICHAEL JOSEPH
an imprint of
PENGUIN BOOKS

MICHAEL JOSEPH

Published by the Penguin Group
Penguin Books Ltd, 80 Strand, London WC2R 0RL, England
Penguin Group (USA) Inc., 375 Hudson Street, New York, New York 10014, USA
Penguin Group (Canada), 90 Eglinton Avenue East, Suite 700, Toronto, Ontario, Canada M4P 2Y3
(a division of Pearson Penguin Canada Inc.)
Penguin Ireland, 25 St Stephen's Green, Dublin 2, Ireland (a division of Penguin Books Ltd)
Penguin Group (Australia), 250 Camberwell Road, Camberwell, Victoria 3124, Australia
(a division of Pearson Australia Group Pty Ltd)
Penguin Books India Pvt Ltd, 11 Community Centre, Panchsheel Park, New Delhi – 110 017, India
Penguin Group (NZ), 67 Apollo Drive, Rosedale, North Shore 0632, New Zealand
(a division of Pearson New Zealand Ltd)
Penguin Books (South Africa) (Pty) Ltd, 24 Sturdee Avenue, Rosebank, Johannesburg 2196, South Africa

Penguin Books Ltd, Registered Offices: 80 Strand, London WC2R 0RL, England

www.penguin.com

First published 2008
1
Copyright © Fern Britton, 2008

All rights reserved
The moral right of the author has been asserted

Pictures are reproduced by kind permission of Fern Britton, unless otherwise noted.
Every effort has been made to trace copyright holders. The publishers would be pleased to
rectify any unintentional omission in subsequent printings. Page 166, and inset no. 44 © BBC Photo
Library; inset no. 45 © PA Photos; inset nos. 60, 61 and 79 © Ken McKay/Rex Features

Set in Monotype Bembo
Typeset by Rowland Phototypesetting Ltd, Bury St Edmunds, Suffolk
Printed in England by Clays Ltd, St Ives plc

Hardback: 978-0-718-15461-5
Trade paperback: 978-0-718-15484-4

www.greenpenguin.co.uk

I dedicate this book to my wonderful Phil,
whose love has turned my life around, and also to
Jack, Harry, Grace and Winnie, who *are* my life.
I love you all.

Contents

If I didn't have any of this life, it was taken from me, I would go out and find a proper job. I'd make a very good cleaner – I wouldn't want to be a nanny because that would be too much like hard work – but I'd be a very good domestic, a very good housekeeper. I love making things tidy.

Of course, I'm happy doing what I'm doing at the moment, but Phil and I often talk about what we'll do when we stop. There is so much life to live, and so many things I want to do while I'm still young enough, while I still have the energy. In the summer I often wake before the alarm. The dawn creeps in through the curtains and I lie, listening to the birds, dozing and thinking. This is my only quiet time of the day, and it doesn't last long.

'Fern, it's half past five.'

The sound of Phil's voice, muffled by the pillow, makes me laugh. How does he always know it's time to get up before I do?

'Do you want a cuppa?'

A grunt. I'll take that as a maybe and give myself ten minutes more. Phil's been my husband now for seven years, eleven months and four days but he never ceases to surprise me, and – in spite of his pillow talk about pigs and hams – he's as romantic now as when we first met.

'I'd like to renew our vows every five years,' he said, the day of our wedding, and I said, 'How lovely. Yes, please!' So we got to five years, but it just went by the by. It was no big deal, it was like, 'Ah – we didn't quite get that organized.' Then yesterday, out of the blue, he said, 'Let's do it now – and in fact I've already spoken to the vicar.' He'd set it all up: eight years, minus one day, to the

I

minute – midday, 23 May 2008 – at St Michael and All Angels in Hughenden Valley, which we'd got to know as it's the church nearest the children's school. They go there for their little ceremonies, nativity plays and so on, and the vicar baptized Winnie and he's a very nice man. So in just over three weeks, for the first time in my life, I'm going to be saying my vows in church. It will be completely private. Just us, and the children. No one else.

I remember hearing Bette Midler talking about her husband of many years, and she said, 'As much as I love him, I'm not always in love with him!' And it does go like phases of the moon. But I will never take Phil for granted. I've been through too much for that. There have been times when I haven't wanted to live another day, when just getting through the hours was more daunting than anything I would ever face again. And the shadow of that fear, that the darkness will return, never really leaves you. It's there to remind you never to waste a moment, never to lose sight of the joy.

Slipping out of bed, I pull on my dressing-gown, go downstairs to put the kettle on and let out the hens. We have two: Sam and Ella – wittily named by the producer who thought they'd be perfect company for Edwina Currie during her stint on the studio roof last September.

A few mornings ago I saw Mr Fox slink away as I opened the back door. He'd obviously been eyeing up their ladyships. Phil is all for sorting out the ginger gentleman himself, but I've put my foot down. No guns in the garden. No exceptions. He has a whole wood where he can blast away to his heart's content, and farmer friends are always imploring him to sort out the foxes and rabbits and even deer who create havoc on their land.

It's going to be a glorious day. Spring is definitely here and it's hard to imagine that the blue sky will ever darken. I am so incredibly lucky, leading this idyllic existence, a job in a million, healthy and happy children, a husband who loves me just as I am, and who regularly reminds me of what he promised nearly eight years ago on *our way to the register office: 'I'll always look after you,' he said. The night before we married I'd been incredibly jittery, thinking even then that it wouldn't happen after all. How did he know, I wonder, just how much that meant to me? My life is full of ghosts, and it is only now, looking back from this place of safety, that I can finally lay them to rest.*

The sun tips the trees across the field, and the dew seeps between my toes as I pad back to the kitchen. I'll wear something summery, I decide. A pair of white leggings, and a silky bit of Kate Moss from Top Shop that I bought on-line. (I love internet shopping.) Which reminds me, I'll have to think about what to wear for the ceremony . . .

I bring in the milk – six pints a day – in time to see the silver Mercedes come glinting up the track on the dot of six thirty. Tony has been driving me to and from ITV's London Studios on the South Bank for the last ten years and, rain, shine, hail or snow, I could set the clock by him. Once I've heard his tyres on the gravel, I take two mugs of tea upstairs for my boys – an excuse, really, to give them a hug and ruffle their hair, and whether they like it or not, I'll be doing it when they're grown men. As for my girls, Goosey and Miss Mouse, I kiss their sweet heads and let them sleep on.

Me and Mr Holly

1. Beginners, Act One, Please

In 1957, the year I was born, my father made his third film, ironically named *The Birthday Present*, with a very young Sylvia Syms as his leading lady. He was thirty-three and it was his first starring role. Tony Britton was on the way up. The previous year he had made *Loser Takes All* with Rossano Brazzi. Unusually for a British film of the period, it was shot entirely on location in Monte Carlo. My mother didn't go with him. On his return he went straight into the West End, playing the romantic lead in *Gigi*, opposite Leslie Caron. One way and another he was around less and less. In the early days, when Dada's career was just beginning, my parents had been inseparable, living in a succession of theatrical digs and longer-term lets, but once theatre gave way to cinema – he was under contract to British Lion Films – a stable home took priority, my sister Cherry then coming up for eight.

Renting the top floor of my grandmother's house in Ealing must have seemed the perfect solution: close to the West End, not far from the studios and company for my mother when Dada was away, not to mention schools and cousins for Cherry. It was while they were living in Ealing that I came along. (A breech delivery and I was two weeks late.) But within a few months, our little family had moved, my father's film-star status demanding something rather grander than a rented attic flat owned by his mother-in-law.

In the post-war years, film studios clustered in west London like mushrooms, and the names, even now, evoke nostalgia for the glory days of British cinema: Ealing, Teddington, Shepperton, Denham, Pinewood and Elstree. Gerrards Cross, in Buckinghamshire, was equidistant between Denham and Pinewood and the address of choice for directors and actors on the up, and we were soon ensconced in the first home I can really remember. 'Steeple', white-painted stucco enlivened with blackened timbers, dated from the twenties and boasted latticed windows and Gothic gables. It sat on a large triangular plot, a steeply sloping peninsula between two roads that joined at the bottom.

The garden had once been an orchard, and each autumn we had more apples, plums and pears than Mummy knew what to do with. There was even a mulberry tree, laden with sweet, sticky fruit in the summer, whose leaves we would strip from their branches for a lady who had silkworms. She gave me a cocoon, I remember, which I took into school for 'show and tell', and the class all stood around and marvelled as the gossamer thread unwound, unbroken, seemingly for ever.

With its four bedrooms, french windows, wall-to-wall parquet and oak panelling, Steeple was the ultimate in home-counties chic. 'Substantial' and 'characterful' is how an estate agent would probably describe it now.

My first clear memory is of being propped in my pram while my mother did things in the garden. There's an old photo of exactly this situation, complete with my bear Mr Holly, so perhaps the memory is only borrowed. Other memories lead on from that one: staring at the world upside down through my legs, the smell of new-mown grass, my mother bent double in the flowerbed weeding, my big sister teaching me how to roly-poly down the lawn.

The corner of memory set aside for my father, however, is empty. A complete blank. He did live at Steeple from time to time, my mother assures me, so I must believe her, but I have no memory of it. There were dinner parties, she says: Bob Monkhouse and his wife were among their friends; the boxer Freddy Mills was Cherry's godfather. Mummy loved entertaining and did it brilliantly – she always has done. Our neighbours seemed all to be witty and eccentric. I remember one couple who drove an open-top vintage Bentley, their Irish wolfhounds lording it in the back complete with goggles.

After nine difficult and sometimes rocky years of un-certainty and little money, this house and the life that went with it were the least my mother deserved. I think she hoped that moving into their own home, with its sprawling garden, bordered by thick, high hedges, would mark a fresh start, especially with the new addition to the family. It was not to be. My father was handsome and talented, and was now moving in a world far removed from post-war Weston-super-Mare, where he and my mother had first met and fallen in love one sultry summer night, the sound of the sea in their ears.

It was June 1947, and my father, soon to be demobbed, had been persuaded to wear his uniform one last time to escort Weston-super-Mare's newly elected Rose Queen to a gala dinner at the end of the pier – the pier which has only recently been destroyed by fire. His parents had moved to Weston from Birmingham at the outbreak of war, when he was about fifteen.

The Britton family had once been well-to-do, with a mansion in Aston, Birmingham, complete with servants, chauffeur-driven cars and eleven children. They were nineteenth-century industrialists and, in classic style, the money came from a brass foundry. In addition to manu-facturing machinery, they made die-cast replica cars, and my great-grandfather patented the Britton bicycle pump. The family fortunes never recovered from the slump that followed the First World War. By the late thirties my grandfather Edward Britton – who served as an infantry officer at the Somme – was employed as a travelling salesman for Oxo and Fray Bentos.

I have very little memory of Prampa, as we called him, from my childhood – I only really got to know him later in life – but he was a jolly man, a former publican. He had once run a pub in Edgbaston, which was where my father was born. My paternal grandmother, Doris Jones, had been working in a theatre box office when they met. That would seem to be the only theatrical connection as far as my father's future career was concerned, although there was an aunt – another of the eleven children – who it's claimed had a wonderful singing voice but whose dream of going on the stage remained unfulfilled as she was considered 'too ugly' to make the grade – the tyranny of the beauty police operating even in the twenties. I knew none of this then. It wasn't until 1977 when my father was surprised by Eamonn Andrews brandishing a large red book and intoning, 'This is your life,' that the picture of this other family began to emerge from the developing tray. Many years later when *This Morning* ran a feature on family trees, I took the opportunity to delve a little deeper.

My father remained a glamorous if shadowy presence throughout my childhood. There were no pictures of him in the house. I only knew what he looked like because I'd seen him on television when I would wave to him madly. I understood enough about acting to know that he couldn't wave back, but obviously he could see me, just as I could see Mummy when we did plays at school.

One afternoon in midsummer, when I must have been

about four, I remember very clearly being put down for an afternoon rest and informing Johnson – the teddy who had displaced Mr Holly in my affections, and I still have – that I was 'too old for an afternoon sleep'. It was one of those brilliant summer days that childhood memory is filled with, and I wanted to be outside in the garden playing. Although the curtains were drawn the window was open, and it wasn't long before I heard voices. I got up, stood on a chair and peered out. There, sitting on the swing seat was my mother, my sister and a man. Instantly I knew who it was: Dada! Mummy must have thought I was asleep and didn't want to disturb me. He was there, it turned out, not to see me, but to take Cherry away on holiday – she would then have been about thirteen – and my mother hadn't wanted me to know what was happening, fearing – rightly – that I would feel left out.

I don't know why he didn't keep in touch. Maybe he felt he had forfeited the right to interfere. Maybe my mother wanted to keep me to herself. But from his perspective, while he barely knew me, Cherry had been his golden girl. It must have been hard for him not to watch her grow up. The journalist in me would love to know what happened, but as a daughter I have no wish to stir up ancient hurts. What good would it do? Parents have a right to keep their private lives private. And I love them both.

Dada's departure so soon after my birth hit my sister much harder than it did me. Cherry knew what it was to have a father. They had lived as a proper family for eight and a half years before I came along. She still remembers the starry 1954 season in Stratford, and the house they rented at 61 Waterside. She went to school there with Anthony Quayle's daughter. Laurence Harvey bought her a pair of red slip-on shoes after she was mocked for only having brown sandals.

9

Margaret Leighton would drop in for tea and a chat, and there were the two Australian actors who always made Mummy laugh, Keith Michell and Leo McKern.

For me it was different. To all intents and purposes I never had a father, or the life that went with it. Divorce was rare in those days. School friends might have had fathers they rarely saw – bankers who worked in the city, or film directors away on location for long periods of time – but at least they were a presence in the house. Their coats would be hanging in the hall. Their shoes would be by the door. There'd be a toothbrush and a tooth-mug in the bathroom. I didn't even know what fathers did. It came as a great shock later to discover that men washed their hair! I mean, how girly! They had so little of it, what was the point? Even odder, they didn't shave under their arms, which, given they all had razors, struck me as ridiculous.

If I lacked stories about my father's family, my mother's made up for it. They were positively exotic. Great-grandfather Hawkins had been a clergyman, the rector of Holy Trinity parish church in Stroud, Gloucestershire – later to retire to Bristol as a canon of the cathedral there. They were obviously a clever lot. Gerald, my grandfather, read Classics at Oxford. When war broke out in 1914 he volunteered, went to France and was badly wounded, though where or how I don't know. It was while he was recuperating back in England that he met the woman he would marry, my grandmother Winifred Carter Fitzgerald, known as Beryl. It's said that she had originally been engaged to his older brother who had been killed in the war. For whatever reason, even though my great-grandfather conducted the marriage himself, it's probable that the Church of England vicar didn't relish his son marrying an Irish temptress called Fitzgerald who wore red lipstick. Or perhaps they'd heard rumours about an illegitimate child. As it was, immediately after the wedding the newlyweds left for Penang, Gerald taking up a post in the Malayan Civil Service.

My grandmother appears unlikely casting as a colonial wife. From my own knowledge she was a spinner of tall stories. She claimed, for example, to have been a spy during the First World War, regaling us with tales of being landed on the coast of France by submarine, a courier of top-secret messages. A secret that she never divulged in her lifetime, however, lay closer to home. She'd had a child out of wedlock, whom she'd given up for adoption. The first we knew of his existence was in 1980. I was working in Plymouth for Westward Television, and a letter arrived addressed to me, care of the studios. Was I the daughter of Ruth Hawkins, the stranger wrote, who had married Tony Britton? If so, then he was my uncle, as he was Ruth's half-brother, the child Beryl had had before she married Gerald.

His name, he said, was John Cass, the surname being that of his adoptive parents. He had kept in touch with his mother, at least for a time, meeting up with her for a few days whenever she returned to England. It was an extraordinary story and yet something about it seemed to make sense. Nana having died fifteen years earlier, I asked Mr Cass to send me evidence of his claim before I broached this inevitably painful subject with my mother, his half-sister. He did: his birth certificate and letters from Nana herself soon followed, sad little notes to her son and his adoptive mother (perhaps only fostering him at the beginning), enclosing money and asking how her firstborn was keeping. He also sent photographs and even I could see the family resemblance. When my mother finally met him, she said he was definitely a Hawkins. He himself never knew who his father was, Nana having so brilliantly covered her tracks. But the general consensus was that he was probably the son of her first love, Gerald's brother, who had been killed at the front.

In the meantime, in Penang, legitimate children had been born. First to arrive was my uncle Paul in 1919, followed by Ruth, my mother, in 1924; Peter was born in 1929 in Kuala Lumpur. Grandpop, as we called him, was eccentric even then, my mother and her brothers being brought up to speak nothing but Malay, which would prove a stumbling block when they returned to England. To this day my mother is known as Adek (pronounced 'Addy'), Malay for 'baby'.

When they were five and ten respectively, the two elder Hawkins children left the Far East, ending up – for some unknown reason – in Port Isaac on the north Cornish coast. It proved a complete disaster. Speaking little or no English, and wandering round barefoot, they were little more than savages, as far as the head teacher of the little school was concerned, and were soon expelled as unteachable. Next stop Eastbourne, where they had more luck, boarded out with a kindly and God-fearing couple called Mr and Mrs Skallen who ran a school overlooking the sea. My mother remembers her father's last words at the front gate, 'Goodbye, old thing, see you soon.' She didn't catch sight of either parent again for four years.

When they did eventually return on leave in 1934, Beryl didn't recognize her daughter, by then ten years old. Further separation, a doctor told her, would have a devastating effect on her children, particularly Paul. She was advised not to return to Malaya. If she did, he said, she might not have a son to come back to. So, when Gerald set off on the six-weeks-long passage back to Malaya, Beryl stayed in England, buying a small house in Weston-super-Mare (60 Chelswood Avenue), which she named Segamat after a region in Malaya famous for its fruit. The sea air would be good for Paul's health, it was decided, and the two eldest could go to the local grammar school. Adek, meanwhile, took on the job of teaching her little brother English.

There was another reason for the choice of Weston. It was close to Bristol, where Beryl's father-in-law was now a canon at the cathedral. Any notion that proximity to her husband's family might make life easier, however, proved wishful thinking. Once a year the Canon and his daughter would make the twenty-mile journey, staying at a smart hotel, and Beryl would invite them to Segamat to tea, and that was that. No one was really surprised. During their four-year stay in Eastbourne, Paul and Adek had never once been to stay with their grandfather, nor had he even visited them. As my mother now says: 'They didn't want to know.' Her paternal grandparents – those pillars of the Anglican church – considered their son's children 'mongrels': they didn't have the Hawkins blue eyes, Paul, Adek and Peter having inherited their Irish mother's (lesser) brown ones.

When war eventually broke out, Adek was sixteen. Twenty was the call-up age for women, and seventeen the earliest you could volunteer. In 1941, as soon as she could, she joined the ATS (Auxiliary Territorial Service), as the women's branch of the army was known. She spent the next four years working on 'heavy ack-ack' – anti-aircraft artillery, plotting enemy aircraft trajectories – stationed in Hull, Bristol, Salisbury, Sheffield and London, rising to sergeant. They were, she says now, the best years of her life, and on 10 August 1945 she took part in the Victory Parade from the Cenotaph down the Mall to Buckingham Palace.

Her brother Paul, meanwhile, had joined the air force, learning to fly Lancaster bombers in Florida, before being posted to Bomber Command at RAF Scampton in Lincolnshire. He did two tours of duty, equating to sixty operational

13

sorties as a pilot sergeant, for which he was awarded the Distinguished Flying Medal. Like everyone in my mother's family, he was exceptionally tall and had been turned down for flying Spitfires because of his height.

Uncle Paul was undoubtedly the most important man in my life when I was growing up. Unassuming, generous to a fault, he was a great bear of a man, a gentle giant, and I adored him. When I asked him why he had wanted to be a Spitfire pilot he replied, 'Well, if I was shot down, I'd be the only one killed, but in a Lancaster you've got seven crew to think about.'

There had been no word from their father, Gerald, since 1942 when the Japanese had taken Singapore. He had been captured and was held in Changi camp – not where the notorious prison now stands but in a former British Army barracks on the site of an old rubber plantation. Beryl wrote to him weekly but, during the four years of his captivity, only one postcard got through, from his daughter, my mother.

From what is known of conditions at Changi – my grand-father had all his fingernails removed, for example – it's possible to understand how nothing could ever be the same again for him. As someone with an education he suffered terribly, yet he was also able to help fellow internees survive. When the war finally ended, he returned to England – and Weston – a very different man. He couldn't stand the food or the climate, he said, and was going back to Malaya. He nurtured no thought that Beryl should go with him.

'We're not compatible,' he told his wife.

'No, we're not,' she agreed. It was as simple as that.

I met him years later, and to an eleven-year-old girl he presented an extraordinary figure – seated in a suburban sitting room wearing only sandals and a loincloth in the middle of an English winter, looking like Gandhi's taller brother. The University of Malaya in Singapore now houses his extensive library, which includes sections on wildlife and trees as well as politics, public administration, education and social sciences. He spoke seven languages, including Greek, Latin, Malay and Mandarin, and in 1953 wrote the definitive work on the country's history, leading up to independence in 1957, of which he was a staunch supporter. It is there he is buried.

Once demobbed, choices for a young woman like Adek Hawkins were thin on the ground. It was either 'factory, laundry, nursing or prison service,' she remembers. Being unconventional even then, she opted for the prison service but was turned down as 'not being mentally suitable'. 'They said I'd be helping them escape!' Eventually she settled on a job in Clarks' shoe factory in Street, about thirty miles away, where she found herself billeted in a Nissen hut. 'I couldn't believe it. I thought, I've had four years in a Nissen hut, now the peace has come I'm still in a Nissen hut!'

But not for long. Now that Beryl was without support, she sold the house they'd lived in throughout the war and bought a small hotel on the seafront – St Bridge's – overlooking Sand Bay, her plan being to run it as a family concern.

Rationing and post-war austerity had kicked in with a vengeance and what better way to cheer the population up than a bit of escapist nonsense? Weston's Rose Queen was not a beauty competition in the swimsuit-parade sense, it was to find the most beautiful girl in Somerset and was sponsored by British-Gaumont, owners of the Odeon chain of cinemas, who would then use the footage in their newsreels.

With a couple of friends Adek decided to enter 'just for a laugh'. While the other two failed to get beyond the first round, my mother made it through to the last fifteen. The finalists were then filmed walking gracefully around the municipal gardens sniffing roses, wearing nothing more revealing than an evening dress with never a hint of cleavage. The key word, she remembers, was 'demure'. To her intense surprise she came second. My father played no part in the selection procedure. As an up-and-coming local celebrity, already making a name for himself as an amateur actor, he'd simply been comandeered to escort the winner, sitting beside her at the gala dinner which was held at the end of Weston's famous pier. The Rose Queen's attendant, however, proved far more alluring to him than the Rose Queen herself.

'Aren't you going to drink your champagne?' he asked the young woman sitting opposite.

'No,' she said.

'Right. You won't mind if I have it, then.'

In spite of First Lieutenant Britton's officer's uniform, former gunner Sergeant Hawkins was not impressed. Although attached to the Royal Artillery since 1942, he hadn't seen active service (the first question she'd asked) while her brother had risked his life night after night over Europe.

'Tony hadn't even got his knees brown,' as she puts it. Then he asked her to dance.

'I think you'd better ask her first,' she said, nodding towards the Rose Queen. He shrugged, got up and came round to my mother's side of the table. He was handsome and fun. They lived within cycling distance of each other, were the same age. They had performing in common: Adek had done her share of entertaining in the army, from impromptu concert parties in the Naafi, right up to three-act plays when she was stationed in Salisbury. Before long the die was cast.

At this juncture my father hadn't yet made the break into professional theatre, but Weston's amateur dramatic societies were better than most and Tony Britton was beginning to get good notices in the Bristol press. His first professional engagement was as an acting assistant stage manager at the Manchester Library Theatre, and it was while he was there that he and Adek married. His first London engagement was at the Embassy Theatre, Swiss Cottage, which would later become important in my life. Then came a season closer to home at the Bristol Old Vic, followed by the Gate Theatre in Dublin. Finally, in 1952, came the big break: being cast as Rameses in the West End revival of Christopher Fry's *The Firstborn*. In Edinburgh he was seen in *The Player King* by Glyn Byam Shaw, artistic director of the Royal Shakespeare Company. My father stayed in Stratford-upon-Avon for two seasons cast in major roles, including Mercutio in *Romeo and Juliet*, and Cassio in *Othello*, and then came the contract with British Lion.

By the time I was born, on 17 July 1957, Nana had sold the hotel in Weston and bought a large house in Denbigh Road, Ealing, west London. Uncle Paul – now working for the Post Office – had married his WAAF (Women's Auxiliary Air Force) sweetheart and, with their two children, bought another house in the same street, also with plans to let: they would live on the ground floor themselves and let the top. Whatever the tensions in my young life, I remember those two houses as places of warmth and love. Just the smell that hit you as you walked through the front door was enough, the wood darkened by years of cigarette smoke.

To have held her little family together without a husband, not knowing whether he was alive or dead, demanded a special kind of personality, and my grandmother certainly had it. During her colonial years she had learnt to play contract bridge to what must have been a very high standard. As a way of making money, she'd go on cruises, earning enough through her winnings to pay her way and then some. Much depended on creating the right impression, in other words gentle deception, to which end she'd take us with her: a little old granny, travelling with her grand-daughters and their mother, was unlikely to set off warning bells. She would happily tell people that she was eighty when in fact she was twenty years younger, anything to get a slight advantage.

I have picture-postcard memories of our ports of call – Naples, Casablanca and Capri. These were the days of severe money restrictions and I remember on one occasion queuing in Southampton's vast Customs hall, having just dis-embarked from some great ocean liner. Nana was trying to smuggle through a musical box in which she'd hidden the cash she'd made playing cards, and her plan was simple. We were to stand in different lines and, at the appropriate moment, Nana would 'faint'. Mummy, Cherry and I would then rush to her side with cries of 'My poor mother!' and 'Poor Nana!' In the ensuing mêlée, we would all be waved through.

My grandmother was a woman of many talents. Knowing that there was always a fancy-dress competition on board (with a substantial cash prize), Nana would come prepared, having already made the outfits back in Ealing. One year Cherry went as half-bride/half-groom, with her costume sliced down the middle. Another time she was a mermaid. As for me, I remember wearing a frilly dress, my face white with huge eyelashes painted on my cheeks and my head encased in cardboard: a dolly in a box. Favourite of all was when Nana and Mummy went as Siamese twins, Nana having made a huge pair of trousers and a jacket – they took one side each. Naturally you were supposed to conjure your costumes from what little was available on the ship, but Nana contended that with no written rule to that effect, no one could stop her.

During the build-up to the cruise, costumes would be stored under the rug in front of the fire in her sitting room, to keep them flat. I have an enduring memory of lazy Saturday afternoons lying on the carpet, going through Nana's button box, while she stitched and snipped, a cigarette in the corner of her mouth – so placed, she told me, to avoid the smoke getting into her eyes. She and I shared a passion for wrestling, and in the corner of the room, the black-and-white television had us both transfixed as we shouted for Mick McManus – 'the man you love to hate'.

I don't think I ever saw my grandmother without a cigarette except when she was eating. She would smoke each one through to the bitter end, the paper adhering to her red lipstick and the ash remaining in place, even while she talked, growing longer and longer until I was completely mesmerized. She always smoked the same brand, Kensitas, and my big cousin Michael and I would regularly be despatched to the tobacconist for supplies. By the time I knew her, Nana was comparatively old but she had clearly been very beautiful and still carried herself as women do when they know what it is to be the belle of the ball. Even though my mother is now well over eighty, she has this quality and always will. It's there in photographs of the time: tall and willowy, jet-black hair caught in a bun at the nape of her neck, she might easily have been a *Vogue* model as captured by Cecil Beaton. She had the look of Kay Kendall, timeless elegance, with an hour-glass figure that was made for the small-waisted, wide-skirted look of the fifties, and skin like porcelain. She and my father must have cut quite a dash – they made an incredibly glamorous couple – and it's no surprise that he went after her. Just a sadness that they couldn't stay together.

I couldn't do this job without my helpers, though even after all these years I find it hard to delegate. Karen and I were neighbours at my last house and one evening, when things were particularly stressed, she happened to drop by and asked if there was anything she could do. Seven years on she's still here, arriving at six thirty just as I leave, doing breakfast, organizing packed lunches and getting them all off to school. Jack and Harry walk to the bus; Grace and Winnie she takes by car. Every morning I sit by the Aga in my rocking-chair, mug of tea to hand, and write her a list for the day. I ought to do it before I go to bed, but somehow I never do. Then, when Tony arrives, it's like a switch in my head and I'm in work mode.

Every night a large padded envelope is delivered to Tony's house in north London so that it's sitting on the back seat ready for the drive into the studio. This is my script for that morning's show and usually runs to about fifty pages. Much of it is technical stuff: which of our little sets will be used, details of cameras and timings. Once the car gets going, I am aware of nothing but the script, the words that will come up on the autocue – the cunning device that allows us to read the text while looking at the lens of the camera. I read through it all. There may be words or phrases I want to change because I don't feel comfortable saying them, or occasionally I'll spot a spelling error that might trip me up if it's not put right.

Then there are the briefing notes. Each programme will involve a handful of interviews, from human interest, to fashion, to film stars – anything the producer feels our viewers would want to see. Although I try to keep myself up to speed, I can't know everything about the guests who are coming and these notes — compiled by our fabulous team of researchers — do it for me. What they don't do, however, is formulate the questions. So where do I start? First with what I personally would like to know and then what I feel our viewers would like to know. Fortunately the two strands usually coincide. I scribble notes to myself down the right-hand margin of each page.

As viewers of live TV know only too well, things don't always go according to plan. To make a success of it, whether in front of the camera or behind, the ability to think on your feet is crucial. You need to be able to turn on a sixpence, and to keep your head when all around you — particularly the voices in your earpiece — are losing theirs.

In a pre-recorded show, lines can be run again and naughty bits edited out, but on live TV there is no such safety net, which is why Phillip Schofield, who can go off-script without anyone even noticing — ad-libbing for twenty minutes, if need be — is worth his weight in gold ingots. I knew of Phillip long before we eventually met. Overworked as the phrase may be, Phillip Schofield is a television legend.

His start in broadcasting was unconventional. At an age when most small boys were happy playing cowboys and Indians, Phillip was playing announcers and presenters in a make-believe studio he'd evolved in his bedroom in Cornwall. As soon as he was old enough, he joined the BBC. Not surprisingly, the reality proved rather different from the fantasy, and his first job involved signing equipment in and out. It gave him a BBC pass, however, and early on he spent a whole weekend exploring Television Centre on his own, working out what happened where, and who did what, when and how. Shortly after this his family took off for New Zealand and he was soon where he had always wanted to be, behind a microphone. In an unbelievably short time he was fronting a teenage music programme, called Shazzam, *and generally learning the ropes.*

Two years later, back in the UK, he joined the BBC again, in 'the broom cupboard' as the Beeb's first in-vision continuity announcer for children's television – the person who tells you what's coming up later and generally fills in the gaps between programmes. The broom cupboard was an under-the-stairs home-from-home hung with postcards, drawings and paintings, all courtesy of his young viewers. And, to help him cope with it all, he introduced a sidekick – a glove puppet named Gordon the Gopher. Twenty years later it seems that I have taken the place of Gordon in Phillip's life, the only difference being that he doesn't put his hand up my skirt – well, not that often.

With a wife and two gorgeous girls of his own, nothing in the female line on This Morning *fazes him. Unlike many presenters, he doesn't perform on camera, he just is. What you see is what you get: an empathetic, intuitive and genuinely sincere guy, who is bloody good fun and has a filthy sense of humour – all the things you want in a partner, really, and I absolutely love him. We rarely discuss an interview together before it happens, we just go in there and let instinct take over. We don't even decide which of us is going to start, or what the first thread will be, but it's surprising how often we plan identical questions. Having someone with whom you feel so comfortable is a luxury: the strain isn't all on you, and – when a show is live and extends over two hours – it makes a real difference to your energy levels at the end. When he's not around for any reason, I feel amputated, as if I'm missing a limb.*

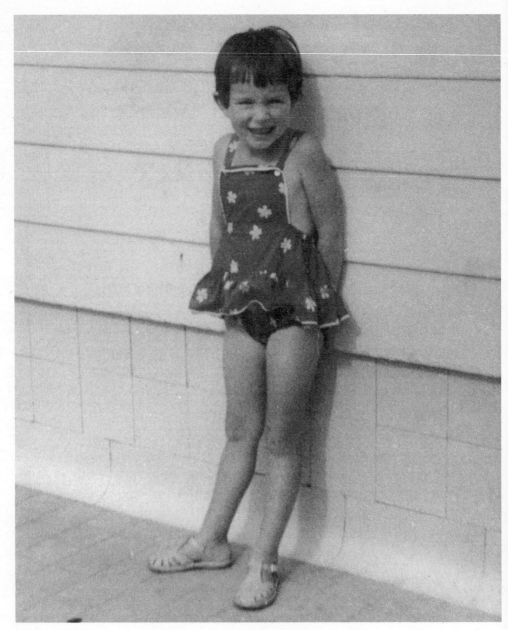

On one of Nana's cruises

2. Glints of Flashing Blue

I first fell in love with Cornwall when I was little more than a toddler. From the age of about three until I left home (minus a blip in the middle), our fortnight in Looe was a fixed point on the calendar. In all those years, nothing ever changed. We stayed in the Dolphin Apartments, halfway up an alleyway at right angles to the quay. We'd set out as soon as it got light as the drive would take the best part of ten hours. We'd go in two cars: Uncle Paul driving his, and Mummy hers. Cherry and I would sprawl across the bench seat in the back, passing the long hours reading books and comics and eating sweets, while Nana and Mummy colonized the front, chain-smoking from start to finish. The fug only dispersed when we crossed the river Tamar into Cornwall. Then the windows would open and a cheer would go up as Mummy said, 'Can you smell the sea?'

Before the bridge was built in the early sixties our route would take us over Dartmoor, a mist-covered wilderness of legend and terror, past the prison, where Mummy would warn us to keep our eyes peeled for escaped prisoners, or the headless horseman galloping, galloping. Then it would be wiggly roads for another forty minutes, till the road began dipping and turning, through tunnels made by overhanging trees, so dark you could hardly see, then glints of flashing blue, and suddenly the river would be there on your right-hand side and you'd see it all laid out before you: the sprawling harbour, the first glimpse of a seagull, the little bridge and boats lining the quay, and everything else was forgotten.

This was a family holiday in the traditional sense of the word. Uncle Paul and Auntie Elsie, our cousins Michael and Gerald, Mummy, Nana, Cherry and me all squashed into one apartment: children in one bedroom, Uncle Paul and Auntie Elsie in another, Mummy and Nana sharing the third.

No matter how late it was when we arrived, we would dash down to the beach, and just stand there, listening to the waves and staring at the dark satin sea. The last straggle of holidaymakers would have left and with them the sun, so the sand would be cold rather than warm under our bare feet, but it was full of the promise of tomorrow, and the day after that and the day after that.

Looe was the perfect little seaside town. The smell never changed: fish and seaweed and Ambre Solaire. It had everything, sandy beach, rock pools, cliffs and a long quay bordering the river lined with brightly painted fishing-boats. Although there were plenty of summer visitors like us, it was a proper little port, famous for its shark fishing, and I loved every last alleyway and tarry rope.

The first morning was the same as every other morning. Under my shorts I'd already have tugged on my red-ruched swimsuit and would be hanging around the kitchen, watching our sandwiches being made, the Thermos being filled and staying as close as I could to my cousin Michael, whom I idolized and wanted to marry. (He was Cherry's age.) Finally, after what seemed an age, the sun cream would go on and we'd head for the beach. My mother, Auntie Elsie and Uncle Paul all loved the sun, and becoming as brown as you could – watching the swimsuit marks getting deeper and deeper – was all part of the ritual.

Looe was where I learnt to swim. Hanging on to my rubber ring, I'd run down the beach, trying to keep pace

26

with my uncle's giant strides. Hand in hand we would wade out into deep water till my feet couldn't touch the bottom. With shrieks of pleasure I'd cling to his neck, while always in danger of losing my grip as his shoulders were slippery with Ambre Solaire, and he would bounce me up and down and throw me into the air before the serious business of swimming began.

Of the eight of us, only Nana failed to remove her clothing. She was always extremely careful in the sunshine and would never appear without her parasol. Arriving on the beach after lunch, she would sit in the shade on her chair, parasol up, a completely Edwardian figure who would preside over her family like a queen, dispensing biscuits or sixpences for cornets while stubbing out her cigarettes in the sand. She came into her own on our visits to Polperro, the next village along, where she'd treat us to a cream tea in a posh hotel on a balcony overlooking the main street.

Nana was the perfect shopping companion and Pixie Halt, back in Looe, was the perfect holiday emporium, a cornucopia of souvenirs, with racks even hanging from the ceiling. Right at the back was an indoor pixie fountain, with little gnomes fishing in it and lit with fairy lights; you'd throw in a coin and make a wish.

Occasionally Uncle Paul would hire a little putt-putt motorboat and we'd go up and down the river with a mackerel line. Once I hooked a pollock – the first and last fish I ever caught – which Nana gutted and grilled for me back at the apartment. Far from it being the treat I was expecting, I hated it and have never been able to eat fish since but, oh, the pride.

The lure of the water was magnetic. Another treat was taking the little ferry across the river. My first career decision was to be one of the ferrymen. Later I wanted to be a speedboat driver, just like Vicky. She'd been driving those speedboats for ever and – certainly at the time – was the only fully qualified and certificated woman speedboat driver on that part of the coast. She's still there now. We were allowed a set number of goes every holiday but I'd save up my pocket money and try to inveigle Michael to come with me, though more often we'd make do with a pedalo. But speed-boats remained the ultimate excitement for me: bumping over the waves and other boats' wash, the spray in my face, the sheer exhilaration of the wind whipping my stringy damp hair, the hairs standing up on my arms and legs, the sting of the salt in my eyes – I would go endlessly if I could.

My memories of those summers are of eternal sunshine, happiness and freedom, of making friends on the beach, of building endless sandcastles – a paper flag on every turret – of sauntering off on my own adventures, without a care in the world.

As a July baby, I was always one of the youngest in my class, but as Mummy and I were having such a nice time on our own, I didn't start my first school until the September after I turned five. Little Turret was what would now be called a pre-prep and, situated in the heart of Gerrard's Cross, it had a full quota of show-business offspring.

My first shock was being called Fern. I was Fifi – I had always been called Fifi and didn't even know my name *was* Fern. My mother had been convinced I would be a boy, and had decided on Charles Edward Fitzgerald (Fitzgerald being Nana's maiden name). When a second girl emerged, she was at a loss for ideas. Then she had a brainwave: Canon Hawkins, my great-grandfather, had been an amateur botanist of some note and had had a fern – a genuine green thing that grows in damp places – named after him at Kew

Gardens, so Fern it was. However, Fifi soon became the name I was actually called, as opposed to the one in the register – it was that kind of school.

The second shock was discovering that the other children – some of whom had arrived several months before me – already knew their letters and numbers. For a few weeks I was completely at a loss but can still remember the moment when the penny dropped and I realized I could read!

I may not have been a boy, but I was definitely a tomboy. There was nothing I liked better than tumbling about in the grass, or running round with no clothes on, or standing under the hosepipe in the garden. If anyone was going to fall into a river or a fishpond, it would be me. While Cherry was a real little girl with long blonde plaits she could sit on, my hair was kept short and, until I was about fourteen, those who didn't know were always saying, 'Hello, sonny!' It stopped when I developed bosoms.

Only now do I appreciate quite how eccentric Little Turret was. The headmistress, Miss Elsie Bird – known to everyone as Birdie – exuded glamour. Resplendent in a tight skirt and high heels, she was rarely seen without a cigarette and you had the feeling that a gin and tonic wasn't too far away. The names of the classes were Pollies, Wallies, Doodles, Poodles and Bigwigs. My two best friends were boys: Jonathan Beecroft and Alan Rosedale, whose speciality was swearing. Our favourite game was Robin Hood with me as Maid Marion, Jonathan as Robin and Alan the Sheriff of Nottingham. As we galloped around the playground on our pretend steeds, Alan's voice would ring out: 'Damn, blast, bloody hell, those are the words I like to hear.' Unusually for the time there was no smacking at Little Turret. Punishment was standing in a corner with a dirty black-board duster draped over your head. So how was it, we asked, after Alan had been made to suffer this indignity for his continuing profanities?

'Bloody awful.'

One day Birdie asked if any of our mothers knew anything about woodwork or drama. I duly passed the message on. Next thing I knew, my mummy was a teacher at the school! She knew nothing about woodwork, but her experience in ATS concert parties and her connection with actors no doubt stood her in good stead on the theatrical front. She turned out to be a natural and continued to teach there for years, long after I left. Her sense of humour and fun fitted in perfectly with Little Turret's eccentric nature. During my last year I was head girl and one afternoon towards the end of the summer term I was helping set up Sports Day with Mummy.

'Mrs Britton,' said one of the teachers, 'have you got the balls for the fathers' race?'

'I think they'll have brought their own!' my mother quipped, at which everyone fell about laughing, while I stood there, a po-faced seven-year-old thinking, How very rude, and surely she can't have understood what she was saying.

Sports Day at Little Turret was like Ladies' Day at Ascot, with the mums dressed in their finery, picture hats and Bond Street dresses, matching shoes and handbags. These, after all, were film people, and this was Gerrard's Cross!

The guillotine on our charmed existence came down shortly before Christmas 1963 when I was six and a half. There was undoubtedly a large mortgage on our house, and undoubtedly my father was having to fund his other life at the same time. My mother fought to retain the status quo – to keep the house and the lifestyle that went with it – but ultimately it was Dada who had to pay, and when the money ran out, he had no option but to sell. My mother accepted it with good grace – at least in terms of how she relayed it to Cherry and me at the time. She never said a word against Dada.

I will never forget our last night at Steeple. It was a Sunday. The furniture had all gone, except for two single mattresses on the floor and the piano, because Cherry had her grade-four piano exam the following morning and needed to practise. At the last minute it turned out that Dada hadn't signed the necessary documents, so that completion – planned for the Saturday – had had to be postponed. Nana and I slept on one mattress and my mother and sister on the other, the two lined up side by side in Mummy's old bedroom. I treated it as a huge adventure because my mother *made* it into an adventure, even though she was probably going through hell.

The following morning I set off for Little Turret as usual but went 'home' to Chalfont St Giles, three miles to the west. Our new house was literally new, having only just been built in a style that could best be described as sixties box, and in my eyes it was tiny, certainly compared to Steeple. But there was one big plus. My bedroom was now next to Mummy's rather than up another landing. The way things were done in those days, legally it belonged to Dada and would do for some time to come.

'The address is The Bumbles, Three Households,' Nana told the bus conductor, the first time she came to visit. 'Perhaps you would tell me when to get off.'

'Don't you worry, luv. The Bumbles, three arseholes ain't something I'm likely to forget.'

On a day-to-day level, the move to The Bumbles changed very little for Cherry and me. We continued to go to our schools and see our friends as we always had. Life for my mother changed dramatically, however, although what little spare cash she had, she spent cleverly and continued to look wonderfully glamorous. Shortly before we moved house, she'd got a new car – a treat, I think, from Nana – a Triumph Herald in a colour known as Monaco blue, which in fact was purple. It was the latest thing and the height of female motoring chic. I remember one afternoon the two of us driving along the A40 – already a dual carriageway – returning from a visit to Nana in Ealing. It was winter and Mummy was wearing a big white Cossack hat, the *Dr Zhivago* look – so it must have been around 1965, when the film came out. In those days there were no seatbelts and children sat where they wanted. I would sit next to Mummy and she'd say, 'Light me a cigarette, will you, Feef?' so I would, taking a quick puff before handing it over. On that particular day, just as I'd got it glowing, another car drew level.

'Look, Mummy,' I said. 'There's a man pointing at you!' I stared at him, but he only smiled more and mouthed, 'Nice hat,' then followed us all the way home. Whether she'd known him before this encounter I've no idea, but he was soon a regular visitor – and he was a nice man.

It was hardly surprising that Adek was in demand because she was both beautiful and fun. From time to time she'd be asked out on a 'date' to a country pub and she would always take me along. In those days children weren't allowed inside so I'd stay in the car and they'd bring me out a packet of Smith's crisps, with the blue-paper twist of salt, and a bottle of Coke complete with straw. I remember one wonderful Vauxhall with a big leather back seat and a radio with push-button tuning, which I would fiddle with endlessly and always succeed in messing up the stations. Eventually Mummy and her friend would come out, and we'd set off home again. I never felt abandoned: it would be a summer evening, and locked in that great tank of a car I'd be perfectly safe and it felt like an adventure.

I was used to being around grown-ups, both men and women, and they certainly didn't seem to mind me. I'd wander behind Mummy and her friends on the golf course being helpful, lifting the flag out of the hole on the putting green so the ball could plop in. I enjoyed listening to their conversations, trying to decode what was being said, though understanding little.

What I loved most, however, was having Mummy to myself, and the times we went shopping for clothes are stuck in my memory, like the way she always smelt of Chanel No. 5. We would usually go to one of the big department stores. These weren't just huge buildings on the outside, inside they were equally vast. The days of pile-'em-high, sell-'em-cheap had not yet arrived and they exuded a real sense of glamour. Suter's in Slough and Murray's in High Wycombe were the ones we went to most often, Murray's being both the nearest and my favourite. I was transfixed by the big yellow clock, like a sun, with a face on both sides, which went up and down the stairwell like a yo-yo on a chain, the staircase curving round it, so shoppers could see the time from wherever they were. At ceiling level there was a labyrinth of pipes, which led to the main accounting office somewhere out of sight. Your money or your cheque would be put in a cylinder with the bill, and – whoosh – with much rattling and hissing it would disappear along the tube. A few minutes later, further hissing would announce its return and the receipt and change would arrive as if by magic.

It was in Murray's that I first experienced the speed of God's retribution. A miniature Ferris Wheel laden with pick-and-mix sweets was a feature of the ground floor and I would spend happy minutes watching the baskets going up and down, round and round. On this particular day, when Mummy was otherwise engaged, I sidled over, watching until my favourite peppermints came within reach, then helped myself. By the time I turned back, Mummy was nowhere to be seen. She had gone! Tearful and distraught I eventually told a shop assistant that I'd lost my mummy. What I didn't tell her was that it was God's punishment for being very wicked. Eventually a voice crackled over the loudspeaker. 'Would the mother of Fifi please come to the glove counter where her daughter is waiting for her?' Of course, she had only ever been a few feet away.

The change in our fortunes once we moved to The Bumbles was dramatic. At Steeple there'd been a gardener and a housekeeper. Now when the fire had to be laid, it was Mummy who raked the ashes and brought in the coal. She had to shop, cook and clean. My jobs were to sweep the stair carpet and take the pop bottles back to the paper shop and collect the deposit. For the next few years, lack of money shadowed her life like a permanent cloud. The first thing she did was to get a lodger – a French student, learning English on some kind of exchange at ICI – for which she pocketed four pounds a week in rent, at a stroke doubling her income from teaching.

Next she took a course with Beauty Counsellors, an American version of Avon and, once again, proved a natural, adept at giving facials and generally showing people how to make the best of themselves while selling the company's products on commission. She also did hair. After school, or during the holidays, I'd tag along and spend hours gazing at women in face masks or smelling of perm solution. There was one old lady, I remember, who thought she was Marlene Dietrich. She lived in Little Chalfont and was known as Miss and was a great knitter. In her youth Miss had been on the

34

stage – a chorus girl – and was really rather beautiful. Her bungalow was all peach-satin bedspreads and lace curtains, photographs and books. While Mummy was giving her a massage or a facial, or just talking about something private, I'd be sitting quietly in her lounge, having been told not to move, looking through her bookshelves. Miss had proper books I would never have come across elsewhere, and I'd pull one out and start reading it until it was time to go.

Just as at our old house, the garden at The Bumbles had once been an orchard. This time only a cherry tree survived. Officially it was my sister's, because of the name, but among its branches was my tree-house, more accurately a rope-ladder, the 'house' bit being simply where I wedged myself to eat sweets and read. My favourite book at that time was *The Magic Faraway Tree* by Enid Blyton. A family of children find a door in the bottom of a tree-trunk in a nearby wood. The tree is inhabited by an array of unlikely and magical folk: Saucepan Man, who is deaf from all the clanging, and Dame Washalot who likes nothing better than to do laundry and the dishes day in day out. As well as animals who wear clothes (rabbits and squirrels) it's a place of elves and pixies, and although things go wrong – the Angry Pixie sees to that – calmness is always restored by the end of a chapter.

It fed into everything I loved and craved, friends, family, adventures, animals, the countryside and, of course, climbing trees, or anything else that presented a physical challenge. If there was something to climb, or cling to, or a river to hop across, be it over rapids or stepping-stones, then I would do it. And if there was any chance of falling, I would do that too. I was always filthy or wet, my knees liberally decorated with scabs and fresh grazes.

One day, without warning, a little over a year after we moved, my world was transformed into a much darker place.

Cherry had a school friend staying whose parents had gone to America for a few weeks, so while Denise had my bed, I had moved in to share with my mother, another wonderful treat. Early one morning – it could only have been about seven o'clock – the phone rang. It lived on her dressing-table, and I watched as she got out of bed, walked across to the window, lifted the receiver, said, 'Hello,' then fell to the floor. The only sound was a woman's voice saying, 'Hello! Hello!' coming from the dangling receiver, just like in an old film. I jumped up, put it back in its cradle, then tried to get Mummy to talk, but she just lay there on the carpet, looking waxy and yellow with her eyes closed.

'Come quick,' I said, running through to Cherry. 'It's Mummy!'

My sister got straight out of bed and I remember hanging back by the door as she covered her up with a blanket.

We were used to my mother fainting. It happened on a reasonably regular basis – I have no idea why, perhaps just low blood pressure combined with stress. For years she had lived under enormous strain and there had been times of desperate unhappiness: the collapse of her marriage, the worry of being perpetually financially stretched, and the sheer loneliness of bringing up two daughters on her own.

My next memory is of sitting in our neighbours' kitchen having breakfast, their son, Carl, being a friend of mine. I must have got dressed at some point and someone must have taken me to school because halfway through the morning Birdie called me into her study, which was less like a study and more like a comfortable lounge.

'Now sit down, Fifi,' she said, patting the chair beside her. 'As you know, your mummy's not very well. In fact, she's very ill indeed. She's being looked after by the doctors, but it may be quite a long time until she's better.'

36

I spent the rest of the day trying not to show how frightened I was. I didn't cry, I just kept on smiling. If I didn't cry, it would all be all right.

I got back home, not knowing if Mummy was going to be there. Cherry opened the door.

'Is Mummy all right?'

'The doctor's been and she's having a sleep.'

'But she's all right?'

I didn't wait to hear the answer but rushed upstairs to see for myself. She was lying slightly propped up, with her bed-jacket on. But something was wrong. Although her eyes were open, she didn't turn her head towards me. In fact, she didn't move at all. I can't remember now what I felt, but the shock, the sight of her lying there, not responding in any way, must have been terrifying. This was my mummy . . .

Later that evening the doctor returned, and when he came down from seeing his patient, he took me into the lounge for a chat. Mummy had had a stroke, he said. He explained how electricity makes our brains work, and that it crosses from one side to the other, like a ping-pong ball, and that Mummy's had stopped in the middle, which meant she couldn't move either side of her body or speak. She needed a lot of rest, a lot of me being a good girl.

I can only marvel now at how Cherry coped. She was only fifteen, and in all likelihood even more upset than I was because she would have known what 'stroke' meant, whereas I was blissfully unaware. Denise, Cherry's friend, continued to go to school, but Cherry stayed at home. Every morning she lit the fire (The Bumbles didn't run to central heating), got us breakfast, did the shopping and the cooking, as well as dealing with callers and keeping Mummy comfortable. Our neighbours Roy and Dorothy Davies, Carl's parents, made it possible for us to stay at the house, coming

37

over with food, having me to play and generally taking care of anything that needed a car. As far as poor Cherry was concerned, the timing couldn't have been worse. Her O levels were imminent and suffered as a consequence. For me, on the other hand, it was a surprisingly happy time. For a few days I had this mute and immobile person all to myself, feeding her, giving her drinks, brushing her hair and generally playing nurse. She recovered her speech comparatively quickly, while regaining her mobility through crocheting dolls' clothes and knitting blankets to keep them warm.

When Nana arrived to take over, it was as if a fairy wand had been waved. Normal service had been resumed. Or nearly. In fact, she wasn't at all well herself, but with the insouciance of youth I had no idea. She was Nana and she could do anything. There were things she couldn't do, of course, and one of the local farmers would regularly come over in the evening and carry Mummy downstairs to watch television, then carry her back up again.

It was a full year before Adek was back to her old self, but in time she made a complete recovery. Nana, however, was not so lucky. She had always had a nasty smoker's cough – given the number of cigarettes she smoked that was hardly surprising – and later that year she was taken into hospital. It was cancer through and through, too widespread, it seems, for the doctors to be sure even where it had started. She was discharged from hospital when there was nothing further they could do. She never returned to Ealing but stayed with Uncle Paul and Auntie Elsie in their new house at Ickenham, until she died, a little over a year after Mummy had had the stroke.

As usual I spend the hour and a half it takes to drive in to work in the morning reading through the script and making notes, looking up occasionally as my concentration is disrupted by a horn, a white van carving somebody up, a Sikh scratching his head beneath his turban. I also have the newspapers to go through, the Mirror *and the* Mail, *which Tony always brings with him. Everyone knows that this time is sacrosanct, so it doesn't occur to me to check my phone, which I keep on vibrate. Only when I get to the studio do I find out that Phillip has been trying to call me. His father is ill, and he won't be coming in. I have met Brian, his dad, many times and I know just how strong the bond is between them.*

When one of us is absent they usually find someone to fill in. Recently I've shared the sofa with Michael Ball and John Barrowman – both terrific all-round entertainers with whom I have a good relationship – but this morning I'll do the show alone. As I sit in Makeup, Lyn and I catch up. We met on Ready Steady Cook *more than fourteen years ago now, and by luck she was asked to join* This Morning *around the same time as me, so we're friends rather than simply colleagues, and she could do me blindfold. It's when she transforms me for one-offs that we really have fun. Over the years she has turned me into the Queen, Mary Poppins, Princess Leia from* Star Wars, *and a schoolgirl. She's a TV veteran, having started in BBC drama way back when. She calls herself 'Granny Makeup', and jokes she's been around since the time of Elizabeth I – who else, she points out, could have devised that white-faced look? As for Cleopatra, well, suffice to say that without Lyn's dab hand with the eye-liner, history wouldn't have been the same.*

While we're joshing – Lyn's great age, my swanlike neck – Carole from Hospitality comes in with my breakfast: Muesli Ryvita – yes, I really do eat it – with peanut butter and slices of banana. Usually Phillip would be here, having us in stitches with some outrageous story even at nine in the morning, and his absence hangs heavy, not least because it means that things must really be bad with his dad. Although he's been very unwell for some time Phillip hasn't missed a programme, so things must now be serious.

But I'll be fine on my own: This Morning *is such a smooth machine. We know each other incredibly well and, over the years, we have learnt to trust each other's ability. We know what we're supposed to be doing and get on with it, which goes an awful long way to making it work. If past experience is anything to go by, I'll be so busy I won't have time to think till it's all over. And then if anyone asks me how I coped, I'll say, 'Oh, I enjoyed it.'*

'Let's hope he's back for Thursday,' I say. It's just been confirmed that Kate and Gerry McCann are coming in then, it being nearly a year since their daughter Madeleine was abducted from Praya da Luz on 3 May 2007. The professional part of me is proud that they have chosen to come on our show. The personal part knows it will be intensely emotional, and I can only hope Phillip will be there too.

Party girl, c. 1963

3. Rubber Boots and Greasepaint

One concession wrung from our father was that Cherry should continue at her private school, St Mary's Convent, in Gerrard's Cross. In other circumstances, I should have followed her there. As it was, I left Little Turret shortly after my eighth birthday and the following September started at Chalfont St Giles village school.

The transition was far from easy. There would be no more concessions to my name and the teachers no doubt considered I was being insolent when I failed to respond to 'Fern!'

Fern? Who's Fern? I was Fifi.

Making new friends had its problems too. Not only had the children known each other since they were five, they sensed I was different. At first they thought I was American: there was a definite Buckinghamshire 'burr' in those days, which I didn't have. At Little Turret how you spoke had been important – indeed, it was what the well-heeled parents paid for. I had the opposite problem. To survive in my new environment I learnt to adopt a more 'village' voice.

New friends did eventually materialize. I already knew Carl from next door. Although he was a year or two younger than me, we would play together after school and at week-ends. But my first real friend – unrelated to where I lived – was Sarah Toll. Our situations were in some ways similar, which may have played a part in bringing us together, though hers is a tragic story. Like me, her parents were divorced. Her

43

younger brother had been killed in a road accident and she lived with her mother, a beautiful woman called Dawn, who had cancer of the eye. Sarah's grandmother also lived with them, but in an independent way.

Sometimes I would stay at Sarah's overnight, and although Dawn was often really unwell, she would always rouse herself, get out of bed and make us grilled tomatoes on toast with cheese on top, or mouli up fresh peas for pea soup. I remember, too, how she introduced me to Rose's lime marmalade. Dawn was both kind and beautiful and I would give her back and neck massages, which she said relieved her pain. I loved going over there even though, compared with The Bumbles, it was very dark inside. It was probably Victorian or Edwardian, and at the back you'd walk out onto a veranda that looked over the garden. With its metal pillars and its own miniature roof, it reminded me of a station platform. Standing there, you really felt that a train might come in at any minute. There was a trapdoor leading to a little loft and, having nicked a few of her granny's cigarettes, Sarah and I would climb up there and puff away, feeling naughty and grown-up at the same time.

When Dawn died, Sarah went to live with her father and we lost touch. We must have been ten or eleven by then, so we would probably have split up and gone to different schools whatever had happened, but it was a terrible, terrible time. During my teenage years I continued to see her granny: after Dawn died, she was allocated a flat in the village and I would drop in on my way to the library on Saturday mornings and take her cakes.

I was about nine when I first met George, the man who would eventually become my stepfather. He was balding, with silvery-grey hair round the sides, always neatly brushed, and with a neatly clipped moustache. Everything about him was neat: he looked exactly like the military man he had once been.

George was the father of a friend of my sister's. It was a tragic story. He had had three children. One son had died in childhood and the second – Cherry's friend – had just turned twenty-one and was about to start medical school when he was killed in a car accident. It was around this time that he and Mummy met. His marriage was all but finished and he fell in love with her very quickly.

At first I liked George coming over – it was nice having a man around the house – but it wasn't long before I realized things had changed. From being Mummy's little girl I felt suddenly displaced in the pecking order. Until then our house had been surprisingly free of rules. Now rules were everywhere. I had to knock every time I entered a room. I wasn't allowed to sit next to Mummy on the sofa. I had to go to bed on my own and there was no more tucking up. Worse, my glamorous mummy had turned into some-one else. The familiar clack-clack of her heels was silenced overnight (he wasn't a tall man, while she was five foot ten). From then on it was brogues, hand-knitted suits and bobbly cardigans, made by Miss whose hobby it was. As for makeup – well, George didn't like it. And this was a woman who did facials and gave demonstrations, who never dreamt of leav-ing the house without her 'face' on. Hair, nails – everything that seemed part of her pre-George identity was abandoned.

Children rarely welcome change, especially when that change concerns their mother, their very own living, breath-ing security blanket. I don't remember now if I showed how unhappy I was or whether I simply confided everything to the ever-faithful Johnson, dealing with it by popping my first Fern Britton pill, as my husband calls it, radiating my

45

broadest smile, while inside falling apart. And, of course, I read. It was around this time that I discovered C. S. Lewis: I sat in bed reading the Narnia books and wept and wept.

Throughout my childhood I had regularly stayed with my aunt and uncle, first in Ealing and now in their new house in Ickenham. I adored Auntie Elsie. She was always very 'with it', slight and slim with cornflower blue eyes, and a great believer in a good perm, kept in condition with a weekly shampoo and set. As a young girl she'd had TB and still suffered from a bad chest, not helped by smoking – but in those days everybody smoked. I was always very happy there and even now the smell of Wright's Coal Tar Soap brings it all back to me.

Auntie Elsie didn't have a job: she was a traditional old-fashioned housewife. Just like Uncle Paul she would be up before anybody else, making breakfast, getting Michael and Gerald off to wherever they were going. Every morning, taking a proper wicker basket, we'd walk to the shops to buy whatever she needed for the day. The butcher, the greengrocer, the people in the dairy, everyone knew her by name.

The day was marked by a succession of little rituals. On our way back there was a playground, so she'd sit on the bench and I'd have half an hour on the swings and the roundabout, before setting off home. The moment we got through the front door she'd make a lovely mug of milky coffee and settle down to read the paper while I'd sprawl on the settee and watch a bit of telly. My favourite programmes were *Take the High Road*, a soap set in Scotland, and *House Party*, where a group of women would discuss hot topics in what looked like a suburban house.

'Now tell me, Bunty, how's your husband's hernia getting on?'

'Very well, thank you, Sylvia, but I thought today we'd ask Mary about amusing things to do with raisins.'

Later in the afternoon I'd help Auntie Elsie in the garden, or we'd chat to the next-door neighbour, or take one of her apple pies to the 'old boy' down the road where we'd have a nice cup of tea and some squashed flies or custard creams. Then it was quick march home to make sure everything was ready for Uncle Paul and the boys. It was all very ordinary and comforting, and very different from the situation at The Bumbles, where George's determination to save money led to some strange situations.

George was a public-health inspector. He'd left school at fourteen and had worked hard to get where he was and had done very well for himself, buying a large house in a very smart road in Little Chalfont. During the war he'd been a physical-training instructor and was still very fit. For ten minutes every day, he would stand on his head, after which he'd say he was 'tingling with health'. The blood going to his brain, he explained, would 'perk up his intelligence'. His conversation was peppered with such sayings. When it wasn't 'tingling with health', it was 'Empty vessels make most noise' or 'Put not your faith in princes'. His great aim was to achieve 'a champagne lifestyle on beer money'.

'I'm just going to go and buy a spare part for the car,' he'd say, and come back with a wreck he'd just saved from the breakers' yard. About six or seven such wrecks were a permanent feature of his drive. The idea was to break them up himself and cannibalize them for one of his own cars. In fact, I quite liked George's house, which we would go to at weekends. Called Three Trees, it was much bigger than ours, with a rambling garden and a wild wood across the road that seemed to belong to no one. It offered plenty of scope for climbing and making dens.

George was an early fan of DIY. He didn't believe in employing tradesmen: electricians, carpenters, garage mechanics, Gas Board men were all 'twisting bastards'. On one occasion he decided the fireplace in the lounge could do with being bigger. Next thing we knew there was a howling gale coming through the house. He had attacked the wall with a little too much force and knocked through to the garage. The resulting hole was there for years, his way of dealing with it being to sandbag the door to prevent us using the room at all.

One thing we could never do was point out these foibles. A few years later, when the chimney was finally fixed, we duly trooped in for the ceremonial lighting of the fire. Of course it smoked like billy-oh. Eventually Mummy quietly got up and opened one of the windows, this on a bitterly cold winter's day. Nothing could be said and nothing was. We simply sat there freezing to death. At some point he cut another substantial hole into the same wall to make an alcove. In the end Mummy got me to help her paper it over.

'Whatever you do,' Mummy would say to guests, 'don't lean against it or you'll end up in the garage.' They would laugh politely, little knowing it was literally true. Over the years we became dab hands at making 'a feature' of George's quirky building efforts.

Perhaps George's most eccentric way of saving money was in the area of food. Part of his job as a health inspector was to visit supermarkets whose freezing systems had broken down. In order to claim on insurance, the food had to be officially condemned. George would bring back whatever he thought was still edible. There was nothing wrong with it, he assured us. He only brought back stuff that hadn't started to thaw. As for a freezer to keep it in, ours was one he'd found on the local tip. Obviously chucked out by a shop, it was branded Coca-Cola and had a sliding top. It kept us going for years, as indeed did the salvaged food. For weeks we might live on boil-in-the-bag cod, or Bird's Eye orange mousse, or chicken supreme.

George was at his happiest when he was tinkering: lying underneath a car, or with a radio in parts on the kitchen table. One day, after I had left home, I came back for the weekend to find my mother standing at the twin-tub washing-machine with one hand behind her back.

'What are you doing, Mummy?'

'Taking care I'm not making a circuit.'

'What on earth do you mean, not making a circuit?' I asked.

'Well, George says the washing-machine's live.'

It was another piece of equipment he'd rescued from the tip. The situation was getting ridiculous and – I must have been reasonably old by then – I went to remonstrate with him. 'Look, George,' I said. 'You can't let her use a washing-machine that's live. This isn't right.'

'Don't worry,' he said. 'I always make sure Mummy's wearing her rubber boots when she's doing the laundry.'

In the mid-sixties Rex Harrison left the West End production of *My Fair Lady* to make the film version and my father stepped into the role of Professor Higgins. At some point it was decided that we'd go to see him. I must have been about nine and I had never been to a proper grown-up theatre before and, from beginning to end, I was mesmerized, though I couldn't believe Dada could be so horrible as to call Eliza a squashed cabbage leaf. After the curtain came down – to thunderous applause, and quite rightly because he was bloody brilliant – we waited until the audience had left, and then somebody took us through the pass door, which connects backstage with the auditorium. Suddenly there I was, standing in Professor Higgins's study! Looking out at the auditorium I felt this incredible warmth, both from the lights and the recently departed audience. Standing there, in this pretend world, with rows of empty seats in front of me felt strangely secure – perhaps it was the smell: the smell of a theatre is like nothing else in the world. Dada was still in costume, but I knew it was him and he let me walk up the library steps to the bookcase. On his desk were the pebbles he put in Eliza's mouth to get her to speak properly. I went over and sneaked a look at them.

'You can have one if you like,' he said. 'Go on, put it in your mouth.' So I did, and it was a chewy mint sweetie! Then we went back to his dressing room, which was like entering Wonderland. I remember it as being huge, though it probably wasn't. The mirror was covered with lipstick messages of good luck, cards and telegrams stuck into the corners. Below, on a built-in bench, there was a bunch of wilting flowers and, of course, all his makeup laid out on a towel. There was something truly magical about that box of mismatched tubes, and sticks of Leichner greasepaint, with the paper peeling down, like wax crayons. There were tufts of hair that looked like caterpillars, eyebrows, he told me, and squidgy bits of flesh-coloured Plasticine – putty for ears and noses – everything coated with a fine dusting of powder. And stretched out on his divan, like an expensive rug, was Cleo, his Afghan hound, a theatre dog through and through, a floppy-eared creature, very elegant and aloof, watching us disdainfully.

We sat there chatting as he took off his makeup, smearing his face with handfuls of Pond's cold cream from a big tub. Behind him were the costumes, the tweed Higgins suit, and the black pumps he would wear with white tie and tails for the ball scene – they struck me as so funny. That a man should wear ballet shoes! As for Dada himself, he smelt of cologne and whisky and tobacco. Gradually other people began to flutter round him, each one smelling of something different, each one smoking – Gauloises, Rothmans and cigars – and Dada pouring out tumblers of whisky. And, oh, the pride when I was asked, 'And who might you be?'

'I'm Fifi. That's my dada . . .'

I had seen my father on television, but now he went soaring up in my estimation. TV tries to give the impression it's real, but the theatre was sheer imagination and I was transported. Everything about it exuded glamour, or used to – sadly, much of that has gone. Audiences don't dress up any more and actors no longer have that aura of difference. Indeed they seem to revel in being 'jobbing actors', taking excessive delight in being able to travel on the tube. No mystique left at all.

Whatever I might privately have wanted, I knew that contact with my father would be little and far apart. Seeing Dada at the theatre was a treat, but a difficult one. He and my mother would embrace and there would be tears of regret, of emotion, and I knew it was hard for both of them. As I watched, I told myself they did love each other. It was simply that they were not allowed to be together. There had to be an outside force: only an outside force could have kept them apart. It was nothing to do with them. This positive picture was sustained by my mother who never once said anything like, 'Your father's a bastard.' All I was told was that there was another lady, whom he'd met before he met Mummy, and that he'd had to go back to that lady. Whether that was true or not, I still don't know.

At school, when children talked about their fathers, I would say, 'My daddy's an actor.' The next question was inevitably, 'So where is he, then?' as I was obviously making it up. All I knew was that he wasn't a daddy in the way other children had daddies: there at your birthday party to organize the games, or on Bonfire Night to light the fireworks and hand out the sparklers.

Once George had arrived on the scene, there were a few more trips to the theatre but then the door somehow shut. I didn't see or hear it shut, but shut it was.

I can still recall the bleak sense of dislocation and power-lessness that would overwhelm me. Mummy was mother and father, friends and security to me. Now her time and her affections had to be split between me and George. I'd spend hours alone in my room, reading and listening to plays and comedy shows on the radio. Everything would be all right, I decided, if I could find Dada and ask him to come home. If only I could get hold of him, if only I knew where he was . . . On the outside, I'd continue to smile.

About half a mile down the road from The Bumbles was Milton's cottage, where John Milton, the blind poet, had lived, and I'd wander down there, spending hours some-times alone in the garden, reading or closing my eyes and just imagining what it must have been like to be him. On Saturdays, on my way to the library, I'd pop in to see Sarah Toll's granny. On Sundays I'd go to evensong at our local church. Nobody else in the family went, just me. I liked evensong as it meant I could walk back in the dark. To stop myself being scared I'd pretend I was walking with a toddler, holding their hand tightly in mine. As soon as the evenings grew longer, I'd be riding my bicycle along the lanes that criss-cross the Chilterns, not too far from home but far enough to give me the thrill of fear and adventure.

Taking on somebody else's children requires a com-bination of blind faith, courage and a thick skin. Of course

George was jealous – just as I was: these things are rarely one way – but he was essentially a good man, if an unreconstructed one, not unusual for the time. And he worshipped my mother and made her happy, all of which she deserved.

George's presence wasn't unremitting gloom, however, and his camping holidays were wonderful – if as eccentric as every other part of his character. I know now how incredibly lucky I am to have seen Europe like that, not a plane or coach or tour guide in sight, apart from George.

'Put that bloody book down and just look at the view,' he'd say, as we crested some pass in the Alps, while I said, 'Mm,' and carried on reading.

There would always be four of us, George and Mummy in the front and us girls in the back. Cherry came the first year when we went in the Triumph Herald, but after that I would take a friend. (By now Cherry was living in London and had a life of her own.) The tent would go in the boot, followed by the portable stove and pans, not forgetting the badminton net, racquets and shuttlecock. Whatever else remained was jammed around us until the back of the car resembled a padded cell. The route was always much the same. We'd sail from Dover to Dunkirk (cheap) and, standing at the rail as we approached France, George would tell the story of the flotilla of small boats and Our Brave Boys, the one story of his I never grew tired of hearing. Then, wending our way through France, we'd stay the first night in a hotel in Rheims, then drive on to Switzerland, Austria (stopping in Germany, even for petrol, was to be avoided at all costs) and down through Italy until we reached Rimini, our destination.

In those days Rimini was known as the Adriatic Riviera and the amazing beach went on for miles. Every hundred yards there were swings on which you could soar right out over the sea. Pizza was a revelation – there was no such thing in England then. There'd be a man walking around the market with a metal baking tray strung round his neck, and he'd hand you a square of this thick dough oozing with squishy cheese wrapped in a piece of paper. As for the ice-creams, they beat Wall's hands down.

The campsite was like a great big back garden, with families of every nationality pegging out their individual patch. But we children, no matter what language we spoke, all seemed to understand each other and just get on. This was when the badminton net came into its own. Put it up, and everyone came running.

Although Rimini was always our ultimate destination, there would be different stop-off points on the way. One year we camped on the shore of Lake Geneva; I also have a memory of setting up the tent beside Lake Como. Once we made it as far as Naples to see Pompeii, and on the same trip crossed over to Capri, which, as with most places we went to, George claimed to know 'like the back of my hand'. Short-cuts were his speciality, yet however many dead ends we ended up in, nothing was ever to be said.

George's local knowledge was put to the test when he insisted on negotiating the back-streets of Naples. It was already dark when suddenly the car jolted, as if we'd gone over a kerb. I peered out of the window to find we had left the road and were bumping along the main Naples-to-Rome railway line . . . While Mummy and George behaved as if nothing unusual had happened, in the back we were snorting with suppressed laughter, locked together in a state of near hysteria. Thankfully, it only lasted a few minutes and, after another bump, we returned to the more conventional route. The incident was never discussed.

Us girls would usually sleep in the back of the car – on this occasion a borrowed Volvo estate – while Mummy and George slept in the Igloo, a state-of-the-art tent whose struts were air-filled; it was always my job to pump it up. That year, hearing an ominous noise, I called George over.

'Listen,' I said. 'The air, I'm sure it's escaping.'

'No, it's not, and stop showing off.'

At around three in the morning we awoke to shouts and oaths: the tent had collapsed on top of George and my mother. More silent hilarity as we stuffed our faces into our sleeping-bags to avoid being heard.

I don't remember now why we had borrowed the Volvo, possibly because none of George's current wrecks had been considered up to a drive of two thousand miles, at least by the mother of my friend, whose car it was. George would never have made such an admission, and Mummy wouldn't have dared even hint at the possibility. The night before we'd set off, he'd have had the engine and the gearbox out on the lawn and be putting it all back together again. Problems were usually not long in appearing, however. On one famous occasion we had a puncture barely twenty minutes after we'd left home. With the spare tyre being under the boot, everything had to be unpacked. Smart Alec cracks were out of the question – anywhere within hearing distance of George was a smirk-free zone. Also we were petrified. Cars flashed by at seventy miles an hour while we huddled together on the non-existent hard shoulder – he'd managed to stop on the White City flyover . . .

By now I had left Chalfont St Giles primary, and had moved on to Dr Challoner's High School in Amersham. Although housed in a modern building – concrete and glass surrounded by greenery – Challoner's was an old-fashioned, single-sex girls' grammar. It was soon apparent that I was not a high flyer. My average mark was C. My reports (I still have them) were peppered with remarks such as 'Fern must develop consistency in her work', 'Fern needs to develop perseverance and concentration' and 'Fern must adopt a more serious attitude to work.' The truth was that I had a serious attitude to work, simply not the kind of work we did at school.

Three Households boasted a little parade of three shops, one of which was the newsagent. It was less than fifty yards from The Bumbles and we'd always known the family who ran it, so shortly after I turned fourteen I began working there. At first it was just Saturdays, then Sunday mornings were added and eventually school holidays. Saturday afternoons were my favourite, particularly if there was a football match on television, as there'd be hardly any customers, and those who did turn up were locals coming to pay their paper bill or to pick up a box of Cadbury's Milk Tray for 'the wife's birthday'. Then there was Queenie, who'd pop in for her *Radio Times*, a quarter of pear drops and 'me fags'. The cigarettes were ranged on the shelf behind my back. Piccadilly, Guards, No. 6, Senior Service, Marlboro, Rothman's, Benson & Hedges. Their positions never changed so I could reach round and get the right packet without taking my eyes off the counter. A regular had only to come in through the door and I'd have their usual brand ready by the time they opened their mouth.

There was a big chest-type freezer for ice-creams and lollies and it was while I was reaching for a choc ice that I became aware for the first time in my life that I was being stared at. It was a young farmer I knew by sight, because he came in quite often, though not his name.

'I was wondering,' he said hesitantly, as I gave him his change, 'if you'd like to come out with me?'

He was about twenty, good-looking and wealthy, as I knew from the MG parked outside. So what did I say? Naturally I turned him down ... It was the first time I had ever been faced with such an invitation and I was overcome with confusion and shyness. I did see him again, but this incident was never mentioned. And he was lovely ...

Chalfont St Giles was like a twentieth-century version of Cranford. The tiniest incident became the talk of the village for days, and our shop was the hub. I remember the time a car crashed into the pillar-box just outside with such violence that it was completely uprooted and lay across the pavement like a felled tree. Needless to say, the story had to be told and retold whenever anybody new came in. We had one old lady who couldn't stop swearing. Regulars used to her unique vocabulary took little notice, but if strangers were in earshot you could see the amazement on their faces, not only at her language but that nobody was reacting. In fact, her 'swearing' was some of the most inventive I have ever come across. One afternoon she came in having just fallen over, and instead of her usual 'arse over elbow' said she'd gone 'ACAS over NALGO', this being the seventies, time of union strife and the three-day week.

My job at the paper shop gave me an excuse to get out of the house; it also gave me a sense of purpose and taught me key lessons about the world of work: you can't be cocky, you can't be late, you have to speak clearly and learn how to listen. It also, of course, gave me money. Over a few weeks I could earn between eighty and a hundred pounds – a fortune in the early seventies. Living not far from London, and with easy train links, I wasn't limited to shopping locally. The new buzz word was 'boutique', and there were two places to go: the King's Road in Chelsea and Kensington High Street, where the huge Biba emporium had just opened. Biba had revolutionized the whole business of buying clothes. Gone were individual changing rooms of the kind I would go to with Mummy in Suter's or Murray's, where there would be a shop assistant to help you, fetching different sizes, suggesting this and that. Now there was just one big space. You dumped your things in a corner, stripped off and got on with it, and so did everybody else. As for the clothes, they were fabulous – wild prints and wild colours, with new things coming in all the time, hung on hat-stands rather than rails and at prices that meant I could treat myself. I'd spend the whole day in London – having my hair cut, trying on shoes and hats and jewellery and generally having a splurge. I no longer wanted to be Vicky the speedboat driver, I wanted to be Mary Quant and invent makeup.

Watching me roll up at the house laden with bags emblazoned 'Biba' and 'Bus Stop' must have been difficult for George, whose watchword was frugality. Electricity at Three Trees was all off-peak, which meant that, at the very time you had to have it – like for lights in the evening – it would go off. Hot water from the tap was a waste of money as it would lose half its heat in the pipes. Much better to boil a kettle when you needed it, such as first thing in the morning for a wash.

In the spring of 1971 my mother, Uncle Paul and Auntie Elsie had arranged to fly to Penang to see Grandpop. As for me, I would stay at Three Trees with George. They were gone for a month. George drove them to Heathrow and I went with them. Mummy's last instruction – called as she disappeared into Departures – was that I should 'be helpful'. I did genuinely try, but somehow never got it right. When I peeled the potatoes, I did either too many or too few. 'Empty vessels make most noise,' George would remind me, if I attempted to speak over dinner.

One evening he arranged for a couple of his Masonic friends to come over. In my efforts to be helpful, I had hoovered and generally cleaned up before his guests arrived; at the sound of the doorbell, I'd gone up to bed. The moment I opened my door, my eyes nearly fell out of my head and my heart hammered. The bed was covered with a mound of what looked like snow. The previous year George had insulated the loft with Vermiculite, tiny pieces of balsawood. There had subsequently been a slow leak from a water pipe and the resultant weight had been too much for the ceiling to bear. I stood there absolutely petrified. How was I going to tell him? To embarrass him in front of his friends . . .

I stood outside the door of the lounge for a good minute before I went in. Eventually I knocked.

'This is the youngest girl,' George informed his fellow Masons when I went in. 'What do you want?'

'Could I have a word, please, George?'

'Just say what you've got to say.'

'I'd rather not.'

'Come on, speak up.'

'My bedroom ceiling's fallen in.'

At least, he didn't claim this to be my fault, although as I stood outside that door, I was convinced I would get the blame.

One day he said he'd pick me up from school. I waited and waited until one by one the shops in the little parade had begun to close. By the time he arrived it was dark. He opened the car door from the inside to let me in but said nothing. There was a terrible atmosphere. What I wanted to say was, 'Why are you late?' What I actually said was, 'What have I done?'

'It's not what you've done, it's what you didn't do.'

'What didn't I do?'

'You failed to kiss me goodbye this morning when I dropped you off.'

He didn't speak to me for more than a week.

The final straw was when my mother's car, our lovely Monaco blue Triumph Herald, went. One day he just took it to the breakers' yard and that was it.

Knowing that Gerry and Kate McCann were coming in today, I stayed up last night beyond my usual nine o'clock bedtime and watched the documentary marking the anniversary of Madeleine's disappearance. This morning, reading through the notes in the back of the car, the full horror hit me again. Where do you start? What can you say in a situation like this? It's nearly a year and there's nothing. Just as they think they're getting somewhere and people are listening, it all goes quiet. The frustration can only be imagined.

At least I wasn't on my own. Phillip is still caring for his dad, so John Barrowman is standing in. There is nothing John can't do, but as something like this was outside his experience we talked it through, agreed where we wanted to go and what we wanted to ask. I would have done the same had Phillip been there. However confident I might be feeling, I'm a great believer in two brains being better than one; I don't have a monopoly on the best line of questioning.

To find yourself face to face with two people you feel you know yet you don't is a surreal experience. So much about the McCanns is familiar, from the way they walk to the way they dress, and suddenly there they are, sitting in front of you, and you're talking to them about the most unimaginable thing in the world.

They wanted to discuss what in America is called the Amber alert and their efforts to effect a change in European law to incorporate it over here. Modelled on hurricane and tornado alerts that are broadcast nationwide across the States, it is named for Amber Hagerman, abducted, raped and murdered in 1996 in Arlington, Texas. However, children go missing all the time and ninety-nine times out of a hundred, it's not an abduction. The fear seems to be that not only will time and money be wasted unnecessarily, but there's a real risk that the public will become desensitized; for both these reasons the European authorities are not yet convinced that such a scheme is warranted on this side of the Atlantic.

An interview such as this is difficult. Kate McCann's tight face and Gerry's stoical sense of 'doing something' are heart-breaking. For them Madeleine is not just an icon, a face on posters, she is their little girl, their daughter. But there are questions the viewers need to have answered. Yet I don't want to be intrusive, and I'm not prepared to interrogate them gratuitously.

There are people who deserve a grilling. The most obvious of these is the coughing major – the man on Who Wants to Be a Millionaire? *who won a million but who was denied his 'winnings' because the jury found that he had cheated and indeed he was given an eighteen-month suspended sentence. Halfway through the interview I asked him, 'Why don't you just admit it?' He took a beat – fractionally too long in my view – then said, 'Because I didn't do it.' There are those who are prepared to tell you everything. You give the door a push and it opens wide and it's 'Oh, my God!' and off you go, and 'Thank you very much.' At other times the door remains firmly shut, and you think, Fair enough, I can see that that's a no-go, and I'm not about to put you on the spot for something that isn't that important. That's how I feel about the McCanns.*

As I talk to these two, brave, dignified people, the thought running through my head is, There but for the grace of God go I. What parent could claim that they have never let their child out of their sight for a second? Certainly not me. I only have to think of what I do when I fill up with petrol. Do I really take my children with me across the busy forecourt when I go to pay? One question I know I have to ask concerns blame. With the best will in the world, you're always going to remember the one who said, 'Don't worry. It'll be OK.' So I put it to them. But they say no. They don't blame each other at all. It was something they both agreed on, both thought out, and both felt that there was no risk.

The chance of something so terrible happening is one in several million. But what mother – or father – hasn't experienced that moment of panic when you think your children have disappeared? I will never forget an afternoon when the twins went missing. We'd gone down to the Rye, the local park, and they'd sped off on their bicycles while I pushed Grace on the swing and Winnie toddled around. The boys were then about ten. The moment I realized I couldn't see them, I felt my mouth go dry and my heart begin to pound. Without really thinking I rang 999, and was trying to stay calm, trying to remember exactly what clothes they had on, when next moment there they were – happily pedalling away, totally unconcerned. I was still on the phone, talking to this police lady when I saw them and I remember saying over and over, 'I'm so sorry. I'm so, so sorry.'

And she said, 'No, please, it's absolutely fine. No problem at all. I'm glad they're back.'

You think about the pressures young mothers are under. Sometimes they are little more than children themselves, living in isolated rooms or caravans, lonely, with no one to share the frustrations and the tensions. Human-interest stories are a staple ingredient of This Morning, *and over the years I have found myself interviewing people in very distressing circumstances. We want to give them the opportunity to tell their story, but it needs to be told as straightforwardly as possible, without wallowing, sentimentality or gratuitously sensationalizing. Wherever we can we try to give everyone who comes to us more than just the interview. When they make that first call, their initial contact is with our counsellors, some of whom will be in touch with people for years, and not just those who have appeared on the programme. I met one little girl whose family were finally charged and sentenced for serial abuse. Somehow she had found the courage to telephone; she was listened to and what she said was acted on. She never appeared on the programme, and neither should she have done. Nor was the case ever referred to on air.* This Morning *helps people constantly without anyone really knowing.*

Portrait of the milkmaid on her eighteenth birthday

4. The Milkmaid

I can't now remember when Dada started to write to me – perhaps it was after Cherry left home and he could see something of her away from Mummy and George. But at some point letters began to be exchanged and the sight of that elegant handwriting on the doormat would fill me with excitement and I'd keep the envelope in my school bag and read and reread its contents. My letters to him were full of the usual teenage stuff, including updates on boyfriends. His letters had a lightness and wit that I'm not sure I appreciated back then. One line, commenting on some young man I'd written to him about, is etched on my memory: 'How's Young Lochinvar, that poor love-crazed fool?' Much as I longed to see Dada, however, I never did.

By now I was old enough to baby-sit. I had always been considered very sensible – and I had become ultra tidy, which my mother found very hard to understand. In her eyes, my tidiness was an illness. Until I was fourteen, I'd been a total slob, but once I was buying my own clothes, I saw that hanging them up made sense, if only to enable me to find what I wanted without wasting half an hour and then having to iron it.

Sensible baby-sitters are always in demand, especially someone happy to spend the night away from home. One of my regulars was an American family; the husband was based at the US air base in Uxbridge, although they lived just down the road. So when, in 1974, they asked me if I could baby-sit for the whole week of half-term, I didn't even think about it. They left money for shopping and food, the boys were happy and I loved being their stand-in 'mom'. I had a freedom there that I still didn't have at home. I could open a door without knocking. I could use the phone without being watched or listened to.

One night, after the boys were fed and bathed and tucked up in bed, we talked about their dad and I began thinking about my own father. He was in a play in the West End – at Wyndham's Theatre – called *The Dame of Sark* about the woman who was head of the feudal government of Sark, and who had stood up to the Germans when they occupied the Channel Islands in 1942. He'd told me about it in his latest letter. Slowly an idea formed . . . I knew where Dada was, and if I had a good enough reason, I could even telephone him.

The next morning, I got through to Directory Enquiries, who gave me the phone number for the theatre, and I called the box office. The show started at seven thirty, they said, so if I rang the stage door about half an hour earlier . . . Feeling sick with excitement I got the boys off to bed in good time, watched the hands of the clock move slowly round until they reached seven o'clock and then, my hand shaking, I dialled the number.

'Stage door, Wyndham's.'

'Oh, good evening, er – may I speak to Tony Britton, please?'

'Depends who wants him, luv.'

'His daughter.'

'Sorry, miss. Just a tick and I'll go and get him.'

I waited, listening to the slow sound of his feet receding, brisk footsteps returning, and then the clearing of a throat.

The next voice I heard was my father's.

I told him how I was thinking of coming with some

friends from school to see his play, which, from what he'd told me, sounded really interesting. Good idea, he said, and I must be sure to let him know when. And of course, after the show, we should go backstage . . .

As soon as I was back at school after half-term, I put the idea to our English teacher, Mrs Calf. I made it sound as educational as I could. It was a true story, the only time the Germans occupied British land. It was all about the Second World War, I told her, written by the well-known author William Douglas-Home with the veteran actress Wendy Hiller playing the Dame. And so it was arranged. During the days leading up to that fateful Friday I was a mass of nerves and one night I had a terrible dream. I was sitting in the stalls and, for some reason, Dada made his entrance through the auditorium, but he walked straight past me because he didn't know what I looked like.

There were seven of us in the end, plus Mrs Calf. We had never done anything like this before so it was a real treat, a total one-off, and as we bowled down the A40 in the minibus the others were as excited as I was. As for the play, I savoured every second, bursting with pride. All the other girls knew Tony Britton was my father and there was lots of nudging when he appeared on stage, and a great deal of twittering in the interval at the idea that we were going backstage. My excitement had now turned into terror. How would he know which one of these seventeen-year-olds was his daughter? The last time he'd seen me I was about a foot shorter. As I sat there in the dark in the second half, I thought about the other girls – did any of them look like me? In fact, I realized, with a sense of dread, we all looked pretty much the same.

The stage doorman escorted us up to my father's dressing room, and at the last minute I pushed myself to the front of our straggling line. As long as I was first through the door, and said, 'Dada,' he would know it was me. So that was what I did, and the moment he saw me, he reached out both arms and pulled me towards him.

My father treated us like royalty, grown-up royalty. He offered everyone a glass of wine and a cigarette from his packet of Rothman's, flicking his silver lighter to light each one. It was all so glamorous and sophisticated. My friends stood around in a state of shock, wonder and semi-flirtation, and left it to Mrs Calf to do the talking. After about twenty minutes we made our goodbyes and left, though not before I got another hug and a kiss. On the way home, as the minibus took us back to Amersham, I looked out into the night, unable to stop grinning. All those years of hearing about everybody else's dad and suddenly the dad they were talking about was mine.

The Dame of Sark proved a turning point. Whatever had been blocking the channels of communication was finally dislodged, and not long after I was invited to Dada's house in Chelsea for Sunday lunch. I knocked tentatively on the door and a boy of about fourteen opened it.

'Hello,' he said. 'I've had to scrub myself with Vim to meet you.' My half-brother, Jasper: the lovely Jas. For the first ten or twelve years of my life, I hadn't even known of his existence. In fact, Jas had opened the door not to one person but two: I had not gone unprotected into the lions' den. Holding my hand, both literally and metaphorically, was my boyfriend Nick.

Nick Smee and I had met through a friend from school called Tina. Tina was a friend of Nick's then girlfriend, who they knew was two-timing him. The plan was to get him off her and on to me, but first we had to meet.

This party they were going to would be the perfect

opportunity, Tina said. 'Don't worry, he's a really nice guy, honestly.' I didn't have any great hopes. My experiences on the romance front so far had not been particularly inspiring. Boys might have been keen on me – and they were – but the feeling wasn't mutual. My first kiss was on a skiing trip to Switzerland when I was fourteen, where the most radical thing you could do was drink Ribena by the pint. There we were, playing pool and listening to the Beatles on the jukebox when Trevor kissed me and I thought, This is cool – but it wasn't the thrill I'd been led to believe it would be. Over the years, I'd gone to the cinema with one or two – but no one who'd got my pulse racing. However, I did like a good party.

I wore a Laura-Ashley style dress (blue denim with a lot of white lace) and Biba shoes (peep-toe brown satin wedges with an ankle strap) – a combination that no one with any visual sense would put together, so I shouldn't have been that surprised when the guy with the beard started laughing the moment we were introduced. 'Well, if it isn't a milk-maid!' he chortled. He and his friend then fell about at this witty and perceptive remark. I didn't think it was funny at all, but the more I insisted I looked nothing like a milkmaid, the more they laughed.

The friend finally got bored and mooched off, leaving Nick free to discover that I wasn't anything like a milkmaid; on the contrary, I was really quite nice and quite interesting. He was tall with long, flowing hair, beard and moustache, not the Jason-King-style droopy moustache, but that was the general look. In fact, we fell for each other more or less immediately, and it became very serious very quickly. He was the first man who told me he loved me, and I have never forgotten just how wonderful it made me feel. We were sitting in his car outside The Bumbles saying goodnight one evening, and he just came out with it. He was a true romantic – I was his 'princess': he wrote me lovely letters and sent me little surprises, which would just drop through the letterbox, like a Snoopy dog and little books of Snoopy poetry.

Compared with other boys I'd gone out with, Nick was the height of sophistication, or he certainly seemed so to me, aged all of seventeen. He wasn't even a boy; he was a young man of twenty-two, with a proper job and a car. He worked in a gentlemen's outfitters in Amersham called Masculine and he always looked the business. He was adventurous and fun, and gave me my first real taste of freedom and the means of escape.

Shortly after we met I gave up working at the paper shop and Nick got me a Saturday job at Masculine. Life couldn't have been better. We'd spend the day flirting – even more fun when customers were there – and once the 'open' sign had been turned to 'closed', we'd roar off in his car, a two-litre soft-top Triumph Vitesse, to whatever the evening held. Sometimes he'd have made us a picnic, including a bottle of champagne, which he'd have sitting in an ice-bucket in the footwell. Nick was already on the up. By the following autumn he was managing the St Albans branch of Odile, a chain of unisex fashion shops that sold records at the back, so there was always trendy music playing. Getting there wasn't easy – it involved two buses, and I'd have to leave an hour and a half to be sure I wasn't late – but it was worth it. The other staff were good fun and then there were the customers themselves, young people like us who wanted reassurance and even help getting into jeans a size too small, accomplished by hooking a coat-hanger into the tag of the zip and heaving. I didn't get commission, just a wage, but it was nice to be the boss's golden girl.

Working in a shop was great for a while, but I never imagined it was going to be my life. When it came to a career, though, I hadn't a clue. Children of actors often become actors themselves, if only because everyone else assumes they will. I had no interest in that at all. At school I had been made to feel self-conscious about acting. I was certainly never cast in anything, my teachers making it clear that, as an actor's daughter, all I'd be doing was showing off.

My report from Little Turret (Upper Pollies, average age six years seven months) notes, 'Fifi can mime quite convincingly.' This is the only reference in all my school reports to anything in the drama line. Cherry had acted at her school and had been very good, but to me it felt faintly ridiculous, which was one reason I didn't care about not being in the school plays. Once I reached the sixth form, however, I became involved in the Christmas revue and the end-of-term revue, performing and writing scripts. These were basically comedy sketch shows, an extension of the jokes and gags my friend Sally Cree and I were always doing on the school coach where we'd hog the back seat. I remember one sketch involving a waiter, two customers and a murder. It was completely ridiculous but brought the house down.

I had always loved comedy and the sixties and seventies really were a golden age: Morecambe and Wise, Dick Emery, the Two Ronnies. My all-time favourite is Eric Sykes. He and Hattie Jacques consistently made us rock with laughter and he was a true childhood hero. I remember a sketch we did – pure Eric Sykes – which involved a cucumber. I'd walk on with this straight cucumber and say, 'Just look at that, ten inches long and not a kink in it.' This was for the annual school drama competition, and the judges tore into us, along the lines of 'disgusting, unamusing, puerile'. We thought we were brilliant, as did the rest of the school. We knew exactly what we were doing, but what the hell? It was a game to find out what we could get away with, how far we could go.

During the spring term of the upper sixth everyone had their interview with the careers' mistress when we had to turn up prepared with ideas. Mine were nurse, bank manager or river policeman, the last one being my favourite. Going up and down the river all day long would be rather lovely, I decided. Nurse had joined the list when I'd had my appendix out. As for bank manager, I'd discovered that I was rather good at managing my money. Earlier possibilities, by now rejected as childish, were elephant or dolphin trainer. George, of course, wanted me to follow him and become public-health inspector. 'A jolly good job for a woman,' he claimed. I don't remember now whether I included it in the list, but I suspect not.

The girl before me emerged from the careers office in a state of shock, chanting, 'I don't believe it, I don't believe it!' having been advised to give lampshade-making a try. Then it was me. One by one I went through my list.

'Thank you, Fern. Very interesting. Now, your father's an actor, isn't he?'

'Yes.'

'Wouldn't you like to be an actress?'

'No.'

'Well, what about a stage manager, then?'

'I don't know what a stage manager is.'

'I shouldn't worry about that. Here are some brochures for drama schools that offer stage management as an option. Fill them in, apply for the technical course, and let me know how you get on. I'm sure you'll do very well.'

On the way home on the coach I considered it. I was

vaguely aware that there must be people other than actors involved in putting on plays but I had no real sense of what those people might do.

My mother soon put me straight. 'It's a terrible job,' she said. 'At two o'clock in the afternoon they'll say to you, "We need an elephant here, fully trained, for five o'clock," and you've got to get it.'

'How fantastic!' I'd never forgotten the first time I'd gone through the pass door into the magical world that lay on the other side of the curtain. It was *The Magic Faraway Tree* and Narnia rolled into one.

The careers' mistress had given me three prospectuses. The syllabus offered by the Central School of Speech and Drama sounded the most interesting, so I didn't bother with the other two. Had I known just how slim my chances were of getting in, I wouldn't have been quite so cavalier. Every year Central got between two and three hundred applications for twelve places.

The form had to be countersigned by a parent, and Mummy thought it might be diplomatic to get Dada to do it rather than her. So I posted it off to him, and the next day he phoned. 'What's all this about the stage-management course? Why on earth don't you do the acting?'

'No, no, Dada, I can't. I really don't want to.' He didn't understand, but he signed anyway. In point of fact he was going against the advice he later gave Jas. 'You should only take up acting if you're burning for it,' he cautioned. 'Otherwise you won't cope with the knockbacks, the rejection.' But Jas *was* burning for it, and if he's experienced any rejection, he's yet to tell Big Sis.

For all her reservations, when it came to the interview Mummy prepared me well. She got me to memorize all my hobbies and achievements, and said, 'No matter what question they ask, always get back to the answer *you* want to give.'

The interview was in June 1975. I had just finished my A levels, and as Nick was working on the day, Tina came with me. We spent the morning shopping at Biba, then took a taxi up to Swiss Cottage; Tina looked after my Biba bags while I went in. The only real preparation I'd done was to make sure I looked great – Miss Selfridge from top to bottom. It never occurred to me that they wouldn't want me. I was 'Oh, this will be fine.'

Central – as it's always called – is built round the old Embassy Theatre where my father made his London début all those years ago. Cherry was still a baby and they were living in an attic bed-sit across the street. Mummy still remembers bumping the pram up and down four flights of stairs, washing nappies by hand and living on tins of baked beans. The Embassy is still a working theatre, but only for students.

Central was then the biggest of the London drama schools. It not only taught acting and stage management, but also ran a speech-therapy course and a drama teachers' course where Dawn French and Jennifer Saunders met – though we didn't overlap.

The interview was held in a rehearsal room. When my name was called I walked in to be faced with about seven people sitting at a trestle table and in front of them this one little chair. The first question took me completely by surprise.

'What television programmes do you watch?'

The truth was that I didn't watch much television. I was too busy either working or going out with Nick. What I thought was, Oh, shit, I don't know. What I said was, 'Documentaries, drama and comedy,' while looking suitably earnest. The only programme I mentioned by name was *Coronation Street*.

Next question: 'What films have you seen recently?'

'To be honest, I don't have much time to go to the cinema. The last one was probably a Clint Eastwood.'

'And what newspapers do you like to read?'

'It's probably not the right answer, but I only really like tabloids!'

By now I was on a hiding to nothing and I knew it. My only chance was to make them laugh. One way and another I had spent most of my childhood and teenage years being embarrassed, and how do you cover your embarrassment? By laughing. And, goodness knows, I was embarrassed now.

And so the torture continued.

'Have you done any amateur dramatics?'

'No.'

'Have you ever done any stage management?'

'No.'

'Have you . . .?'

'No.'

'Have you . . .?'

'No.'

Then there was silence as they looked over my application form. Eventually someone said, 'It says here that your father is Tony Britton.'

Finally a question I could answer. 'Yes,' I said.

'Which Tony Britton?'

It was the ultimate put-down. According to the rules of Equity, the actors' trade union, there can only be one actor with that name. If a young actor coming into the business happens to have the same name as an existing actor, they have to change it. And I thought, If this is to tell me that using my father's name to open doors won't work, fair enough I'll take that on board. I never mentioned him again until four years later when I worked with a director called Jonathan Lynn. One day he came up to me looking puzzled. 'Are you Tony Britton's daughter?'

Asked straight out like that I was hardly going to deny it. I'm incredibly proud of him, and very proud to have him as my father. 'Well . . . yes, I am, actually.'

'Why didn't you tell me?' Jonathan went on. 'I've just written a play for him!'

When I met up with Tina after the interview I was not quite the chirpy bird she'd left at the entrance. From the sheer numbers of would-be students I'd seen milling around, I'd realized that the odds were stacked against me. As for the interview, it had not gone quite as I'd planned. In fact, I had made a complete idiot of myself (though I still didn't see why I should be expected to know much about stage management. Surely that was what they were going to teach me).

Two weeks later the fateful letter plopped onto the door-mat and I opened it with a sinking heart. I could no longer live on hope. Mechanically I began to read. 'Dear Miss Britton . . .' Only when I came to 'We are glad to offer you a place' did I grasp what it was. I'd been accepted! A grin, a genuine, honest-to-goodness, split-your-face grin, was spreading from ear to ear. It was like, 'Wow! This is my new life. I'm leaving this place!' It was 'Wow, drama school!' Glamorous or what! And with the letter in my hand I saw then how perceptive the careers' mistress had been. She had found something that was not academic yet would interest and excite me and, most importantly, I knew I could do because I was practical and organized! (Although I didn't know quite how practical and organized I was.) It was perfect for me. Absolutely perfect.

'Mummy!' I called upstairs. 'I've done it! Central have accepted me!'

'Marvellous, darling. Why don't you put on the kettle and we'll have a nice cup of tea?'

The summer between leaving school and your next step is the last summer of your life when you have no responsibilities. Although, as it turned out, I had some, but not many.

Our neighbours, the Davieses, had an apartment in the Algarve and invited me to spend the summer with them as a kind of nanny to help look after Carl's baby brother André, who was then about five. Naturally I said, 'Yes, please,' and 'Thank you very much.' I was to join them after my eighteenth birthday, on 17 July 1975.

On the previous Sunday Mummy had given me a very nice party. It was a perfect English summer's day so we were out in the garden at The Bumbles and had all the aunts and uncles, except Uncle Pete, Mummy's younger brother, whom we hardly ever saw because he was a seismologist, concerned with searching for oil in the furthest reaches of the world. In fact, Uncle Pete's absence was nothing to do with being abroad – he was very ill with lung cancer, but I didn't appreciate just how ill. In those days cancer was a taboo word and people generally kept such things from you.

On the seventeenth itself no special celebration was planned – I just wanted to spend the evening with Nick. Nice as the idea of summer in Portugal was, I knew I was going to miss him horribly. As we drove up to the house in Chorleywood, which he shared with his widowed father, he went beep-beep on his horn.

'What did you do that for?' I asked.

'I'm just happy!' he said, flashing me a smile. But when

I opened the door to the lounge, I was deafened by shouts of '*Surprise!*' and '*Happy birthday!*' There were balloons everywhere and all my friends. Needless to say, I burst into tears, overcome by the thought that this nice man would do this for me . . . And we had a great party. Tina, who was a really good cook, had done the buffet and it was lovely, in the way only teenagers pretending to be grown-up know how.

That summer was overshadowed by the death when I was in Portugal of my uncle Pete. The last time I had seen him was two years previously – still just as I remembered him, tall and thin and always at the other end of a cigarette. I had never known him well because most of the time he was abroad – another of those distant but glamorous figures in my life. But he was a wonderful sender of postcards, which for some reason he always signed, 'from the intrepid explorer Johnson'. It was to him I owed the bear named after him – he'd actually belonged to my sister originally, but as she already had Teddy, I snaffled Johnson.

My A-level results came through in August, sent out to Portugal. Luckily my place at Central was unconditional, so the fact that I'd done abysmally didn't matter. Abysmal barely describes it: I had failed them all. With hindsight it's not that surprising. My revision timetable had been a masterpiece of time management, and I'd spent hours perfecting it – so much so that I barely got on to the revision itself. The first thing I did was write a grovelling letter of apology to the person I had really let down: my mother. I knew I hadn't done well, but I hadn't expected to fail everything. At the end I wrote: 'Oh, and could you please send off the form for my grant, not that I expect I'll get one now!' But I was wrong. I did. And thank goodness, because I don't think I could have gone to Central without it.

The Davieses were very kind and my summer in Portugal

was lovely – swimming-pool, beach, general lazing about and lots of laughter, but there was the sadness of Uncle Pete and I missed Nick like crazy. He was my first true love and I had left him behind. What could I have been thinking of? But every post brought something with his handwriting on it, including little books of *Love is* . . . and every time I heard Cat Stevens singing, 'Wild World' my eyes filled with tears. It was our song. Little did I know that he was already breaking my heart.

A quality that Phillip Schofield and I share with doctors and under-takers is a black sense of humour. Never far beneath the surface, it bubbles over when the tension becomes too great, and suddenly we're helpless with laughter. It's a safety valve. It helps us cope with the insanity of the job, with the insanity of life.

On This Morning we get more than our share of hard interviews, people who have very difficult lives: maybe they are dying, or maybe they have just watched their child die. And I'm often asked, 'How can you do something like that and the next moment be falling about when somebody mentions horn or pork, or how you quite fancy a muffin?' The important thing for us is that we treat people with respect. And I believe that we do. These ridiculous remarks aren't scripted or planned. They just fall out of our mouths and then we're helpless and it's 'Let's go to the break!' Sadness, happiness, rudeness, ridiculousness – sometimes we look at each other and think how lucky we are to be doing this now. In the olden days the executive producer would have marched onto the floor and given us the sack. We're no longer the only ones with the tendency to 'corpse', as it's called, but it's fair to say that we were the pioneers, and so far we have got away with it, with no one wagging fingers. Recently we were hysterical for two and a half minutes non-stop. Apparently it gets the endorphins up, and if laughter makes you live longer then we must've added another ten years to our lives.

Phillip has definitely got a naughty pixie streak in him. You can see when the magnesium is lit: there's this bright light in his eyes and I know he's ready. It makes me go just one step further . . .

Now it's like a dare between us, like playing chicken. We bounce off each other and get as close as we can.

Of course, when the guys on the floor know you're going, that's the end. You can see them begin to shake behind the cameras, and you can hear directly in your ear what's happening in the gallery: there's the scrape when the director pushes his chair right back to get away from the mike, and he's even been known to go into the corridor because he's laughing so much.

Really, it's only an extension of everyday life, like when you visit someone in hospital. The situation can be far from optimistic, but seconds later you're falling about because you've noticed that the consultant on the gynae ward is called Mr Studd, or the urologist is called Mr Tinkle. (Both true . . .) Laughter and tears are the two ways humans have of releasing tension, and at the beginning of an interview I have no idea how it will affect me. There was a fantastic man who told us the story of his gruesome childhood. He'd been abused and beaten and starved at home but – like so many children – he remained full of hope. On the morning of his birthday, he went downstairs and his mother said, 'Come with me, I've got something for you.' He followed her, but instead of handing him a present she put his hand through the mangle. I had read the research in the car coming in that morning, so I knew what to expect, but hearing it from him, hearing his voice break with the pain that had stayed with him down the years, and seeing him weep in front of me, I wept too. With a story as harrowing as that, you can't help it, at least I can't. I don't remember now what followed it – inevitably something lightweight because that's how the show works. Shakespeare knew all about it. Comic relief, it's called. From light to dark and back again.

Stage managing Guys and Dolls, *1977*

5. Grubby Tech

'Hello, Princess.'

At the sound of Nick's voice on the other end of the phone, whatever suspicions, or feelings of jealousy, I'd been nursing were banished, and the month we had together before I started at Central was a time of unalloyed happiness. It was because of Nick that I didn't make a fuss about not living in London. That was what I'd always imagined happening, of course – a room in a trendy flat in Primrose Hill with other students. It wasn't to be: Mummy and George said no. I tried to explain that it wasn't like studying something ordinary, like typing or bookkeeping, that I'd be working on shows late into the night, returning home on the last tube or even later. And how was I to get from Chalfont and Latimer station to Three Trees? (We had basically left The Bumbles by now.) It was a good mile away, and the lane was unlit and overhung with trees. Did they really want me walking back at gone midnight? Financially it didn't make much odds. The grant came to around three hundred pounds a term, which just about covered my season ticket. Although I kept my head above water, I was always skint.

What it did mean, of course, was that much of the time I stayed at Nick's. He would pick me up at Chorleywood station, then run me back there in the morning. Sometimes he'd even drive all the way to Swiss Cottage to get me. I see now that it was asking for trouble: I came to rely on him, making myself dependent and therefore vulnerable, because he didn't always turn up. Naturally there was an excuse but, as time went on, his excuses began to wear very thin. In fact they became totally transparent.

He was a good-looking young man with a car and a regular girlfriend who was regularly not around. Perhaps, too, he was jealous, though he had no reason to be, yet from the outside my life must have appeared much more glamorous than it actually was. We were only twelve on my course, an equal split between girls and boys. We didn't mix with the trainee drama teachers or speech therapists, who were much more numerous. Once we started working on plays, we were wholly involved with the actors, but they were a different breed, considered a definite liability and to be kept clear of. The truth was very simple: I loved Nick with a passion, and when he let me down, as he did again and again, I didn't go seeking revenge by playing the field myself, I would curl up in a ball and sob until my eyes were baboon-bottom pink. I was paralysed, overwhelmed with intense, unremitting jealousy.

I could never get hold of him on the phone and it didn't take a genius to work out there was somebody else on the scene. Only when I saw him with his old girlfriend outside the station one evening did I realize who it was. I ran towards them and took a swing at her with my tool-bag, the stage-management equivalent of a briefcase, which contained a monkey wrench, hammer, screw-driver, hacksaw, Stanley knife and tape-measure.

Dark days followed. I would cry for no reason, claiming it was exhaustion. My friends were worried but I'd fob them off, saying that the constant travelling up and down to London was doing me in. When I went to the college doctor – for something else entirely – he was so kind and concerned about me that I broke down completely. Because

1. My parents made an incredibly glamorous couple. My mother had the hour-glass figure of a *Vogue* model.

2. Living the film-star lifestyle before I was born: Mummy, Dada and Cherry (*second, third and fourth from right*).

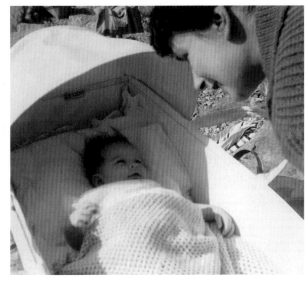

3. In the garden of Denbigh Road, Ealing, a few weeks old. Poor Mummy didn't have an easy time: I was a breech birth.

4. With Mummy and Cherry in an exotic location. One thing we were never short of was holidays, thanks to Nana and her money-making cruises.

5. Both my grandparents fought in the First World War. Here, Prampa, my father's father, poses for a snap with fellow officers in Taranto, Italy, 1919.

6. Uncle Pete and Mummy pose on their new bicycles in the garden of Segamat as Nana and Grandpop hold them steady. Shortly after this picture was taken in 1939, my grandfather returned to Malaya, only to be interned by the Japanese at Changi.

7. Uncle Paul, Grandpop, Uncle Pete and Adek (Mummy) holding Mickey the cat *c.* 1938.

8. The wonderful swing seat at Steeple: Mummy, Dada, me and Cherry. This picture is proof that Dada would sometimes be there, but I have no memory of it.

9. 1962 on my blue and yellow trike. My love of cycling begins ...

10. Mummy, Nana and me in Casablanca, on one of Nana's cruises *c.* 1962.

11. Cherry and Dada at the seaside, before I was born.

12. My childhood was full of wonderful British beach holidays: here I joined family friends the Canns on the Isle of Wight. (*Left to right*: Susie Cann, me, Ricky and their mother Betty.)

13. Cherry, me and Nana at Looe in Cornwall, the perfect little seaside town and my favourite place. The smell never changed: fish, seaweed and Ambre Solaire.

14. With Mummy and Cherry in the sitting room at Steeple, the first home I remember.

15. My sister and I pose with our cats Ellie and Ginger as our stepfather George looks on. At fourteen I had caught up with my sister in terms of height.

16. Mummy in the garden of The Bumbles, *c.* 1973 with our family dog. Even in a hand-knitted suit and flat shoes, she still manages to look glamorous.

17. George mends a puncture at the start of an epic European holiday.

18. My stepfather would do anything to avoid going to Germany. Here we are in Austria on our way down to Italy.

19. Mummy and me back in Looe at the end of the sixties.

20. Another of George's epic trips took us to Rome when I was fourteen.

21. Cherry and me in the garden of Three Trees in the early 1970s – so chic!

22. Sally Cree and me in Leningrad on a school trip, 1974. Sally and I devoted our energies to writing and performing for the Christmas revue.

23. Out of school I was really quite trendy, though you wouldn't think so from this, taken around the time I applied for Central.

24. Larking around on the last day at school, I'm sitting on top of my friend Jackie Edwards: my body, her feet, her hands.

25. My first love, Nick Smee (*right*) as he was when I first met him in 1975: a dedicated follower of fashion.

26. … and three years later in Cambridge when our romance was on its last legs.

27. Although not an undergraduate, I nevertheless learnt the basics of punting.

28. In Portugal, on nanny duty in 1975.

that's how it is with depression: the minute somebody's nice to you, you're on the floor. And depression it was, he said, and put me on Valium.

There came a point when I knew that, for all the passion, for all his many good qualities, I'd have to end it with Nick once and for all. I still melted at the sound of his voice on the phone, saying, 'Hello, Princess,' but I remember lying in the bath and it was like a light-bulb going on: no one has the right to make me feel like this. I hopped on the train and took myself off to Brighton for a few days, found myself some digs, slept on the beach in the sun, had fish-and-chip suppers in my room and came back feeling renewed.

And I'll always be grateful to him. The agony of betrayal by your first love can never be matched, and once Nick and I were finished, it was as if all the jealousy in me had been played out. I vowed that no one would ever make me feel like that again and nobody has. If a man said he didn't want me, or perhaps didn't even have the balls to say it but made it obvious that I wasn't enough for him, I'd say, 'Fine. Goodbye.' I'd been given a very strong inoculation and from then on I was immune.

The first few days at Central had been terrifying. We had all recently emerged from school where life is governed by rules and routine. 'Why do you sit in the same places?' Mr Streuli, our head of department, wanted to know. 'Why do you feel you need that security?' But we did, and we stayed in more or less the same places throughout the year – three tables arranged in a horseshoe around a blackboard. I remember so clearly that first day and the welcoming talk. You sit there, knowing that these strangers are soon going to be your friends, and that you'll have some of the best laughs of your life with them. But you also think that every single one knows more than you do, has more experience than you have. You, meanwhile, are zero: no confidence, no knowledge, no nothing.

At the end of two years we'd be qualified to work as assistant stage managers, but after that the sky was the limit: any branch of the theatre would be open to us.

An ASM, as you are called, is the lowest of the low in a theatre company. You are there to do what the director tells you, what the stage manager tells you, what the actors tell you. You run errands, make cups of tea. Your job goes from sweeping the stage to sourcing props. Not only do you have to find whatever it is, you have to bargain on the fee because your budget is tiny. Anyone who has been a stage manager could do *The Apprentice*, no problem. You can never throw a hissy fit. If the leading actor sticks his hand up your skirt you have to smile sweetly and let it go. *Nothing* can upset an actor. As an ASM, if you're doing the job right, you go unnoticed. If you *do* get noticed it means you're doing it wrong.

Much of this can only be absorbed over time. Inevitably there was a certain amount of theory, starting with the history of theatre right back to Grecian times and right up to the present.

Then came the practical side, with tongue-and-groove and dovetail joints and how to put up flats. A flat is the pretend wall of the set, basically a wooden frame with painted canvas stretched across. To make a series of flats look like the wall of a room, they have to be joined together, using sash cord. Cleats are set into the top of the flat, so you have to flip the cord up, get it round the cleat, catch it, then tie it at the bottom. During a scene change you might have two minutes to get all the flattage out and the next scene up, so time is crucial and you can't afford to miss in your throwing efforts, so we'd practise and practise.

We learnt how to put up a set, how to take down a set, how to build a set, paint a set, wallpaper a set. We learnt how to measure a set to make sure it would fit the space available – critical if you're touring. We learnt how to read the floor plans of theatres. Some might have the wide opening familiar in old-fashioned theatres called the proscenium arch, which would usually have curtains (or tabs, as they're called). We'd work out the sightlines of all the entrances and exits so that if an actor was waiting in the wings he couldn't be seen by the audience. Working this out can only be achieved through trial and error, by getting another ASM to sit in the stalls, or the upper circle, saying, 'I can see you, I can still see you . . . now I can't,' then marking that place with white tape.

We learnt to mark out a rehearsal room, putting coloured tape on the floor to show exactly how big the set is, where the doors will be, where the furniture will go. If it's a three-act play you'd use three different colours, so blue for Act One, red for Act Two, yellow for Act Three or whatever. We'd learn how to fly things. In those days, particularly on tour, it was all done by pulleys. Now the ropes are computerized. You'd have to haul up scaffolding bars heavy with lighting or scenery or cloth by hand. It would take three of us in a line and I remember one day a girl let go and I flew up ten feet in the air, thinking, Fuck, I'm going to die.

We learnt how to set up a props table at either side of the stage, exactly as the actor wanted it. Maybe there's a plate of sandwiches. So who gets to make the sandwiches? Correct. Matches would always be set with the box almost closed but the matches sticking out so they didn't have to fiddle with them. To conform to fire regulations there had to be wet sand in the bottom of any ashtray if there was smoking on stage. As the ASM you had to put fresh water on the props tables in both wings so that actors could have a drink if they needed one. Then there were the 'personals', props they needed in their dressing room to take on stage: a handbag, wedding ring, driving licence or keys. It all had to be checked before every performance by the ASM – after that it was the actor's responsibility. Everything was about organization and lists. Lists, lists and more lists.

As we were getting to grips with all this, the actors were rehearsing their plays. During the first-year shows we operated as minions for the second-year stage-management students, learning as we went. Once elevated to the second year, we were involved from the start, exactly as you would be in an actual show. We'd have read the script, been at rehearsals and worked like a proper stage-management team. We'd each be allocated a specific job: wardrobe, lighting, sound, stage manager, deputy stage manager (DSM) and ASM. Each show would run to three or four performances.

It was a very good system. By the end there was nothing you didn't know. To build up our strength (all that hauling on ropes and shifting furniture) we joined in music and movement classes with the actors. We learnt how to trust each other with falling-back exercises – you'd close your eyes, fall back and know that somebody would catch you. We learnt how to give each other massages to deal with the unaccustomed aches and pains. We joined in voice classes, learning to project: like actors we had to be heard from the back of the stalls. No use saying, 'Watch out, number-one lighting bar is about to fall on your head!' if you've the vocal range of a mouse. As for the actors . . .

'In real life,' we were taught, 'actors are perfectly normal

92

people who can open doors, turn on taps, take photographs. They can even answer the phone. But as soon as an actor is on stage he can do none of these things, and when he can't do them, it's your fault.' And it was brilliant. You think, OK. I accept that. So whenever they were going mad and shouting at us, you'd just think, Ah, yes. Actors ... It was like a disability, as in 'Ah, bless, they can't help it, poor things.' As for us, we were known as 'grubby techs' because that was exactly what we were: backstage in a theatre is like being in a dust factory.

Carrie Fisher was a student at Central when I was there, though she left a year early to do Princess Leia in *Star Wars*. With her mother being Debbie Reynolds and her father Eddie Fisher, Hollywood was always going to claim her – she had already been in *Shampoo* with Warren Beatty. She always wore a cloth cap and tried to pull it down over her head, and was generally quite grungy, in the don't-whatever-you-do-mention-Debbie-Reynolds kind of way, but because of that she had an air of fabulous glamour and mystery.

Then there was Roberta Taylor, who now is Gina Gold in *The Bill*. She was always sweet and kind and so bloody good. We still meet up occasionally at dos, and it's always lovely to see her, and her husband Peter Guinness. But then there were far too many others who I haven't seen since we parted company, so many of whom were super-talented.

Looking back, the range of plays we did over those two years was incredible. Chekhov's *The Three Sisters*, *Uncle Vanya* and *The Cherry Orchard*, Ibsen's *The Dolls House*, Pinter's *The Homecoming* and Sherriff's *Journey's End*. Then there were musicals. *Guys and Dolls* was our final production and for that I netted the job of stage manager, and, once again, it was like, Wow! I've got the gig! Mrs Big at last!

The interest in musical theatre came directly from the head of the acting course George Hall, a wonderful man who believed in giving us as broad a spectrum of experience as possible. He loved musical theatre and loved old music hall and he introduced us to Mrs Shufflewick (in real life Rex Jameson), one of the true music-hall greats, who died a few years later.

Guys and Dolls was an amazing show to bow out on. From a stage-management perspective it was highly complex with live music to add to the usual mix. My prompt copy – the copy of the script on which everything related to the technical side of the show is written in, the Bible for any production – was a work of art, every colour under the sun and more notes and instructions on it than any I had later.

Even when you're working with fellow students theatre discipline has to be preserved. You might have actors as mates and sit together over cups of coffee, and they might be Cathy or Bill in the pub over the road, but once you're working it's Miss Thing and Mr Thing. It doesn't matter how senior or junior an actor is, that's how they're referred to, either in person, or in calls made over the Tannoy. On one level it was practical – but it also meant that everyone knew their place. I would hear directors (the gods of the theatre world), having listened to actors complain that their lines had been cut or their part diminished in some way or another, say, 'There is no such thing as a small part, only a small actor,' or 'Twinkle, twinkle, little star, what a fucking bore you are.'

The theatre, of course, is where 'darling' comes from, and I'm a real 'darling' user. It's easier to say to an actor, 'Darling, just move back a couple of feet, will you, before that light falls on your head,' than 'Mr Fortescue, would you mind . . .' particularly if Mr Fortescue is a twenty-year-old pain in the rear end and you can barely remember his name. The funny thing is that, in spite of my 'darling' habit, people don't think of me as having a theatre background. Guests come on the show and they say to Phillip, 'Saw you in *Dr Doolittle*,' or during an interview an actor will turn away and start talking to Phillip with 'Now, *you* know about the stage,' and I think, Yeah, mate. So do I.

My two wonderful years were up. All I had to show for it was a small piece of paper: 'This is to certify that Fern Britton, having completed a course of training extending over 2 years, is awarded a diploma in stage management, 18 June 1977, John Allen, Principal, Peter Streuli, Director of Technical Course.'

I had loved doing *Guys and Dolls* just as I'd loved the whole course. I didn't have time to get too emotional because a couple of weeks before we left a few theatre companies did the rounds, looking for cheap ASMs. One of these was the Cambridge Theatre Company and they took two of us, me and Michael Townsend, who had previously been Michael Langton: ASM or actor, the Equity rule remains the same. Not surprisingly, that wasn't a problem with Fern Britton.

Lying in bed this morning, watching the dawn light flicker across the ceiling, Phil knew I was awake, as he always does.

'I'm so excited,' he said.

'Mm,' I replied. We were doing Paul O'Grady together after This Morning. He's a great chat-show host and a really nice man, but excited? No.

'My pigs are coming! They're arriving at four o'clock!'

This is his third batch, ten or eleven of them, but they'll all catch up with each other.

He started with just two, kept them for nine months then killed, cured and salted them, collar, joints, doing everything himself. Our piggies have a nice life. They live on the side of a hill in the woods in huge pens. They're fed on specially formulated natural pellets but they also tuck into what's available in woodland that's been there for thousands of years. There's beech and oak and hazel and blackthorn, which for them means beech nuts, acorns, cobs and sloes. Part of the wood is cherry and we get a lot of wild morello cherries, so they're eating what their ancestors would have had. Although there aren't many of them, we don't give them names. That would be a bit much, even for me. Phil does talk to them, though. I hear him wandering around, saying, 'You'll make a nice ham ... You'll turn into some nice bacon, and you're a bit little at the moment but you'll be fine in a few months.' The ones up there now will be ready for Christmas.

And it's not only Phil. Just the other week I heard Winnie telling one of the piggies how he would soon be bacon. And I'm fine with that. As Phil says, 'If one day my daughters turn on me and say, "Dad, I'm not going to eat meat any more," I'll say, "No problem. At least you've seen how to do it properly."' Food is not only Phil's livelihood, it's his life, and he's been shooting both predators and game since he was a boy in rural Kent where – growing up next to a farm – it was a natural progression from the catapult. Give him a shotgun, a full moon, a clear sky and an empty freezer and he's in clover.

Above all, my husband is a countryman, and where game is concerned, he shoots it, cooks it, eats it. According to Bob the window-cleaner, who tried some unwittingly, Phil's barbecued grey squirrel is a delicacy reminiscent of duck. The children are already under his influence: an evening's shooting with Daddy is greatly to be preferred to a bicycle ride with Mum. I have no fears on any count. Not only is Phil an expert shot, but the welfare of all animals – farm or game – is of paramount importance to him.

Our wood is Phil's dream come true. One morning, shortly after we moved, Phil was taking Winnie to school when he saw a man nailing a for-sale sign to a post. He stopped and said, 'How much do you want?' The man told him, and Phil just said, 'I'll have it.' The man said, 'OK,' and took the sign down there and then. Naturally he asked the man why he was selling.

'Well,' he said, 'I've got two shops, one in Slough and one in Newbury, and over the past year and a half I've been held up twice at gunpoint, I've been robbed, my wife's just left me, so all in all I've had it. I'm selling up to go and live in Cornwall.'

Over the next few months Phil turned into a tree-feller, fence-builder and hedge-layer. Then he put some pheasants in and finally the piggies arrived. Twenty-six acres of pure bliss, that's my view. Once the girls get back from school, I'll get out the Land Rover and we'll put on our wellies and go and see the new arrivals. I'll make a nice Thermos of tea and we'll have a picnic. The bluebells are out at *the moment and while the girls scamper around gathering armfuls for the kitchen, I'll sit there quietly letting the deep peace of the wood soak into me.*

Cast and crew of The Unvarnished Truth, *1978*

6. Privilege and Magic

The Cambridge Theatre Company had nothing to do with the West End theatre of the same name, it was simply a touring company based in the city of Cambridge.

My interview had been with the production manager, Rodger Neate. To make an impact, I wore a very fifties-looking outfit – big swirly red skirt, tight little bodice and halter-neck top. Whether or not it made any difference I have no idea, but it certainly gave me confidence: I thought I was the bee's knees.

CTC's artistic director was Jonathan Lynn, whom I'd seen as an actor in *The Liver Birds* and Jack Rosenthal's series about London taxi drivers, *The Knowledge*. Later he would became famous as co-writer for *Yes, Minister* and *Yes, Prime Minister* with Antony Jay, before going on to Hollywood, to direct, among other things, *Nuns on the Run* and *The Whole Nine Yards*. Touring on its own didn't really make money: the idea was to take a show on the road, and – if it went down well – 'come into town', as it's called, bring it into the West End. There, our team would stay in place for a week or two to bed it in, then hand over to a permanent West End crew. None of us wanted to be stuck in London.

The first show I did was *The Deep Blue Sea*, by Terence Rattigan. Written in the early fifties, it's about a married woman who tries to commit suicide when her affair with a younger man goes wrong. It's a powerful play, emotionally highly charged, and the cast was equally strong, with Sheila Hancock, Clive Francis, Maggie Jones – now Blanche in

Coronation Street – and a very young Lyndsey Duncan.

We rehearsed at the Irish Club in Eaton Square, Belgravia. It was the first week of July and the big thing that summer was Virginia Wade winning Wimbledon. Next door to the rehearsal room someone had installed a television set so, whenever we could, we'd go in to watch. I can remember it all so clearly, everyone crowding round, the sun pouring in through the high windows, great shafts of light filled with dancing dust, the thud of ball against racquet and the roar of the crowd.

Far from feeling in alien territory and out of my depth, I felt completely at home. Central had taught me everything I needed to know, and the stage manager I was working with was bang on, so if ever there were moments when I thought, I don't know what to do, she was there ahead of me. Everyone knew, of course, that I was a new girl, but I was a quick learner and I wanted to be good and I wanted to be liked. Most importantly, I didn't want to fuck up. Appropriately enough for my first tour with the CTC, our first stop was two weeks in Cambridge itself, at the Arts Theatre, where Sheila Hancock proved a wonderful introduction to all that's best about actors. As ASMs, Mike and I were earning practically nothing, and on a punting trip that had been arranged for the whole company, Sheila paid our share so we, too, could partake of the whole experience – the wine and the cheese and the strawberries, as well as hire of the punts.

The Irish Club, I would soon discover, was very smart in terms of rehearsal space. Usually we made do with dusty church halls where the floor would soon look as if a mother-and-toddler group had been let loose, criss-crossed with every conceivable colour of tape – but only between nine and five. At the end of the day it would have to be removed, in readiness for the badminton, or the Scouts, or whoever had booked it after us. The next day we'd be back, marking up the floor, plugging in the tea urn, nipping to the corner shop for the milk, all before the actors arrived. We'd have to make sure there were enough 2ps in the petty cash for the phone, and coins of larger denomination to feed the actors' parking meters: if they got a ticket it would, naturally, be our fault.

Once the actors were rehearsing, my job switched to hunting for props, which usually meant trawling junk shops and street markets. *The Deep Blue Sea* being set in the fifties, props I needed to find included a period-accurate tin of Cherry Blossom boot polish, and a proper 1950s (whistling) kettle. *Uncle Vanya* proved more of a challenge as we needed a Bath chair and an ear trumpet – turn-of-the-century – both of which I eventually found in the Wellcome Medical Museum. Even with well-honed bargaining skills, some props were too expensive for me to get hold of the real thing, and I remember several happy hours spent hand-painting a map of Russia. When I presented it to the actor, he said, 'Is this it?'

Not being an actor yet being with actors is the perfect arrangement, as you have all the pluses with few of the minuses. However well a script might read on the page, when you see these people bring it to life it's sheer magic. Then there's the technical run when you go into the theatre for the first time and see the set with full lights, full props, full furniture. Suddenly the actresses appear, unrecognizable in their wigs, tight bodices and long, flowing skirts. Sitting in the auditorium in the dark – the stage glowing in front of you – is the most privileged and magical thing imaginable. Your responsibility is to the actors, to make them feel comfortable and safe. You have no responsibility for their performances, but you have all the fun of the fair: the laughter and tension as they stumble through the awful 'tech runs', which can go on for ever, then the first dress rehearsal, then the final dress rehearsal, and suddenly it's the first night . . .

Unlike the actors, who were often cast for just one show – which might lead to intense insecurity and rivalries – stage management remained as a team. Once you'd found your place and learnt to trust the people around you, why change? Actors came and went; we were part of the fabric.

For the next couple of years, this was my life. Every tour was enjoyable for different reasons. The moment I arrived in a new town I'd book myself a driving lesson: most of the actors had cars and I'd seen the difference being mobile made to your sense of freedom. My skill as an organizer was soon put to use outside the confines of the theatre. I became head of entertainments, in charge of setting up a weekly company outing when we were on the road. 'Right,' I'd say, after the first run-through at Aberystwyth. 'After the show on Thursday we'll have a barbecue on the beach and fireworks.' It might only be spring but I knew a shop that had fireworks at any time of the year.

There were rituals wherever we went. At Aberystwyth you had to walk along the promenade as far as you could and kick the metal railing at the end for luck – it was called kicking the bar. At Whitby – the home of Dracula – we had to run up the steps to the church. We never played Whitby (it didn't have a theatre) but it wasn't far from Richmond in Yorkshire, which was a regular stop on the CTC tour. (I had discovered *Dracula*, the original Bram Stoker novel, when I was about fourteen and Cherry and I spent a wonderful Christmas together at Three Trees, drinking George's port and reading it aloud to each other.) We'd go in a convoy of actors' cars and I got everyone to be Dracula's dog, running up the steps from the beach and into the church. Tourists would watch in amazement as this mixed bag of adults charged up the hill like overgrown children.

On Saturday we'd do the get-out, load up the lorry and, to save my train fare (which we were given in cash), I'd often travel in the pantechnicon. There was a little bed in the cab behind the driver and I'd sleep for a bit, then clamber down to have big mugs of tea and lorry-drivers' sandwiches at transport caffs, arriving at the next theatre early on Sunday morning. By nine we'd be doing the get-in.

The actors would turn up on Monday afternoon, ready for the opening that night. Although the set would have been carefully designed to fit every theatre on the tour, they'd need to see how far away the audience would be, and how long it took them to get from their dressing room to the stage. There might be a practical problem, such as getting through the wings in full periwig or bustle. If there was a blackout rather than a curtain, they needed to know where their exit was, while stage management had to be ready with a light on the floor so they could see where they were going – more difficult than you think after the brightness of the stage. It recently happened to my father: because Dada couldn't see the torch, he fell into the orchestra pit, the audience hearing a crash followed by 'Fuck!' He hurt himself really quite badly, damaging his shoulder, knee and hip. Thankfully this kind of accident never happened when I was in charge, but I always had a contingency plan just in case . . .

We'd usually be out in repertoire, which meant we'd play *Charley's Aunt* at the beginning of the week and *Uncle Vanya* at the end. So you'd be rehearsing one show in the morning and playing another that night, and at times I thought I was going bonkers. One day I went to post a letter to my mother, walked out of the theatre and round the corner to where I knew the post-box was, but it wasn't there. Where was it? Slowly the penny dropped. I'd thought I was in Darlington when I was actually in Poole!

During my time with the CTC, making my way up from Assistant Stage Manager to Deputy Stage Manager, I worked on *The Matchmaker* (Thornton Wilder), *Charley's Aunt* (Brandon Thomas), *The Inspector Calls* (JB Priestley), *Uncle Vanya* (Chekhov) and several others I can no longer remember.

On the whole the CTC actors were a pleasure to work with, but occasionally pleasure would turn into misery. As an ASM, as well as the coffee and sandwich runs, I remember being 'on the book' during rehearsals for Samuel Beckett's *Waiting for Godot* with Bryan Pringle and Dudley Sutton, where your job is simply to prompt actors with their lines. The script of *Godot* is incredibly complicated, going round and round in circles, and unless the actors are word perfect, you can easily get lost. In addition, the cast and director were all men so it was very intense and male. As for rehearsals, everything was deathly earnest. I remember how Dudley, in particular, took to exploring the text via selective memories of his childhood. 'It's like when I was a boy,' he'd explain. 'I'd go down to the wood and do a big poo, then return a few days later to see it decomposing'.

Waiting for Godot is known for its pauses. So there'd be this silence and, after a bit, I'd give whoever it was the line I assumed they'd forgotten. Then would come the scream: 'I'M GIVING A PAUSE. UNDERSTAND? THIS. IS. BECKETT!'

So, OK. Fine. In the theatre an overlong pause is known

as a Macready pause, after the Victorian actor-manager whose speciality it was and which we'd learnt about in drama school.

So the Macready pauses would go on and on – I decided to let them run rather than have my head blown off. But then I'd be jerked into life by 'LINE!'

It was so tedious that at one stage I dropped off, waking suddenly at an imperious 'LINE!' at which I leapt up, saying, 'Good idea! I'll put the kettle on,' having no idea where I was or what I was doing.

Years later I bumped into Bryan Pringle and reminded him that we had worked together with CTC. 'Oh, yes,' he said. 'I remember you. The worst bloody DSM we ever had.'

He was not alone in this view. *The Unvarnished Truth* was a farce by a lovely man called Royce Ryton, tall with curling red hair, and a fondness for loud jackets. He was impish yet with a brilliant historian's brain. Not only was he the author, both he and his wife Moira – whom he idolized – were in the cast, while Jonathan directed. As is often the case with farces, it took place in one house, and in addition to the usual leaping in and out of doors and up and down staircases, everybody who came to this place ended up accidentally dying. The central character – played by Tim Brooke-Taylor – spent his time rushing around throwing water over these 'bodies' trying to revive them. It was hilarious, but a bloody nightmare to take on tour, particularly on matinée days, because of the gallons of water that would be thrown. Not only did we have to double up on costumes (they'd be soaking wet) but after every performance we had to go round with our Vax carpet cleaner, which, if you put it in reverse, sucked water in.

By the time we reached the West End, exhaustion had set in. Our producer at the Phoenix Theatre was Michael

Codron, an impresario of the old school who would appear with a camel coat draped across his shoulders accompanied by a fleet of executive-looking men. One day Jonathan introduced me to him as 'Tony Britton's daughter' and then, of course, it was all 'Oh, darling, wonderful, how lovely' – a rare event for a DSM to get recognition. OK, so I would rather have got it for my work, but there you go – and Michael Codron was Michael Codron, the biggest cheese in the West End at that time. So on the first night, there I was in my place in the prompt corner at the side of the stage. Once the show is up and running your role is akin to that of a conductor, co-ordinating the various practical elements that make up the show, lights, sound, scenery, etc., which are scattered around the theatre. It's probably all changed now, but in those days, communication was via a switchboard, which operated warning lights – red for 'STANDBY' and green for 'GO' – and when you flicked the STANDBY switch, your cue would be acknowledged by a couple of quick flashes.

After the first act of *The Unvarnished Truth*, a very fast curtain took us to the interval, so I cued the flyman. Nothing happened. No curtain. Nothing. What was going on? 'GO!' I said, into my mike. No curtain, no sign of any curtain. Just a stage littered with bodies, unable to move because they were in full sight of the audience. So I did the only thing I could think of and called, 'BLACKOUT!' The electrician was fantastic – this was completely off-script – but we went straight to blackout and the cast was able to come off stage and finally I heard the rattle of the tabs coming in . . .

It was now the interval and Codron came through the pass door a few feet from the prompt corner where I was still in a total jitter, thinking, Oh, God, oh, God, oh, God.

'So,' he said, 'you belong to Tony Britton, do you?' then,

without waiting for a reply, stalked off. I did the second act in tears. After the curtain calls, when the final tab came down, I did what I had to do: cleared up, reset for the following day, sorted out the props, said goodbye to the company, then staggered round to the Comedy Theatre to see the only person I felt would understand. My father. He was still there in his dressing room – he was doing a play called *Murder Amongst Friends* – and the moment I saw him I just wept and wept. I had failed. I felt mortified and ashamed and upset. My career lay in ashes. When the word went out I would never work in the theatre again. Later I went to stay with Cherry and future husband Brian Cant, and they were both incredibly kind, calmed me down and said not to worry that Codron was clearly a pig and that 'these things happen' and of course they were right. But looking back, calling for the blackout in those circumstances was the right thing to do.

A much happier experience was *The Relapse* – a classic of restoration comedy by Sir John Vanbrugh – with David Jason, then a reasonably well-known comedy actor but not the star he is today. I will never forget the first time I saw him. Again I was the DSM – which I always enjoyed as the show and the actors would feel like 'mine' – and I'd gone off to make tea as the ASM was out propping. I found him in the corridor leading to the kitchen where the tea urns were kept, holding a bit of bamboo. 'Watch this,' he said. 'I've trained this fly.' And there was a fly, buzzing above his head and he went, 'Hup! Hup!' as he swished the bamboo around and the fly flew backwards and forwards as if over it. And I thought, What a very funny man . . . He wasn't trying to be clever, or even to make me laugh. He was simply enjoying himself. A complete natural.

★

When I began working for CTC I lived out of a suitcase, discovering the joys of theatrical digs just as my parents had done. The company didn't do pantomimes, so Christmas was always free, and I spent it back at Three Trees, turning up at Chalfont and Latimer station laden with presents. That first year I had just returned from Bangor in Wales where it was so cold I'd go to bed wearing all my clothes and my duffel coat, and was still frozen in the morning. North Wales wasn't great when it came to accommodation. I remember one hotel in Mold where you'd regularly come across other people's belongings both under the bed and even in it . . .

Keeping in touch with family and friends was difficult when you were on the road. In those days there were no mobiles, so it was payphones (expensive) or more usually paper and pen. Somewhere I still have a great stack of letters from back then. We'd have a good gossip and a moan – saying if you ever come across such-n-such actor, give them a wide berth – and invite each other to visit if we were going to be in the neighbourhood.

At the end of my first year with CTC I decided to get a base in Cambridge, and rented a little one-bedroom top-floor flat above a lighting shop opposite St John's, on the corner of Bridge Street. It was my first home-of-my-own, and I absolutely loved it. The address was 36c Thompson's Lane, which I could never forget as it was my bra size. Although I wasn't 'up' at Cambridge, I found myself leading a surrogate undergraduate life through friends the same age. I was invited to a May ball, would eat regularly in halls and once went to a very smart dinner at Gonville and Caius. My mates from Central would come to stay for the weekend and we'd go punting on the Cam, have picnics, go out for dinner and generally feel quite the thing.

The two people I kept in regular touch with were my best

friends from college: Ben Sumner – we shared the same birthday – and Vikki Heywood. Vikki wasn't an obvious soul-mate for me in that while I read the *Daily Mail* she'd read the *Guardian*. Her real surname was Taylor – that Equity thing again. Her father, Ken Taylor, was a big television writer, with dozens of *Plays for Today* to his name, and he adapted *The Jewel in the Crown*. The family lived in a big Edwardian house in Muswell Hill, north London, and were definitely political. Anything to do with drama was pre-dominantly left-wing in those days whereas I was unpolitical, middle-English, and middle-class from a Conservative-voting family and I always felt I was being slightly poked fun at. But her parents were very sweet to me, and I didn't mind laughing at myself.

In late 1978 Vikki left Salisbury rep, which she'd joined straight out of Central, and came up to Cambridge to join CTC. We didn't work together. There would usually be two tours on the go, and they would leapfrog, so the stage-management teams would leapfrog as well, so Vikki was brought in to DSM the other tour. But it worked out well. When she was back in Cambridge she would stay with me.

I was now twenty-one but in terms of the theatre still very much a fledgling. Working with Jonathan I had begun to nurse thoughts of directing. When it came to comedy, whether Chekhov or farce, Jonathan Lynn was the acknow-ledged master, and he was extremely generous, explaining, analysing, generally involving me in all the ins and outs, which I hugely appreciated.

One day he had a suggestion, but not one I was expecting. The publicity manager needed help with the marketing side, he said, and he thought I would be brilliant. I don't really know why I agreed. Perhaps I thought it sounded fun. Perhaps it was simply that I adored Jonathan so would have done anything he asked me. Also, of course, being by now passionate about the theatre, I completely understood the need to get bums on seats. Actors hate playing to empty houses; as the DSM I'd go round the dressing rooms before each performance and the only question I'd ever be asked was 'Is the house full?'

Realizing I was a total novice, Jonathan packed me off for a session with Antony Jay, his co-writer on *Yes, Minister* who proved a fount of really good advice and I can remember some of it even now. On a flyer, for example, never leave the back page blank because people will simply use it as a shopping list. Instead print a booking form – prices, times of performance, anything. He stressed the importance of having a good telephone manner, how you should always smile when talking on the phone as people would hear it in your voice, even though they couldn't see you.

While the publicity manager's job was geeing up the local media, I was in charge of poster and flyer distribution, which meant walking up and down endless high streets handing out bits of paper to people who, on the whole, weren't that interested. I also liaised with the theatre: inspecting seating plans, finding out how many tickets they'd sold and trying to improve the situation by looking at novel ways to 'sell' the show.

In less than a week I knew I'd made a big mistake. I was desperately missing the actors, desperately missing the life. For the first time in eighteen months, I was on my own – no rehearsals to watch, no late-night sessions at the pub, just a succession of dreadful digs and no one to have a meal with or – worse – a drink. Instead I'd spend the day flogging round the streets, followed by a fun-filled evening watching television in a lonely room. I should have resigned there and then but I didn't, largely because I didn't want to let

Jonathan down and, to quote my stepfather George, I knew it was 'character-building'.

I stuck it out for a year, but the loneliness and sense of isolation began to get to me. Nick had gone and, apart from the odd dalliance, nobody else had appeared to fill that particular vacancy. The longer I was on my own the worse it got, and I became terrified of sinking back into depression. I knew I didn't want to go down that road again.

There were some high spots, times when I found myself back with the company, and I remember with delight the production of *Song Book*, a spoof by Monty Norman who wrote the James Bond theme. It was about a fictional American songwriter called Monty Shapiro, but we had led the audience to believe he was real. The songs were so good that sometimes in the interval you'd hear people saying, 'Ah, yes, I remember that one,' and of course they couldn't have. Monty Shapiro was played by Bob Hoskins and he was absolutely brilliant, with Gemma Craven and Anton Rodgers. One day during rehearsals Bob couldn't get his dance routine right. Normally he was an easy-going man but this got him so frustrated that he stomped out of rehearsal, shouting, 'I'm going to ring my agent.' After a pause Anton – a great song-and-dance man – said, 'I don't think *he* can dance either,' at which, of course, the tension broke and we all fell about.

The following March I came down with flu. Vikki happened to be staying and she was wonderful. She bought an enormous jam pan – I still have it – made pints of chicken soup and sat on the edge of my bed spoon-feeding me. But all too soon she was off on another tour and I was alone. I couldn't walk – I couldn't get out of bed. This was not an exaggerated cold, this was the real thing. When I finally hauled myself off to my doctor, I burst into tears. He was an old man, well over retirement age, but kindness itself. It wasn't just the flu, he said, I was depressed. Unlike my doctor at college, he wasn't interested in giving me tablets. 'You need to go home,' he said. 'You're simply exhausted. You need food and rest.' He wrote me a sick note for a month, I packed a small suitcase and went back to Little Chalfont.

My mother couldn't have been kinder, putting me to bed and generally looking after me. All too soon, however, my four weeks were up and it was back to Cambridge again. The job now seemed even more pointless. Nobody in the theatre earns very much but at least when I was with the company we were all in the same boat, and a bit of the Dunkirk spirit could get you through. Although I'd had sick pay when I was off, it wasn't even enough to cover my rent and I was in debt, stuck in Cambridge without the wherewithal to make a phone call. I would take what was left of the milk at work so at least I could have a cup of tea when I got home, and the newspaper so I'd know what there was on television. Cherry, then working at the BBC, sent me a cheque for a hundred pounds. I was so broke it could have been a million, it meant so much to me. All my friends were out on the road. In Cambridge there was no one. I remember lying in bed and thinking of ways to end it all. Paracetamol seemed the obvious answer, but I hadn't the strength to check whether I had enough in the bathroom cabinet to do the job properly.

At about three in the morning I was lying there, unable to sleep, feeling utterly desperate, when I became aware of a white, diaphanous, glowing figure beside the bed. And this person put his hand on my head, and I immediately felt peaceful: the tension and negative feelings had gone.

I accept that many people may think this was some kind

of synapse misfire, but I genuinely felt the figure was very real, very tangible, and thirty years on I still believe I had an angelic experience. I had been heading down a long dark lane when he stopped me in my tracks and turned me round. Within a few weeks my life had completely changed.

In the morning I woke up and knew what I had to do. Resign. So I did. I had to work out my notice, but I filled the time well. When I left Cambridge I had passed my driving test (at the fourth attempt) and written seventy-two job letters to every radio and television station in the UK except Belfast. In the early 1980s Northern Ireland was a very dangerous place to be.

Where the idea came from I do not know. I had certainly watched a lot of television over the past year, but nobody had ever said to me, 'You've got a great voice,' or 'You've got great delivery.' Perhaps it was Act Two of that three-in-the-morning experience, but I do believe I must have been guided.

Perhaps because This Morning *has no studio audience, the building we're housed in is incredibly run-down. They keep saying we're about to have a revamp, but I'll believe it when the men in overalls arrive with their ladders. It wasn't built to be a studio – it's actually a former brewery – but it's a good space and a fabulous location. The view looking across the river – Big Ben one way, St Paul's the other – is simply sensational. Yet when your guests are Lauren Bacall, Goldie Hawn or Joan Collins and there's a little mouse-poison box in the corner of the corridor, it's not great. Of course, we never open the conversation with 'Watch out for the mice!' It's 'Hi, lovely to see you, hope you're being well looked after!' Then we retire to our own home-from-home.*

The sign on my dressing-room door says 'The Spa', Phillip has 'The Club', then David in Wardrobe is 'The Priory', and Lyn in Makeup is 'The Clinic'. Dominating mine is a poster-sized photograph of Marilyn Monroe as a beautiful young woman in a striped dress, her chin leaning on her hand and smiling happily. I've a map of Cornwall (dated 1842) and, in pride of place pinned to the loo door, a picture Winnie did last time she was here. Then there's my little Roberts radio on which I listen to Today *on Radio 4 when I come in.*

When we have really starry guests, Phillip and I move out of our rooms, and it gives me enormous pleasure to think that Lauren Bacall has looked in my mirror and that perhaps – who knows? – it has retained some of her magic. Before she arrived, I gave the whole place a good going-over, a quick blast of air-freshener before lighting the candles, which I always do anyway the moment I arrive in the morning. Well, she was gorgeous, one of those women who spread that Hollywood sparkle about the place – and, to my great surprise, she turned out to be a woman's woman. There are some stars who totally ignore me to the point that I might as well not be there. I can usually spot them straight away: they give me a perfunctory handshake, look me up and down, then gush over Phillip. Fair enough. And I sit back and I smile to myself.

Ms Bacall was nothing like that. When Phillip and I went to say goodbye, we bumped into her coming out of my dressing room carrying my brand-new Jo Malone candle. It comes in its own little glass and I'd lit it for her specially – I love the smell, it's my absolute favourite – and she'd blown it out and the wick was still smoking. 'Thank you so very much,' she said, in the voice that takes me straight back to my childhood, watching black-and-white films sprawled out on Nana's carpet on Sunday afternoons. 'And I love my candle.' She glided off, all graciousness and smiles.

Phillip watched her disappear in disbelief. 'But that's the one I gave you for your birthday,' he said.

Of course, it can happen the other way round. Goldie Hawn left her Armani lipstick on my dressing-table, and I was hardly going to put it in the post, so that was nice.

I include Goldie Hawn among those I thought might be difficult but were charm itself. Then there was Eartha Kitt, who came in just the other week. 'A man's woman if ever I saw one,' I said to Lyn, before she arrived. 'I know just how this will be. She'll direct everything at Phillip and I'll be invisible.'

Before the show she came on the set to familiarize herself with the sofa, barely giving either Phillip or me a glance. We exchanged a here-we-go raise of eyebrows. But then, once the interview got going, everything changed: she laughed, she joked and she addressed us both – a woman's woman, after all. That afternoon we had an email from her and her daughter saying how fabulous it had been, and 'Apologies if I came in a bit grumpy, and PS who won Beat the Stylist?' Now that's what I call a star.

Inevitably there are interviews that simply don't work, and these can materialize from nowhere. Take Maureen Lipman, who I managed to upset without the least intention of doing so. Her husband Jack Rosenthal suffered from an incurable form of cancer called multiple myeloma and he had just finished writing his autobiography when he died. It was published posthumously and Maureen – now his widow, who had written a heart-breaking post-script to the book – came in to talk about it. All very difficult. Towards the end of the interview I said, 'Bereavement is something we never talk about because we don't know what to say and the bereaved doesn't know what to say. We don't want to embarrass each other and we're all very British about it, so it's good you've felt able to come here today.' Then I went on: 'Do you hear him?' Because a lot of people say that they do hear the one who's passed away – as a voice in their head. She shut down immediately; the door closed. Following the programme she wrote to me, querying my motives in putting that question to her, accusing me of trying to get her to cry on air – absolutely not the case. But it was a shame. I appreciate how she felt and I'm sorry that I didn't have a chance to explain. Maybe the truth was that she wasn't ready in her grieving process to be out there facing the public.

I don't know what it is that makes a woman a woman's woman – perhaps it's just that feeling of sisterhood. I'm too young to have been a feminist. I suppose I could be described as a post-feminist in that I haven't had to fight for my equality with men: I never needed to burn my bra. The trailblazers made it easier for my generation. Over the past thirty years – which is how long it is since the term was first conjured up – women's lib has changed its focus. The liberation now is doing what you're happiest doing. If it makes you happy to be barefoot and pregnant at the sink, fantastic. If you want to be a power in a City boardroom, fantastic. If you want to be *somewhere in between and you can juggle that happily, fantastic too. Those tired old battle lines – you should be at home, you should be at work, you can have it all, you can't have it all – are simply bollocks. Women have had a raw deal for such a long time. Why be so hard on each other?*

To me, these powerful and wonderful women who come on the show are the embodiment of woman-ness. Take Joan Collins and Barbara Windsor: you'd think they'd be difficult but they're not, they're just a hoot. As for Dolly Parton, she was in a class of her own. When she left us, we knew we'd been touched by Hollywood glitter. One woman who has said she will never come on the show if I am there is Dawn French. Maybe it's loyalty towards her husband, Lenny Henry, who did not enjoy an interview Phillip and I did with him a few years back. It was reported that he'd had a period of depression followed by a spell in The Priory. During the interview I asked him about it. He would not go there, he kept deflecting it, and the moment the commercial break came on he stood up, said 'This is not a This Morning *interview,' and left. Ah.*

What do people think a This Morning *interview is? But the idea that a* This Morning *interview is all lovely, an easy vehicle for plugging whatever you want to sell without question, is very far from the truth. I may not be Jeremy Paxman, but that doesn't mean I'm a pushover. I remember once Jeffrey Archer was talking about how wonderful his wife Mary was, and I said, 'If she's that wonderful, why were you philandering?' and he went, 'Good question.'*

Angela Rippon had a bit of a funny turn with me. She was promoting a supplement designed to keep you fit after the menopause, her line being that the menopause needn't be an interruption in your life. One of my jobs, as an interviewer, is to open up the debate, to put the other point of view.

'Well, for some women,' I suggested, 'it's about mourning their childbearing years.'

To which her reply was 'You're a disgrace to womanhood.'

I'm afraid my reaction was to laugh. I looked straight to camera and went, 'Oooooh.'

It soon blew over, and whenever we meet now, we're fine. Unlike Robert Kilroy-Silk. At the end of that interview – in which I had argued with him quite forcefully – he stood up and said to Phillip, 'Well, at least one of you is on the ball.' Then, in his Daily Express *column, he wrote that I should go back to my knitting. Some people you can't mentally connect with at all and you just think, I'll ask another question and see what happens. Others have charm enough that you know you're in the game.*

Years ago, when I was still very young and wet behind the ears, Sophia Loren was being interviewed and I was sitting in. Now, there was a woman who had 'star' running through her like Blackpool rock. So I was just listening. Eventually I decided to join in.

'I've heard you're a very good poker player,' I said.

She turned those exquisite almond eyes towards me – the first time she had acknowledged my existence – looked me up and down very slowly, and I thought, Fucking hell, here it comes . . . 'Yes,' she said. 'I am, actually.' And her face broke into a broad, generous smile.

So who is still up there on my wish list? Well, I'd love to meet Richard Gere. A bit hackneyed, I know, but he is gorgeous. It probably wouldn't make a good interview, though, because if Richard Gere was sitting in front of me I wouldn't be able to speak.

Father and daughter, 1981

7. Good Evening

There were no computers back in 1979, or none that someone like me had access to, and although I addressed the envelopes by hand, the letters were photocopied. The names of the radio and TV stations came from the invaluable *Contacts*, published by the same company responsible for *Spotlight*, the directory of actors working in Britain, without which no casting director can function.

My letter was certainly direct, along the lines of 'Dear Whoever, I have no useful experience but I'd very much like to be a newsreader or something like that because I think I'd be quite good at it.' I didn't keep a copy of my original, but being Mrs Organized, I still have the thirty-four replies. Some were 'Thanks for your interest, sorry, but good luck', others more 'No thanks. Who do you think you are?'

Dear Miss Britton
Whilst your background and experience sound admirable, I'm bound to say it does not equip you in any way for work here at Radio Newcastle. Our newsreaders are fully experienced journalists and our presenters are producers. Both positions require a great deal of hard grind for a number of years to achieve. At the same time, I have no wish to spread gloom, so I enclose a leaflet setting out job opportunities on local radio stations, I am only sorry I cannot offer you anything.

The following, from Capital Radio dated 26 January 1980, was particularly instructive:

Dear Miss Britton

Thank you for your photocopied letter of 15 January. I am sorry but I really do not think that we have any vacancies at all, and if I may say so in the spirit of helpfulness, I do not think that we or indeed anyone else would be likely to jump at the chance of employing someone who seems to know so little about the station that they believe we employ newsreaders. I would have thought the IBA handbook would have been a good investment for you. I wonder if you should not try to gain some part-time experience in radio by say offering your services to your local hospital radio service before trying to embark on a radio career. And when you have got some experience may I, again in the spirit of helpfulness, suggest you should write a personal letter to the programme controller of any company you wish to approach, addressing him by name (see IBA handbook), and enclosing a tape of the kind of programme you wish to present. Would you, in the theatre world, have responded to a letter from a would-be actor who admits no experience and doesn't even seem to know what sort of plays you stage? I think not. Please don't be offended by anything here, I write merely in a helpful vein. Presumably you are already reading the various radio magazines that carry radio vacancies.

    Yours sincerely

    Jan Reed

    Press and Public Relations Officer

Ms Reed would doubtless have been astonished to learn that, in response to identical letters to hers, I received four positive replies. They didn't even know that I was a lapsed performer – I hadn't mentioned the Christmas revues I'd done at school. All they knew for certain was that I was young and green and full of optimism.

    Harlech Television (HTV), based in Bristol, was looking

for a continuity announcer. Radio 4 wanted someone to write trails with the possibility of being trained up for continuity. The third was for Westward Television in Plymouth – also a continuity announcer, and I can't now remember what Three Valleys Broadcasting, a commercial radio station in the Thames Valley, had in mind.

The job I really wanted was the Westward one. I knew nothing about the company: my interest related solely to its location. Although Plymouth, where Westward was based, is officially in Devon it's right by the Tamar – from time immemorial the boundary with Cornwall. For twenty years, since I first became aware that this different place existed, the sound of the name alone had been enough to raise my spirits. The idea that I might be able to live there – to have it on my doorstep – was like a dream come true.

I took the train from Chalfont and Latimer into Marylebone, then from Paddington began the life-changing journey down through the West Country to Plymouth. It took all day. My interview was first thing the following morning, so I stayed overnight in a little B-and-B. Yet again, I made sure I looked the part: red tartan Miss Selfridge trousers with a red woolly jumper appliquéd with little blue flowers here and there. (Think Lady Diana Spencer before she married.)

It was the last of my four interviews. The first had been at HTV in Bristol. Brian Cant, who presented *Playaway*, the children's programme, and was my sister's boyfriend, very sweetly drove me down, then allowed me to drive back – my first ever long drive. No doubt I gave him a few hair-raising moments, but he was very kind and it was definitely beyond the call of duty.

The second was the BBC at Broadcasting House, where

I was interviewed by the Radio 4 presentation editor, Jim Black. We sat in a dull grey office and just chatted. Looking back, I suppose he was listening to my voice although the job, he told me, was not in front of the microphone – at least at the beginning: I'd be writing trails, which I wasn't at all sure I wanted to do.

If I imagined that the Westward interview would be equally low key, I was mistaken. This time it was the full Monty, i.e. a screen test. Nor was it just to see how I looked on camera: it was to be a dry run for the real thing. Being a continuity announcer, I now knew, meant the ability to fill the gaps, which might be five or fifty-five seconds – two minutes, even. You've got to understand instinctively how long a second is and how to fill that precise amount of time. There is a clock to help you – in those days this was a large studio clock with a highly visible second hand. Even though you're not looking at it directly, because you're gazing into the camera lens – 'down the bottle', as it's called – you have it in your peripheral vision. This was all explained to me in the interview by the department head, David Sunderland. I was concentrating so hard I didn't have time to be nervous, it was just 'Right, OK.'

Finally he handed me a copy of the *TV Times*. 'Take a look through tonight's menu of programmes,' he began. 'And then I want you to write a fifteen-second fill, a thirty-second fill, a forty-five-second fill and a one-minute fill.'

He left me alone for about twenty minutes and I wrote these four little 'scripts', memorizing them as best I could.

I was then ushered into the cramped continuity studio. First they wanted a few links to camera – such as 'Good evening, later tonight we've got the news at ten o'clock, but now here's *Coronation Street*.' Then it was time for my own mini scripts.

'OK, Fern,' the voice said, over the loudspeaker. 'When the second hand hits the top, you go.'

I smiled at the lens – hoping to exude warmth, authority and confidence, none of which I actually felt – while watching the clock out of the corner of my eye and, as the second hand jumped to the twelve, I began: 'Good evening . . .'

I took a parting look at the Westward building, a seaside version of BBC's Television Centre – the same kind of modern architecture, concrete, steel and glass, but with a hint of end-of-the-pier. 'We'll be in touch,' David said, as he shook my hand.

I walked back to the station in a daze, just one phrase running through my head, repeating itself over and over again: 'That's the job I want. That's the job I want.'

It wasn't my first contact with the world of television. When Cherry left school she worked initially at Pinewood and later got a job as a production assistant with the BBC. Eventually she went on to direct and to write, but she was working then on shows like *Late Night Line-Up* and *Playaway* – which was where she'd met Brian. For a fourteen-year-old like me, it was all incredibly glamorous, and the great treat was going to meet my big sister at Television Centre for lunch at the BBC Club. In those days, they still served alcohol, and the bar would be full of famous faces. In the canteen there would be actors in wigs and costumes, having their spaghetti Bolognese like everyone else. Sometimes, on the way in, I'd pass queues of excited teenagers waiting to go into *Top of the Pops*. Even the lobby struck me as incredibly glamorous, with its view of the courtyard and the tinkling fountain.

Disconcertingly, the first positive response came from Cunard, to whom I had also applied and who offered me the post of entertainments officer. Fortunately their offer arrived in a letter so I had a few days' grace, but it was at least a week before I heard from anybody else. Next was Jim Black. It was incredibly tempting: Radio 4 was the BBC's flagship speech network, and Jim Black himself was personally responsible for introducing some of the most familiar voices in broadcasting: Laurie Macmillan, Susan Rae, Peter Jefferson, Dilly Barlow, Harriet Cass, Charlotte Green and Moira Stewart.

'I know it's a bit cheeky,' I explained, 'but since seeing you, I've been interviewed for a job at Westward and I'm still waiting to hear back.'

'I quite understand,' he said. 'Put it this way, if you haven't heard from them in twenty-four hours, let me know.'

I didn't move from the house. I just hung around trying to avoid George. He hadn't stopped getting at me since the moment I'd got back from Cambridge carrying all my worldly goods. I was headstrong, feckless. Not a sticker. I'd thrown it up. I had to get a job. If I thought I could lie around and live off them, I was very much mistaken. I had to get off my backside and find another job smartish. When I told Mummy and him about my hopes for a career in television I think they thought I was living in fairyland. And, realistically, what chance did I have? Westward must have had dozens of hopefuls on file. I'd just had a late reply from Radio Brighton: 'It might incidentally help you to assess your position if I tell you that recently a junior post involving presentation and production provided three hundred applications, many of whom were experienced in radio work.' Yet I felt I'd done well – in fact, I'd surprised even myself. Every time the phone rang, I caught my breath. But nothing. Neither was there anything on the doormat the following morning.

Twenty-four hours to the minute after Jim Black tele-phoned, I picked up the receiver and dialled the BBC. He'd been kind enough to give me this extra time, and I couldn't risk losing the chance. I thanked him for waiting, and said that if the job was still open I'd love to accept.

I remember wandering round the garden and wondering if I'd done the right thing. For all the kudos of the BBC, Portland Place wasn't exactly Cornwall. Too late now.

Five minutes later the phone went again.

'For you,' George shouted, from inside the house.

'David somebody-or-other,' he said, as he handed me the receiver. 'Westward Television.'

'Sorry it's taken so long to get back to you, but I'm delighted to tell you the job's yours.'

All my tension evaporated and I threw my head back in a silent laugh. Then I remembered. 'Oh dear. The thing is, I've just accepted a job at Radio 4. Do you think I could just ring them back and say, "Sorry but . . ."?'

'I think that's exactly what you should do.'

Jim Black couldn't have been nicer. 'Tell you what,' he said. 'Let's forget we ever spoke. Good luck to you, and well done.'

There was one slight cloud on the horizon.

'If we were to take you on,' David Sunderland had told me at the interview, 'we'd need you to slim down.'

I wasn't totally surprised. When I'd come out of drama school I'd been about eight stone and now I was nine, and although still a size ten I was considered overweight. The food you eat when a show is on the road is hardly the healthiest, consisting of bacon sarnies, fry-ups, and curry – all at entirely the wrong time of day.

As a child I had never had what are now termed 'food issues', being neither a picky eater nor a guzzler. Like most children I lived on fresh air, and when Mummy could catch me I'd sit down and eat what was put in front of me, though I'd always prefer to chew a bone and suck out the marrow. I learnt not to eat between meals, and generally didn't – though, of course, sweets didn't count. However, growing up in a household where both my mother and sister were very body conscious was a mixed blessing. While they were ladylike and slim – attributes generally approved of – I was neither. In reality I wasn't much bigger than they were, but I had bosoms and they did not. When I was growing up, references would be made to my 'puppy fat', which I was told I would grow out of. When I'd emerged from Central, however, the message had changed: now I was 'skinny' and should take care not to lose more weight.

My boss-to-be had specifically mentioned my shoulders and upper arms: they were decidedly 'chunky', he said. I'd need to take care never to wear anything without sleeves as I'd end up looking like a footballer. The business of television making people look bigger isn't an urban myth, it's literally true. In normal vision the brain constructs a single image from the converging viewpoints of two eyes. The camera does exactly the opposite: from a single lens the viewpoints need to diverge to focus on a body or a head, hence giving the impression of something larger. It's been calculated that this adds between ten and fifteen pounds to perceived weight. This had been explained to me by my father when I first told him I wanted to be an announcer. His response was a raised eyebrow and 'You're too fat to be a Sue Lawley.' I wasn't particularly upset. It wasn't exactly new.

So, the moment I walked out of Westward's studios, I put myself on a diet: I lost a stone in a month, largely through eating one meal a day at lunchtime: lamb chop, Bisto gravy, frozen peas, Smash and mint sauce. For breakfast and supper I had Slimfast. I was ravenous, but it worked.

As I had every intention of living in Cornwall, I would need a car. With Mummy's help I bought a little Simca, pale blue and ancient – like a French farmer's car. Nick helped me find it. Although we had both moved on, we were still friends.

My destination that Sunday afternoon was not Plymouth itself, but Liskeard, half an hour into Cornwall where Nick's sister Haley lived with her husband and baby boy. Haley's husband worked on the oil rigs, so she was alone quite a bit and had very kindly offered to put me up until I got myself sorted out.

Before setting off, I made a bet with myself that I'd travel the whole 250 miles in the middle lane as I was terrified of having to pass anything.

'Just think,' I had said, as we sat down to a farewell lunch at Three Trees, 'this time tomorrow, I'll have been on television!'

'Listen to her,' Cherry said. 'She's unbearable already.'

And yet it was true. Whether I went on air during the first shift or the second I can't now remember, but from day one I was on the roster and off I went. It was absolutely fantastic.

Although I had loved my time working in the theatre, what I was doing now was considerably less stressful and considerably better paid. From being on sixty pounds a week with CTC, I was now on a hundred and twenty.

Once I had found my feet at work, the next thing was somewhere to live. All I knew was that I wanted to be in Cornwall, within half an hour's drive of the studios. One morning, Haley handed me the local newspaper with an ad ringed in felt tip in the 'For Rent' section. 'Here,' she said. 'Have a look at this.'

Fursdon Farm was built on a steep hillside leading down to the Tamar, on the edge of a village called St Dominick. It had been divided into two, and the smaller part – known as the cottage – was mine. A door connected the two halves but this was blocked by a wardrobe. Otherwise it was totally self-contained, including its own front door. The owners, Tom and Chris Gorman, were proper Cornish farming people and became like surrogate parents to me. They reared bullocks and turkeys in the autumn and winter, in the spring there were anemones and daffodils to take to market and in the summer sweet-peas and strawberries. They were incredibly hard-working, up at dawn and in bed by nine. When I came out of my front door at strawberry time, there would be a punnet of strawberries on the front step for breakfast. (My newspaper was delivered by Pearl, who'd leave it tucked into a pipe in the hedge.)

St Dominick is a proper Cornish village: narrow deep-cut lanes, primroses smothering the banks in springtime, hedges thick with bluebells and pink campion in May. It stands high above the Tamar – just above the sub-tropical gardens of Cotehele, run by the National Trust. When you stood outside the cottage, there wasn't a sound to be heard except birdsong.

When I wasn't working, I would run down the lane to Halton Quay, with its tiny white-painted chapel like a signal box, and sit there quietly, reading, watching the salmon leap and the fishermen rowing silently out onto the water to lay their nets. When the tide was out, the mudflats would be teeming with rare water birds, like the avocet, with its long legs, black-and-white plumage and upward-curving bill. When the warmth had gone out of the sun – or the rain descended (not an uncommon occurrence in Cornwall) – I would run back up the hill.

There were four of us in the continuity team, which, with the usual swapping around, worked out as one shift a day, five days a week. The day was split into two shifts, nine till six, or six till close-down. Early shifts were nice because you had the evening. Late shifts were nice because you had the day. For several years I didn't get home for Christmas, and Christmas morning was a lovely shift. To be at work and yet with friends was the perfect combination.

After my year of misery in marketing, once again I was one of a gang. As a former backstage girl I felt instantly at home with the crew, and the feeling was mutual as I understood their woes and gripes more than most. Among my fellow announcers I was closest to Ian Stirling, who sadly died a few years ago. He was a great personality, very funny, and used to have me rocking with laughter.

A particularly important member of the Westward team was Gus Honeybun. He had his own theme tune and would appear twice a day, halfway through the morning and then again at teatime; I had a very soft spot for him. Gus was a rabbit. He didn't talk, but he had a wide range of other skills to call on. He blinked, winked, flapped his ears and could even stand on his head, but his speciality was 'bunny hops'.

A parent would send in a picture of Sam, aged three, with a request that Gus do 'three bunny hops', which I – or another of Gus's 'aunties' (or 'uncles') would naturally arrange on Sam's behalf. Gus was a very talented rabbit – it was said that he came originally from Dartmoor, found under a gorse bush by an outside-broadcast unit – and people would send in clothes for him, particularly knitted items. Gus's chief 'handler' (and manager) was Trishy, one of our team of 'loggists' (including Ruth Langsford), whose job involved noting the exact times we were on and off air, what commercials ran, incidence of glitches, etc. Gus insisted on hogging stardom to himself, however, and Trishy was never seen, having to crouch on the floor beside the desk. Gus was much in demand for the opening of fêtes, and his name on the poster would result in thousands turning up, while mine might muster a paltry hundred. Time has inevitably taken its toll and I gather that in 1992 Gus was reunited with his rabbit family on Dartmoor. But I still meet grown-up men and women who say, 'You did Gus Honeybun for me on my birthday . . .'

Our job in continuity was to provide links at each switch between national and regional programming, to fill the gaps, both scheduled and unscheduled. The continuity studio had to be permanently manned in case of the latter. You could nip out to the loo provided you told the control room, but you couldn't go off and have supper. Food – in the shape of a banana or a sandwich – would be brought to you. So, how to pass the time? Obviously you could watch whatever the viewers were watching, and in the afternoons I'd try and catch Mavis Nicholson on *Afternoon Plus*. She was absolutely brilliant and the programme was a forerunner, I now realize, of *This Morning*. Often, however, I'd just read. So, one evening I was sitting there with my cardigan on because it was cold. A film was being broadcast, part of our local output, the reels being physically changed by our guys in Telecine. It was a horrible film and I didn't want to watch so, as images flickered across the monitor in my peripheral vision, I read my book. All of a sudden the lights in my little studio were turned on, and – surprised – I turned round and caught sight of myself on the monitor. No lipstick, tatty cardigan, hair standing on end. I was in vision!

After six o'clock on Friday, Saturday and Sunday, women continuity announcers wore evening dress and sparkly earrings, while the men sported dinner jackets and bow ties, at least from the waist up, which was all that was seen. Beneath it was jeans and I was more likely to be wearing gym shoes than heels. The seventies was the heyday of ITV glamour and we dressed accordingly, inviting our viewers to join us as the curtain went up on a star-studded evening of the biggest names in television.

By far the most glamorous person at Westward was our chairman, Sir Peter Cadbury. He would turn up in a swirl of sophistication, his Aston Martin screeching to a halt in the car park – where he would park with a cavalier disregard for designated spaces, or even parallel lines – sweep in, glad-hand everybody in sight, then put the smallest possible coin in the fruit machine in the bar and promptly win the jackpot. What none of us knew, however, was that his luck was about to run out. Not everyone appreciated his maverick ways.

Just after Christmas that year, during the national screening of Westward's drama *Drake's Venture* to mark the four-hundredth anniversary of the circumnavigation of the globe, and starring John Thaw (pre-*Morse*, post-*Sweeney*), ITN broke into the broadcast to announce that Westward had lost its franchise. I was at home, watching our big drama, when it happened. Everyone was devastated. As for me, I had been there less than a year, but I had been thinking about buying a house. Now everything was in the air. We had been promised continuity but there would inevitably be changes and not only at the top.

That spring TSW – the in-coming company – took over in all but name. In the meantime life – and the Westward galleon (its emblem, the *Golden Hind*) – sailed on.

At the end of July Lady Diana married Prince Charles.

There was a real sense of festival about it, everyone desperate to second-guess what the bride would be wearing, would she have painted her nails, would she have grown her hair. Every little piece of her was dissected and analysed. It was the first time anyone had been subjected to such scrutiny, at least on this side of the Atlantic. She was our Jackie O and Marilyn Monroe rolled into one, yet she was barely twenty.

That evening I was on the late shift so, with the rest of the population, I watched the wedding on television while dashing in and out of the house to hang out my washing – it was a beautiful summer's day. I arrived at the studio around four and the atmosphere was still tremendous. That evening I wore the most glamorous evening dress I had, black and sparkly topped with a sequined jacket. As for Gus Honeybun, he was kitted out in a regal waistcoat a viewer had sent in.

I had even more reason to be excited than the rest of my colleagues . . .

A few days earlier, I'd had a call from David Waine, head of production for BBC South West (Westward's rival), asking me to lunch the following week. He had a proposition to discuss, he said. The current female presenter of their regional evening-news programme was leaving to have a baby. *Spotlight South West* was a two-hander and I'd be working with Chris Denham. It went out daily between six and six thirty. I would be employed as a freelance, at a fixed fee of fifty pounds a day – two hundred and fifty a week, twice as much as I was getting at Westward. Was I interested?

It wasn't a difficult decision. But I will never forget Westward. Although not my first job, it was the beginning of my chosen career and it marked me indelibly. Even after nearly thirty years, I can still remember how we opened up, word for word. 'Good morning, this is Westward Television broadcasting to you from the transmitters of the Independent Broadcasting Authority. Today is the first of May 1980, the time is nine o'clock, and now we go straight over to the ITN studios in London for the latest national and international news.'

The other constant was close-down, where you were allowed a bit more latitude. Whatever time transmission finally ended, a vicar would come in to do a thought for the night. During a film clip of the Queen doing a walkabout in Plymouth on her Jubilee year, I'd jump out of the chair to make room for him. Once he had finished it was back to me.

'Thank you for watching,' I'd say, 'and take care – it's a bit slippery out there tonight,' or 'There's a frost.' Then it would go to black, and a little cartoon of a lion called Looki would come on and blow his trumpet. Then it would go black again and my final words were 'And don't forget to switch off your television, unplug it from the wall, and put those milk bottles out. Goodnight.'

The local elections on 1 May 2008 were always going to be a disaster for Labour, so I wasn't surprised when the news came through that the prime minister was coming in this week; it would be his opportunity to explain to the ordinary TV-watching public what had gone wrong. I interviewed Gordon Brown when he was chancellor and was impressed. On a personal level he was charming and he clearly understood our audience. It was immediately after a budget, and we had people ringing in with tax questions, which he answered with thought and clarity. On a few points when he said he'd get back to the caller, he was as good as his word. Now here I am, about to meet him again under very different circumstances.

Interviewing politicians is a funny business. In their own realm they are all-powerful, but put them in an unfamiliar environment – like a TV studio – and everything changes. In December 2004 I was set to interview the then prime minister, Tony Blair. This Morning had moved out to West Wycombe for the Christmas fortnight. It was very spoiling for me – twenty minutes down the road so lie-ins every day, not to mention two weeks in surroundings a great deal more civilized than our usual mouse-bait-ridden corridors, a glorious eighteenth-century mansion festively decked out in tinsel and holly.

Whether they also thought it would be convenient for Chequers, I don't know, but in the event the prime minister flew in by helicopter from somewhere else. I had never seen anything quite like it. There was an armoured car outside and men with briefcases that seemed to transform instantly into machine-guns, like Inspector Gadget. When Tony Blair duly arrived he was all smiley and

139

asked for a cup of tea, but I was surprised at how unsure of himself he appeared. When he was faced with the sofa, it was 'How shall I sit? Shall I sit forward, shall I sit back?'

Our next encounter was far less cordial. He was promoting some health campaign called, I think, *Healthy Living*, and in keeping with the theme I was to interview him in a London gym. After kicking off the programme at the studio, I climbed onto the back of a taxi-bike and roared off to meet him somewhere in the West End: Racy Fern in her leathers v. Bruiser Blair in his tracksuit.

I started gently, something like, 'So, tell me all about this "Healthy Living", Prime Minister.' He looked at me for a moment to see if I really had asked such a simple question. Satisfied that it was genuine, he began, 'Small steps can make a big change. We can get off the bus a stop earlier and walk. We must climb the stairs instead of taking the lift.' Blah, blah, blah.

He'd answered exactly as I had hoped. Right, here we go. 'But we know that, Prime Minister,' I interrupted. 'We know that from magazines. We see it every day on our televisions. With all due respect, this is nothing new. Why are you wasting your money on this campaign when it's the health service itself that needs the cash?'

His eyes flared and the smile grew more and more rictus-like. He was so angry. Out of camera shot but in my eye-line, one of his advisers was sawing across her throat with her hand, the universal language for 'Stop!' I took no notice. What was I supposed to do? Congratulate him on a novel initiative that would fire the public's imagination?

The interview over, I said, 'Thank you very much,' but he had already gone.

Some time later Cherie Blair was on This Morning. 'I told my husband I was coming on here,' she said, as she chatted to Phillip during the break. 'He groaned and said, "Last time I did that I was sandbagged." I told him, "What did you expect?"'

People have this odd idea about me. 'Oh, Fern, she's soft, she's *chief reporter for the* Bunty, *she'll be all right.' Then it's 'Oh, bugger . . .'*

After yesterday's programme I was handed the brief from Number 10 in preparation for today's interview with Gordon Brown. It was a list of topics the prime minister would like to cover: the economy, the 10p tax rate, etc. – overall much more Newsnight *than* This Morning. *The more I looked at this list, the uneasier I felt. If I stuck to their agenda, I'd be totally at sea before I knew it. It's not difficult to get lost in an interview, particularly in a subject that's not your home territory. So you have to be prepared, to think in advance – how will I handle it?*

Feeling scared is certainly not the answer. The truth is that Gordon Brown is only a man – a clever man, certainly, and success-ful – but essentially only a man. Then I thought, I'm an ordinary woman and I'm living an ordinary life with ordinary children, and I understand about state education because my children are all state-educated. I understand about the NHS because all my children were born on the NHS, and all our general illnesses have been treated on the NHS. In terms of the economy I have the same concerns as the next man or woman: mortgage, savings. I drive a car, I worry about crime. So I said to my team, 'Tell me if this is too naïve, but I'd like to deal with the credit crunch, education, security, hospitals and fuel prices.'

I also wanted the PM to have the opportunity to show his human side, that he wasn't solely an automaton spouting statistics, percent-ages and political bollocks. It's no wonder the majority of the public don't bother to vote. It's because we think, They all talk rubbish, they all talk the same, nothing will change.

My team agreed. His advisers were told, and we assured them it wouldn't be a hectoring interview, that it would be more about how he was handling things – as well as raising issues that concerned our viewers. And they said, 'Fine.'

With Phillip still away, and no stand-in organized, I was on my own – and happy with that. It's like when your husband is gone for the odd night, you think, How lovely is this? I could take it at my own pace and steer it in the direction I wanted without worrying about anyone else.

The prime minister arrived just as we went on air. Before the interview itself we ran a tape, giving a bit of background: his childhood in Scotland, losing the sight of an eye playing rugby as a student, and how he'd started his career as a TV journalist.

'Very nice to see you again,' he said, as we settled down, the videotape still running. 'I don't know if you remember but we met once at Number Eleven Downing Street.'

'I do remember,' I said, 'and well done you for being well briefed . . .'

'No, no . . . I did remember, really.'

And so the interview started. I didn't, as one commentator claimed, 'put him through the mincer', nor was he 'monstered' by me. But neither did I give him an easy ride. At the end of Downing Street's list it had said: 'The prime minister will not talk about Sarah or the children.' And of course I get that. But not to ask about a family member who is known to be ill – when you're dealing with health anyway – is just plain rude. His son John has cystic fibrosis so I felt it only polite to ask after him and I did: 'If it's not too personal a question,' I said, 'how is John doing?'

Next day the Telegraph *reported, 'Downing Street aides are understood to be angry that [Gordon Brown] was "bounced" into answering the questions.' They can't have watched the interview. It was the PM himself who opened the discussion on family when he talked about being a single dad while Sarah and his elder son were away. John is apparently doing very well, and his father was open and warm. It showed him to be very human, which was what I'd always hoped would happen.*

142

Best of all, driving home in the car I had a phone message from my mother saying that she was very proud of me and couldn't believe I was her daughter.

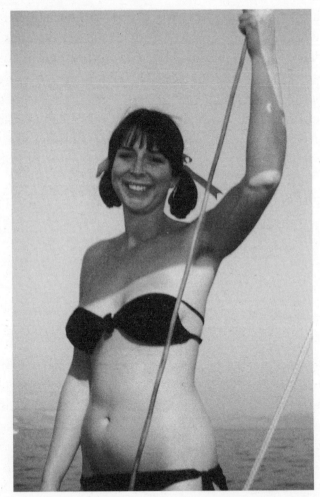

Sun, sea and speed in Cornwall c. 1982

8. Sink or Swim

Working as one half of a two-hander is radically different from working on your own, and its success depends to a large degree on the personality of the other person. In this I was incredibly lucky as Chris Denham, my co-presenter on *Spotlight South West*, was a joy to work with – something I would only really appreciate later. I was effectively now a news magazine presenter. It was definitely a promotion. This was where my journalistic apprenticeship began. I found myself with my own desk in a full-on newsroom. I'd be reading from scripts that would appear on the teleprompter, where the words were typed on a thin roll of paper, installed under the camera and unwound as you read. It worked in the same way as autocue (of which it was an early version) in that the image is reflected by a mirror onto a screen directly in front of the camera lens, the disadvantage being that the paper would sometimes break so you'd always have a copy of the script with you on the desk just in case.

Spotlight was on air between six and six thirty in the evening, but the working day started with the editorial meeting at ten in the morning when stories would be assessed and film crews distributed. Chris and I were backed by a team of reporters and correspondents right across the region that covered not only the whole of Cornwall and Devon but stretched north into Somerset, east into Dorset and across to the Channel Islands. In addition there were the usual specialist correspondents including home affairs, business, sports and weather. The weather man, Craig Rich, was a local institution. As well as forecasting, he had his own late-night show called *That's Rich*, and on one never-to-be-forgotten occasion a director friend of mine, Juliet May, persuaded me to emerge from my presenter's chrysalis to do 'Singing in the Rain', wearing a lilac Lycra catsuit, red tap shoes and not a little bravado. She had only done news before and this was her first foray into the heady world of light entertainment. Knowing I'd been taking tap classes, she thought it might be a laugh, and I wouldn't have to sing, just dance. 'Trust me, darling,' she said. 'I won't make you look stupid.' A video of my 'turn' survives and it's hilarious. I marvel that I had the courage to do it at all: the first time I decide to perform in public, it's to several hundred thousand people and I'm obviously not wearing bra or knickers . . .

The hike in my salary made my financial position much more secure, and when I heard in the village pub that a tiny cottage was for sale, I didn't think twice. It cost fifteen thousand pounds. I managed to get a 100 per cent mortgage, and spent the rest of my pay-packet on doing it up. The old lady who'd lived there hadn't touched it for years and everything needed to be done. One day a great chunk of plaster fell off the wall to reveal a broad metal lintel. Behind it lay a walk-in fireplace complete with the original clome oven – unique to Cornwall now, but used since iron-age times to bake bread. The cottage had a wonderful atmosphere and I'm convinced it sheltered a friendly ghost. My more traditional companions were my two pussycats, Wally (short for Cornwall), who arrived at Fursdon Farm as a ginger kitten, and sleek black Delia, who also adopted me. Called Titch by her original family, I decided she needed a superior name as she was exceptionally refined and partial to Maltesers and Christmas cake.

Baber Cottage was right in the heart of the village and was

tiny: two up, two down, with a curious curved exterior wall. It had once been the village butcher's, and while excavating the floor to waterproof it, Terry the builder discovered all sorts of animal bones. Terry had a proper Cornish turn of phrase: 'I'm as happy as a tom-tit on a pump handle' was one, and that could certainly have described me. House, friends, Cornwall on my doorstep, a job to die for and a wonderful social life. Misery and depression banished for good. Or so I thought.

Not long after I'd moved in, a former colleague asked me to go on a jaunt. We'd leave after work on Friday and stay with friends of his near Truro. He had a brand-new Japanese sports car and wanted to put it through its paces, he said. By the time we set off it was late, so we stopped just beyond Fowey to get something to eat and unwind over a few glasses of wine. His car was indeed very splendid – at least compared with mine – and utterly male, the sort that runs on testosterone rather than petrol and, as we left the restaurant, I was overcome with an urge to drive it. Given I was fully insured on my own car, I told him, legally I'd be covered. So what about it?

The motorcyclist travelling behind us – later a witness – said that I drove perfectly up until the accident. Approaching a T-junction, my foot slipped. I missed the brake, hit the accelerator instead and shot straight across the road into a dry-stone wall. I can still see the grass and greenery growing out of the cracks just feet away from my face. They say your life flashes past in a situation like that. Mine didn't, though I do remember looking quickly from left to right and thinking, Shit, I hope nothing's coming. Luckily, apart from the motorcyclist behind us, the road was completely empty.

I came round to hear a woman's voice. I'd been in an accident, she said, but I was OK. By then an ambulance had arrived – I remember the blue flashing light reflected on the wet road – and there was a low murmur of voices, the sound of professionals getting on with their job.

I was stretchered into the waiting ambulance and, with the inevitable jolting, it began to dawn on me that, fuck, this wasn't a dream, it was really happening.

'Fern?'

I recognized my friend's voice before sinking down into unconsciousness again, worrying that no one would be there to feed the cats. The next memory I have is of a neon-lit room and my head being cleaned up. I had escaped comparatively unscathed. I must have raised my hand instinctively to my face to protect it in the collision because there was a gash where my watch had sliced across my eyelid.

'You're lucky,' said a doctor. 'I've done training in plastic surgery.' I was handed a form to sign but couldn't see anything. I've never been able to see out of my right eye properly and, with the left one swollen, I was nearly blind. Next I was breathalysed, cautioned and read my rights. Then it was back into an ambulance to be transferred to a hospital with a head-injury unit. There, I was put into a side room and, quite rightly, the medical staff were none too sympathetic.

My luck was not limited to the neat job on my eye. In 1981 the seatbelt legislation hadn't yet been brought in: it didn't become compulsory until nearly a year later. However, by sheer chance I was involved in a seatbelt campaign with the Plymouth police, so I'd taken to doing mine up automatically every time I got into the car. If I hadn't been strapped in, I'd have gone through the windscreen, and that would have been that. Later, as part of the campaign, I would show people the scar above my eye and tell them the story.

The day following the accident, lying in my hospital bed feeling mortified and sorry for myself in equal parts, a man came into my room carrying a pineapple. He was a friend of one of our reporters, he said – a good friend of mine – and she'd suggested he drop in to see how I was and if I needed anything. He was very sympathetic, which, in the absence of much sympathy from the hospital staff, I was all too open to. He gathered the police had been involved. What had happened? And I'd been breathalysed, had I? So how did it happen? I told him everything.

The story ran the following day in the local Sunday paper. The bastard was a reporter. No connection with my friend at the BBC at all. My new boss took great exception to this gross intrusion and stood up for me in a way that I didn't deserve but will always be grateful for. When I got back to work a couple of weeks later I was handed my postbag. It did not make pleasant reading: letters from people whose loved ones had been killed by drink drivers; letters pointing out that it was only sheer luck that I hadn't killed anybody. It was a salutary experience and I answered each and every one, acknowledging my wrong-doing and explaining how I was now taking the consequences.

At this time, I had an unexpected boost to my career. Working for the BBC had one huge advantage over working for a commercial company. The regions are viewed as nurseries, where young reporters and presenters can learn their trade away from the glare of the national spotlight. In spite of my personal unhappiness, the 'Fern Britton smile' had not gone unnoticed in Television Centre, and in January I was seconded to London to fill in for someone for a month. I arranged for a friend to come in and feed the cats, and off I went. Thus it was that I became – at twenty-four – the youngest newsreader on national television.

The early-morning news conference at the BBC was at eight a.m. Although I didn't know the individuals sitting around the table, I knew who they would be: the director, producer, news editor, the sub-editors, reporters and news-readers – just as in Plymouth.

'Take a seat,' said one of the guys, pointing to one of the vacant chairs. Then, on the stroke of eight, the double doors swung open and the head of news came in, stopped, glared at me, then barked, 'Get out of my seat.'

Blood surged up to my face as I pushed the chair back, wishing I could put my head down a lavatory and flush it. If that was my initiation test, I think I must have passed as there were no more such jolly pranks and the remainder of my time in White City was incident-free.

I wasn't a journalist, and even at Plymouth no one had ever thought of teaching me the rudiments of how to get a story. It was Moira Stewart who put me right. 'It's really very simple,' she said. 'Who, where, why, what, when. Answer those questions and you've done it. That's the secret!' She was the sweetest woman and wonderful to me and I am eternally grateful: her 'secret' continues to serve me well.

I had one further moment of embarrassment. A date had just been set for my appearance at Bodmin Magistrates' Court. Hardly world-shattering news, but the daughter of Tony Britton being done for drink-driving was worth putting out on the wires, it seemed, and within minutes there wasn't a desk in the newsroom that didn't have a copy.

My time at Television Centre was over all too soon and I was back in Plymouth, this time without a car. For the first few weeks I took the bus. Accompanied by the ever-faithful Wally and Delia, I would leave Baber Cottage shortly after eight to ensure I was at the studios by ten. (I had been used to leaving an hour and a half later.) I would get back to St

Dominick around eight thirty, when my two pussycats would both be by the bus stop. Although spring was around the corner, the nights were still dark. Waiting at bus stops was cold, and there were no beautiful views of the Tamar valley to console me on the journey. I knew I deserved it. I sat staring out of the window, feeling increasingly isolated. Depression was looming again. I had just got myself organized, great new job, my own house – all I'd ever wanted – and I'd fucked it up. Within only a few months I'd gone from financial security to the verge of bankruptcy. While I had been legally insured, writing off a brand-new car was not covered. Somebody had to pay, and as my insurance wouldn't it had to be me – fifteen thousand pounds, the same amount as I'd paid for my house just a few months earlier. Nor did it stop there. Bills continued to mount up, ranging from lawyer's fees to ambulances. The only thing my insurance did cover was rebuilding the wall. My accountant thought my best option, financially speaking, was to go bankrupt, but if I did that, I risked losing my house and, increasingly, it was the only place I felt safe.

I felt besieged and alone. But it was sink or swim, and I decided to swim. Enough of this self-humiliation. I had to stop being a wet blanket. I could just about cope with the work but afterwards all I wanted was to get home, and an hour and a half on a bus was the last straw. So when a freelance photographer, a friend of mine in the village, offered to act as a taxi I accepted gratefully. It suited us both, giving him a bit of extra income and me an end to waiting for infrequent buses late at night. While he and his family did what they could to absorb me into their lives, I turned in on myself. The moment I shut my front door that was it. I'd close the curtains, and if anyone knocked I wouldn't answer. And people did knock – after two years in the village I'd built up a nice social life, with some good friends – a group of us would meet regularly in the pub. But now I didn't want to see anyone. I'd press myself into the wall behind the door so they'd think I wasn't there. It was all I could do to get myself to work, do the job and then come home again.

Although there was a village post office, it didn't run to much more than baked beans so, rather than be dependent on other people, I bought myself a bike and would cycle to Callington three miles away to get the groceries, returning with carrier-bags on either side of the handlebars, clanking with tins of cat food. This was exactly what I'd wanted never to happen. I remembered all too well my mother's precarious situation, never having enough money to be truly independent, constantly having to borrow from Peter to pay Paul. I was acutely aware how important it was to stay afloat rather than risk having the house taken from me. It had come full circle. Although I had a job and was earning, it was all going to pay my mortgage and my debt. So I cut down wherever I could: the TV and the video went back to Radio Rentals.

Fifteen thousand pounds was a huge debt, and it very nearly crippled me, but my bank manager was amazing and, with my father acting as guarantor, he agreed to a loan, and over the next few years I worked my butt off to repay it as quickly as I could. I dealt with it because I had to. Coping in a crisis was something I was learning to do. The fallout would come later, when all seemed safely in the past.

On 2 April 1982, Argentina invaded the Falkland Islands. The initial reaction in the newsroom was mystification. What interest could Argentina possibly have in some islands somewhere around the Hebrides? However, Plymouth being one of the largest naval bases in Britain, it wasn't long before we were better informed. While the UN put its faith in diplomacy, the prime minister, Mrs Thatcher, decided a show of force might prove more effective. Within hours Plymouth had changed out of all recognition. The voyage to the South Atlantic would take six weeks so there was no time to lose. All leave was cancelled and the streets were full of uniforms as young men said their last goodbyes to their girlfriends. This wasn't just an exercise: for the first time since Korea, the country was going to war. What became known as the Task Force was about to set sail.

At BBC South West I was very much a studio-based presenter. I could read an autocue without fluffing, but I had zero experience as a reporter. When the opportunity arose to get out there, however, I grabbed it with both hands. Word came in that local register offices were opening early to cope with a sudden rush of marriages. By a strange co-incidence, a new one had just opened on Plymouth Hoe days before, and at seven thirty one morning – complete with camera crew – I found myself witnessing the marriage of a young marine and his girlfriend. The naval dockyards at Devonport were now working round the clock, fitting out the aircraft-carriers, troop-carriers and warships, as the civilian population got on with the business of loading munitions, taking on supplies and removing all trace of names from the ships with an extra coat of paint. Meanwhile Plymouth Sound lay quietly in a state of readiness for what was to come.

That morning both bride and groom were emotionally confused and I sensed that they didn't really grasp the full meaning of the vows they were making. But make them they did, and immediately the ceremony was over we sped off to Unit Headquarters, 42 Commando. The new husband left immediately to join his fellow marines on the parade-ground, while my crew and I had the extraordinary privilege of hearing the company commander address the troops before they flew out to Ascension Island. Both the scene and the fantastic speech seemed to have come straight out of *Henry V* as the CO laid down the reasons they were going: democracy, freedom of speech, liberating the islands from a foreign invader. They had a difficult job to do, he said, but it was the one they had been trained for. 'You haven't faced war before and some of you may return as casualties, but your comrades will be there to help you, as you will help them.' I've paraphrased what he said – this was, after all, thirty years ago – but his final sentence I will never forget: 'Quick march the South Atlantic.' At that, the huge body of marines turned as one and marched off. Then, pomp and ceremony over, it was time for reality: young people clutching each other, others joshing that they had counted the body-bags and there weren't quite enough ...

While my crew filmed the last embrace of our newly-weds, I stood back and surveyed the scene. I know that I will never witness anything quite like it again. Then, as the buses carrying the troops drove off we went to the bride's flat for a couple of fags and a glass of wine – no honeymoon for her.

Then it was back to the studio with the film – no video in those days. Once it had been developed, I'd join the film editor in the editing suite where we'd put the package together ready for that night's programme. I never saw either of those young people again.

The next few weeks were very strange. Communication was minimal. The country lived in limbo. Programmes would be interrupted with a newsflash and a defence spokes-man would come on air. The first announcement by this grey-suited, sombre-voiced official, that a ship had gone and lives had been lost, brought home to us as nothing else could that this really was war. Six weeks before it had been very gung-ho. Now, with the news of casualties, the atmosphere changed. The *Sun* might have gloated over the destruction of the ARA *General Belgrano*, but the loss at sea of more than three hundred Argentinian lives was greeted soberly in Plymouth, while the sinking of HMS *Sheffield* by an Exocet missile was proof that the Royal Navy was not invincible. Her home port may have been Portsmouth rather than Plymouth, but the effect on morale was the same. It was devastating.

Filmed reports could only be brought back by plane, and sometimes they would be broadcast from the Azores by satellite, but more often we made do with audio accounts. The Falklands was perhaps the last conflict when radio was the prime source of information. Censorship was a huge problem, and when Brian Hanrahan, the BBC's foreign affairs correspondent, famously said, 'I counted them all out, and I counted them all back,' his words were chosen as a way of circumventing the rules about giving direct information. It was a coded way of saying that all the British Harrier jets had returned to their aircraft-carrier without loss.

On 13 June the Argentinian general in charge of Stanley surrendered. During the seventy-four days of the conflict, more than nine hundred lives had been lost. In addition to Britain's 258 dead, there were three times as many wounded. Yet when the Plymouth fleet returned to its home port, this time there was jubilation and it was utterly infectious. At lunchtime, if I could get away, I'd go up onto the Hoe and watch as a bystander. Every time news came through that one of these great ships was on its way in, boats of every kind and size would go out to escort it into harbour. The quays and the Hoe would be lined with people and the little flotilla would arrive, hooters sounding, fireboats spraying arcs of water over the returning heroes with their giant hoses. Then came the quayside reunions, wives, girlfriends, mum and dads, not to mention the babies born while their fathers had been away.

Although I was young and didn't really understand the full implications, I was already emotionally involved. Since I had arrived at Westward two years previously several ships had asked me to be their 'mascot'. It wasn't official but it was generally approved as a way of building links with the community. The Ministry of Defence saw you as a morale booster, the TV bosses as an ambassador for the station. For my part, I was always very touched that they wanted me. I would be treated with all due ceremony and piped aboard but then I'd be whisked off into the bowels as I was usually there at the invitation of the ratings – the sailors – rather than the officers. They would always be keen to show me what they, personally, were responsible for: loading the guns, firing them, or working the radar, none of which I really understood. The sleeping quarters were like cramped dormitories, each berth decorated with photographs and mementoes of loved ones and home. I went down into submarines, up in helicopters, and aeroplanes, including a Hawk, the plane that the Red Arrows use.

Our region was dominated by the sea and one of the most terrible news stories I was ever involved with was the Penlee lifeboat disaster in 1981. It was just before Christmas the previous year when the call had gone out that a Dublin-registered coaster was in trouble near Wolf Rock off the south coast of Cornwall. The *Union Star* had been built in Holland and was on its maiden voyage, heading for Ireland. The weather was so bad that an RAF helicopter was unable to take the crew off. The *Solomon Browne* duly put to sea.

Penlee is a tiny community and only one man from each family was taken because of the danger. Of twelve volunteers, eight were chosen. All were drowned. There wasn't one family in this village that wasn't touched. I was in the studio that night and I remember having to stand in front of a big screen on which were written the names, and having to read out the roll-call of those who had died. I absorbed the blow at the time. It was only later that it hit me.

The sea is an inseparable part of Plymouth's history. The *Mayflower* left from Plymouth as did Francis Drake, in the *Golden Hind*. For every boat that sails across the Atlantic it's the last port of call and has always had a vibrant yachting community. I met Chay Blyth who, in 1971, became the first person to sail westwards – the wrong way, against the prevailing winds – around the world, and also got to know Rob James and his wife Naomi, already a DBE, who broke the world record for sailing single-handed round the world via Cape Horn. One of the great events of the yachting calendar was the *Observer* Single-handed Transatlantic Yacht Race and, in 1980, on the evening before the start, a party was held at Piermasters, the sailors' (and broadcasters') favourite drinking haunt in the Barbican, where everyone would let their hair down. It was an outrageous evening, complete with jazz band and every yachting name under the sun. Over the next couple of years Rob would never fail to remind me of how I'd been dancing on the tables and generally behaving with a total lack of decorum.

Less than three years later, I found myself in a situation that every newsreader dreads when news came through of someone that I knew. On 22 March 1983 Rob James had been lost overboard, not in some outlandish place, but a few miles off the Devon coast. He was sailing a trimaran to Plymouth from Cowes when he fell from the rigging, and the netting between the hulls broke. He was brought out of the water an hour and three-quarters later and helicoptered out, but the intense cold had been too much for him and he was pronounced dead on arrival at hospital. He was thirty-six. His daughter was born eleven days afterwards.

This was back in the days when sporting heroes did die doing their jobs . . .

Ever since my car accident and its aftermath, I had found myself unable to break out of my black fog, unable to move forward. My twenty-fifth birthday came and went and nothing changed. Not even the visit of my father and step-mother – who took me to Piermasters to celebrate – could dispel the gloom. Not that they had any idea as I raised my glass of champagne, and joked and laughed – but it meant nothing. Nor could I lay the blame at anybody else's door. I had done it all by myself. I felt utterly derelict, banished from the happy life I had envisaged when I'd found my little house. I had forfeited this happiness by my own stupid behaviour. I felt I was in limbo, in no man's land – on the outside all smiles and growing professional confidence, and on the inside a pit of despair, dark and unforgiving. How could I feel like this when I had so much? The guilt only made it worse. I hated myself and felt that God was right to abandon me.

Nick's sister Haley was one of the few who saw behind the smile. I had somehow to 'get out of myself', she said. It was her suggestion that I learn to ride and she put me in touch with Carol Hazard. Carol was beautiful, a wonderful wild woman with a fantastically attractive personality and a voice you would never forget. She had a little yard and stables on the edge of Bodmin Moor, at a place called Henwood, about half an hour's drive from St Dominick.

It was too far to cycle and the first time Haley took me up there. After that I inveigled a reporter on the show called John Francis to come with me and we learnt together. On summer evenings we would drive to Henwood after work, saddle up, walk up the lane then – bang – we were on the moor. Occasionally we'd stop at a pub – there actually were hitching posts – and go in for a sausage and a pint. I could hardly call myself a rider, but I loved the combination of strength and gentleness in these graceful and dignified creatures who were prepared to carry me and put up with my ineptitude.

One weekend Vikki Heywood joined us – a fully fledged stage manager now. She put both John and me to shame as it turned out she had ridden since she was a child. One incident sticks in my memory. One evening we came across a couple of distressed sheep that had got out of a field. Somehow, on horseback, we managed to round them up, open the gate and shepherd them back in. I felt utterly exhilarated. I might not have any control over my life, but I could control a horse!

In the spring of 1983, I got my driving licence back but, in one of those cruel tricks of fate, it coincided with the break-up of a relationship. This had been a glow on the horizon, which had promised a different kind of future. Nor was it a clean break. It was messy and, for me, a time of terrible uncertainty. One afternoon I decided I couldn't bear the pain any longer, and I sat down and opened a bottle of paracetamol. It was autumn, the light was already fading from the sky, and I couldn't bear the thought of the interminable evening ahead of me. All I wanted was to sleep, sleep, sleep. The pussycats were with me and I tipped the bottle, poured myself a handful and swigged them down with a glass of whisky. It felt like a brave thing to do, scary but also seductive. I didn't take the whole bottle, as if I didn't know whether or not it was what I wanted to do. That was when the phone rang.

'Hello, Princess. How are you?' It was Nick.

'Oh, you know . . . all right.'

'You don't sound all right.'

Then I burst into tears and told him what I'd done. We talked for a couple of minutes, then he put the phone down. He was miles away in Buckinghamshire, but his sister was only in Liskeard. Twenty minutes later Haley was there, banging at the door. I had bought a new bottle so she could see how many I had taken and decided it wasn't enough to kill me. She did the time-honoured thing they do in Hollywood movies, strong black coffee, keep moving, keep awake, and I was lucky.

Why hadn't I swallowed the lot? Because I was a coward. I wasn't brave enough.

Over the next few days she encouraged me to see the doctor and tell him the truth of how I was feeling. He made sure that, for a while, I saw him once a week for a half-hour chat and gave me my first prescription of anti-depressants. He knew what he was talking about. I found out later that he was a fellow sufferer. Over the next few weeks and months the fog did begin to clear, and while I wasn't in a constant state of bliss I was feeling more like my old self.

Craig Rich, our legendary weather man, said he had a caravan on the north Cornish coast that I could borrow. It was late spring and I drove off, not knowing where I was going, and it was just as he said, a little caravan in a field looking over the sea just west of Padstow. It was a completely amazing place – utterly unlike the south Cornish coast that I was so familiar with. Within ten minutes you were on

Trevose Head, a wild promontory of bleak beauty. For four days I walked, through gorse and spiny trees bent double with the prevailing wind, the crash of the surf drowning all other sounds in my head, then returned, exhausted but exhilarated, to the great horseshoe beach that the caravan overlooked, and sat huddled on the sand, my back to the cliff, watching the sun go down over the Atlantic.

Something I raised with Gordon Brown yesterday was the cost of paying for a chronic illness such as cystic fibrosis. Once he had talked about his son, the fact that it would be there for life, and the importance of exercise ('I want him to be a rugby player like I was'), I went on to ask him why sufferers from cystic fibrosis had to pay for their medication while diabetics, for example, do not. His answer belonged in the 'we plan to change that' category.

This issue hadn't come up via our researchers but from a letter that had been sent to me. There might not be a lot that Phillip or I can do personally, but we can weave case histories into the show if we feel they're relevant to our general audience. Some get channelled through our 'resident' doctor, Dr Chris. He deals with a number of health issues on a regular basis, such as prostate cancer – the symptoms, the test and so on. Another is breast cancer, and we've had a lot of ladies who, having seen Dr Chris examining a topless model in the studio, do it themselves in a way they haven't done before, then discover a problem and go to their GP to get it sorted. One lady recently wrote thanking Dr Chris for saving her grand-daughter's life. When this little girl started choking, her granny knew exactly what to do, thanks to a recent item he'd done on exactly that.

Until two or three years ago I found it difficult to stay dry-eyed when I heard people's stories live on air, particularly when they concerned seriously ill children , wholly innocent about the treatment they're receiving and what the outcome is likely to be. I usually managed to hold myself together while we were on air – but during the commercial break . . .

I don't do it now. It's not that I've toughened up, just realized it wasn't helping. We're not doing open heart surgery on This Morning, *we're not running the country, but in a small way we're giving somebody who is in a terrible situation a fantastic day out and a happy memory. It's hard enough for them to tell their story without worrying that I'm upset.*

It's not about me, it's about them. People like me do live in a gilded world: we have cars taking us in and out of work, we get paid very well. So to start complaining – about feeling tired, or having a headache, or being stressed out – it's like, So fucking what? We're paid to smile and entertain.

Heading to London and the BBC

9. Breakfast at the Ritz

One evening in early August 1983, just after I got back to Baber Cottage after the evening's show, the telephone rang.

It was the BBC in London, to be precise Ron Neil, the editor of *Breakfast Time*. 'We'd like you to come up and do a couple of days on the sofa,' he said.

British television had recently undergone its first major upheaval since the introduction of BBC2. The previous October Channel 4 had been launched, and TV-am – who would only broadcast in the mornings – had gone live at the beginning of February 1983. In the spirit of competition, the BBC had decided to steal TV-am's thunder with a breakfast programme of their own fronted by BBC veteran Frank Bough and the ultra-glamorous Selina Scott, a newsreader poached from ITN. Against all the odds they beat TV-am's *Good Morning Britain* to the finishing post and launched *Breakfast Time* on 17 January, two weeks earlier than their commercial rivals went on air.

Before then, breakfast television hadn't existed in Britain. Morning programming had been entirely educational – Open University, schools or pre-schools. The format was very different from anything that had gone before. The set looked like a living room, with red sofas, low tables and easy chairs, and it was generally very laid back. It mixed hard news with horoscopes; there might be an item on the economy at one minute, the Green Goddess (Diana Moran) doing aerobics at Waterloo station the next, and the family of presenters genuinely seemed to be having fun. It was an instant success and I remember lying in bed watching the first one go out and thinking, This is interesting.

So, when Ron Neil called, I was both flattered and excited. It would only be for two days, he said: Selina was off filming and I'd be standing in for her. I was used to doing a half-hour show – I'd done *Spotlight* now for nearly two years – and I didn't see how it could be that different, just five times longer. So that was what I did – carried on as usual, smiled, and generally didn't betray any kind of nerves or discomfort because I didn't have any.

My stint over, I returned to Plymouth, but it wasn't long before Ron Neil called me again. 'We'd like to give you a contract,' he said. 'We'd like you to come up and you'll have a proper contract for a year.' They wanted me as a floating presenter, covering for Selina 'on the sofa' when she was away, and reading the news when Debbie Rix, the newsreader, was off. In addition I would be doing some of my own reporting. It was a peach. The idea that this might prove the equivalent of bungee-jumping off a skyscraper without a safety harness never occurred to me.

There were a couple of downsides, the first of which was the exceedingly early start. As we went on air at six thirty, I would need to arrive at the studio at around four thirty in the morning, which meant getting up at three thirty. Second, my interviews were inevitably the nimsy, gimsy, nibbly ones, like 'Hmm, the latest mousetrap' – nothing interesting in terms of meatiness, but I understood that and didn't take it personally; in 1983 television was still very male-dominated. As for my co-*Breakfast Time*rs, Selina was wonderful, as lovely as she appears, but Frank Bough was not quite the genial uncle his public persona suggested; after all those years at *Grandstand* and *Nationwide* he was seen as something of a national institution.

Just before I started, Ron Neil arranged a get-together lunch to meet the team. Frank and I sat next to each other at the restaurant and he was quite sweet – after all, we had already done two days together in August, and such was his power that I wouldn't have got the job had he not approved. Then, as it got to the coffee-and-cigarette stage, he leant over to whisper in my ear.

'Well, young lady, I wonder how long it will be before I'm having an affair with you,' he said.

I laughed and then looked at him carefully. *Was* it a joke? I'll never know. We never had a comfortable working relationship. Sharing a sofa with Frank, needing to be smiley and jokey on air, was difficult in the circumstances.

During the interview briefings before the show, Frank would wave me away with 'Oh, hers can wait. Now back to mine.' And, of course, his interviews *were* more important, but I was too raw to say, 'Hang on a minute. I need to be briefed on this one properly, please.'

Selina, meanwhile, was lovely to me. She could see I was unhappy and knew exactly what was going on. Frank was ungenerous to her too. It was perhaps jealousy because she was beautiful, guests loved her and she was filling the newspapers and magazines. The man with the thinning hair and saggy cardigan was not in the same league. Not that Selina was seeking celebrity, quite the contrary. Like Moira Stewart, she was doing her best to be private, trying always to fly under the radar.

One day after the show she asked if I'd like to have breakfast with her. Love to, I said.

'Come on, then, I'll take you to the Ritz.'

And she did, and ordered devilled kidneys for us both and I wasn't brave enough to say, 'I think I'd really rather not . . .' but – well brought up as I was – I swallowed them with a smile and said, 'Mm, lovely . . .'

'So, tell me,' she began, as we settled down for a chat over the Ritz's best damask, 'how are you getting on with Frank?' Because, of course, she was elsewhere when he and I were sharing the sofa.

'Well,' I said, choosing my words carefully, 'he hasn't got a sense of humour, has he?'

She roared with laughter. 'No, he hasn't and I'll tell you something else he hasn't got – he has no ad-lib facility. The best way to muck him up is to ask him a question on air – any question you like. He won't be able to answer it. Try it.'

Shortly after this it was Mother's Day, and Frank and I were presenting the show together. Every morning he would irritate everybody going, 'Yip, yip, yip!' – getting his energy together, he said.

So he'd done his 'yips' and the opening titles rolled, and to ease everyone into the theme of the day we started talking about the price of flowers. This was my moment. 'So, Frank,' I said, 'what are your favourite flowers?' I caught a flash of wild panic in his eyes. He was completely stumped.

'What are yours, Fern?'

And I thought, Gotcha. I know how to do this now.

Though I still had my cottage in St Dominick, for the first time in my life I was living in London on a permanent basis. Cherry had asked Jonathan Cohen, Brian Cant's co-host on *Playaway*, if I could be his lodger, and he'd said yes. Anyone who watched *Playaway*, whether as a mother or a child, knows who Jonathan is, and I was lucky enough to have met him when I was fourteen, when my sister first began working on the show. To me he was family.

Jonathan is a wonderful person to be around. He is very tall with a deep nut-brown voice and is passionate about his music – he started as a classical pianist and joined *Playaway* immediately on leaving the Royal College. He's a typical Gemini, gregarious, outgoing, and with a fantastic sense of humour. He'd be the first person to admit that he has never quite grown up. He tells a wonderful story of how, as a child prodigy, the local paper's caption on his photograph after a recital read, 'Small Boy Dwarfed by Giant Organ'.

I arrived at Jonathan's planning to stay two weeks and ended up staying two years. It was a large three-storey Edwardian house just off Chiswick High Road and I lived in the basement, with my own bedroom and bathroom, sharing the living room and kitchen. Not that there was ever any food. The most you could hope for was the remains of a bottle of milk and a few teabags. Yet it was the most welcoming place you can imagine, always full of musicians and performers – a wonderful counterpoint to my increasingly tense life at Lime Grove.

Having to get up in the middle of the night made for a strange kind of existence. Until I had kids I always tried to get eight hours' sleep, so would usually be in bed by seven. Living in a basement helped, but on a warm summer evening, with Chiswick High Road at its most seductive – young people promenading up and down, spilling out of pubs and bars onto the pavement – it was hard to resist Jonathan's suggestion that we pop out for a drink and a bite to eat. And so the evening would begin, the company funny and friendly, the conversation hilarious. Then it would be, 'Well, perhaps just one more.' And then, 'Well, just one more.' Eventually we'd roll back to the house, the lid of the piano would come up and Jonathan would start to play, somebody else start singing – from Carole King to Motown – till he would begin some beautiful classical piece, then fool around and play it backwards ... We'd all be having an absolute ball. First it was midnight, then one o'clock and then ... 'Oh, fuck. The taxi's coming in an hour ...' It didn't happen very often, but when it did ... Two and a half hours of live television isn't the best environment to nurse a hangover.

The only problem about living at Jonathan's was the pussycats. I couldn't bring them with me – they were used to the freedom of the countryside. Reluctantly I'd decided they wouldn't survive twenty-four hours in Chiswick. But I'd be back at St Dominick most weekends and Wendy, the lady who looked after the cottage, would feed them, and so far it had worked. One morning I had just got back from the studio when Jonathan said I should sit down because he had some bad news. There'd been a phone call, he said. Delia was dead. She'd been knocked over by a car and left at the side of the road. She'd been found and buried by a local farmer. I was devastated. My pussycats were my family. Just their presence in the cottage was guaranteed to make me feel less alone and we'd been through so much together. Luckily it was a Friday and I drove straight down to Cornwall. But I couldn't bid Delia a final farewell because Wendy had removed all trace of her: bowl, bed, catnip mouse, everything had gone. I couldn't bear it, and went upstairs that night after my long drive down feeling very heavy-hearted. But there, at the foot of my bed, I saw the dent she always made. Silly as it might seem, I felt comforted. There was something still left of her.

'I took everything away so you wouldn't be upset,' Wendy explained, the next day when she came round.

'You just missed one thing,' I told her. 'Her dent in the duvet.'

'No, I didn't,' she said. 'I made sure I shook the duvet out.'

Winnie says it was her ghost, and I believe her.

Back at Lime Grove, things weren't getting any better. I was by far the youngest member of the onscreen *Breakfast Time* team but I was being treated in a way that nobody should be treated. I'd regularly get called up to say they needed me to do a filmed report that evening – this at six p.m. on a day when I'd been up since three thirty a.m. Sometimes I agreed – dragging myself out and feeling terrible – but at others I'd explain I was dog tired and simply couldn't do it. Then I'd be hit with 'What do you mean you can't do it?' Suddenly I was everybody's punch-bag.

When standing in for Selina, Frank would pat the sofa next to him, turn to Debbie and say, 'Well, it won't be long before you're sitting next to me.'

One Friday Frank threw a lunch party at his flat in Earl's Court, some end of term occasion. Everybody had been invited and, although I didn't want to go, I thought it might be used against me if I didn't turn up. But the moment Frank opened the door I realized something was wrong: I'd got the time wrong. It couldn't have been worse: the first to arrive was his least favourite person. I sat there, perched on the edge of the sofa, my hands sweating while Frank and a lady friend played house.

'Oh darling, don't forget to put the crisps out for our guest.'

'Of course, darling, they're by the telephone.'

'Oh darling, where's the orange juice we bought, darling?'

'It's in the fridge, darling.'

And then with a flourish the lady friend produced this

plate of crisps and I managed to choose one the size of a tea plate, the sort that explodes all over you and the carpet when you bite into it . . . I definitely got The Look.

Finally the other guests started to arrive, forming cosy groups as far away from me as possible. I got the message and left.

One morning Ron Neil swept onto the studio floor through the forest of cameras. Although he headed up *Breakfast Time* he was not often in the studio itself; that was the province of the Producer of the Day. It was just after eight. After being on air for an hour and a half, we'd have a short break while Debbie read the news. There wasn't enough time to do anything very much, so we'd just sit back, relax and wait for the cue that we were up and running again. That particular morning Ron stood there in front of me – and the guests – and started ranting: 'You are terrible, terrible. I have never seen anything this bad, now get on and do another hour.'

After the show, he took me into his office, locked the door behind him and tore into me. I was appalling. I was useless. I was a bad presenter. I was a lazy presenter. I didn't do my homework, I didn't listen to a brief in the morning.

'Well, I don't get a brief. It doesn't happen. Frank gets briefed but not me.'

Protesting wasn't going to help. Frank was a very powerful character, and he and Ron were best mates. I started to cry. He wasn't impressed.

'I'm not leaving you alone,' he said, 'until I see some grit in you.'

'You'll never see any grit in me if this is the way you treat me.'

By this time my face was a disaster area, my makeup gone, my skin blotchy, my eyes red, my nose running and mascara making rivulets down my face. The confrontation must have lasted about an hour and even when it was clear we were getting nowhere he wouldn't let me leave in case somebody should see.

'Wait here and I'll go and get your makeup,' he said. So I stayed in his office until he returned, and then I had to sit there in front of him while I put my makeup on again.

'Get this straight,' he said, as he left. 'If you don't pull yourself together, you're not going to get your contract renewed.' I couldn't have cared less. I would have liked to say, 'You can stick your job.'

There had been some breaks in the horror. Vikki had introduced me to the joys of riding in Hyde Park – not a patch on Bodmin Moor but a good deal closer and at least I was out in the open. Then my father had invited me to go with him to Hong Kong where he was touring with *The Tempest*. At the age of seventy-three, Sir Anthony Quayle had set up his own touring company called Compass, which enabled him to play some of the great Shakespearean roles for the last time. It was wonderful to find myself with actors again. No jealousy, no rivalry, I could just enjoy the magic.

All too soon it was back to the misery factory. I would sit in the bath at four a.m. sobbing and thinking, Please, God, how long do I have to go on? Then I'd pull myself together, and it was on with the smile. The scene hands knew what was happening, and would do their best to bolster me up, bringing me cups of tea, having a laugh and generally looking after me, as would the makeup lady who regularly had to mop me up.

In spite of my personal unhappiness, the programme itself had confounded all expectations. By pipping TV-am to the post by two weeks it had secured the loyalty of the viewers and TV-am was soon in meltdown. For several weeks presenters changed as if they were playing musical chairs. In April 1983, only two months after it had gone on air, an unknown executive called Greg Dyke went in and turned it round, making the show much more like *Breakfast Time*, replacing the high-profile presenters (David Frost, Anna Ford, Angela Rippon) with two easy-going unknowns, Nick Owen and Anne Diamond, not to mention Roland Rat. He was criticized at the time for taking the programme down-market, but if he hadn't, then in all likelihood it would have gone to the wall. Little over a year later Greg left TV-am for TVS, the Southampton-based commercial television channel, and at around the time I was reaching breaking point, I had a call from his office. Greg Dyke wanted to know, they said, if I'd be interested in having a chat about working with TVS.

The timing couldn't have been better. An initial meeting was arranged in TVS's London office. The interview was with the two people who would be most involved, a former colleague of Greg Dyke's who'd been with him at TV-am called Clive Jones, and Mark Sharman, the producer of the show they had in mind for me. They were making some changes to programming, they explained, and wondered if I might be persuaded to go down there to co-anchor the evening news magazine *Coast to Coast*. They were taking a punt in asking me to go back to the regions, because they made the assumption I was flying high at the BBC. Why would I want to leave a successful national show and work in the sticks? I would obviously need an inducement. They said all the right things and the money they were offering was poaching money. I leapt at it.

Meanwhile, back at the BBC Ron Neil had left and somebody else was sitting in his chair. Within a few days of my meeting with TVS, the new editor called me into his office. He wanted to remind me that my contract was coming up for renewal. 'We're considering whether to keep you or not.'

'I've been offered a job by another company.'

He laughed. 'If you think I'll fall for that old trick . . .'

'It's no trick, I assure you. And in fact you've just made my mind up.'

I worked out a short period of notice and that was it. My leaving party took some beating, no expense spared, straight after my last programme, around the desk and flowers from the garage across the road. Even so, the majority wouldn't come near me because any contact with the Poisoned One was the kiss of death. Frank (and Ron, who dropped in for the 'occasion') didn't even have the grace to say goodbye. My parting shot was, 'This is the happiest day of my life.'

When I joined them in 1985, TVS was three years into its franchise. It was a bigger player than Westward had been and had aspirations to be bigger still. *Coast to Coast* – TVS's flagship programme – had long been hosted by Fred Dineage so I joined an already existing and successful 'brand'. Fred was a senior and highly respected anchorman and it's to his credit that he welcomed me as he did. With his owl-like glasses and combover hairstyle, he was a local institution. My first task was to find somewhere to live. Realistically I couldn't hang onto my cottage in St Dominick any longer – it was simply too far away for weekend visits. But neither could I risk buying anywhere too close to Southampton where TVS were based: what if it all went wrong? Hedging my bets, I bought Mayflower Cottage, one of a little Victorian terrace overlooking the common in a village called Sherfield-on-Loddon, just north of Basingstoke, about halfway to London and a forty-five-minute drive from the studio.

I had taken to Clive Jones, Greg Dyke's colleague, from our very first encounter. He was big and burly and generally avuncular – he reminded me of my uncle Paul. He was used to dealing with presenters so, on that level, we got on very well but in reality we had little in common. In the beginning he thought I hadn't a brain in my head but I soon changed his mind. We were talking about the poem 'Not Waving but Drowning'.

'Stevie Smith,' I said.

'No,' he said. 'Stephen Spender.' And, of course, he was wrong and I was right. He used to mock me for having gone to what he called a direct-grant school. Although it was called Dr Challoner's High School, it was totally state funded. 'Well, you had to partially pay for it.'

'No, we didn't. Nobody paid anything. I grew up with no money in my house – you're not the only working-class hero round here.'

His background had been very different from mine, however. He came from very modest roots: his father was a miner and his mother had clearly had brains though she never had the opportunity to do anything with them. Clive was the classic grammar-school boy made good. He was the first in his family to go to university – he studied industrial relations at the London School of Economics. From working as a journalist on the *Yorkshire Post*, he'd switched to television, becoming a reporter on Yorkshire Television in 1978. He'd then gone via LWT to TV-am with Greg Dyke. Now he was TVS's controller of news and current affairs – to give him his full title – with Greg as director of programmes. He was powerful, clever and, it was soon clear, interested in me.

I can't remember now exactly when our relationship started. I always knew he was married – he'd met his wife at university – but I had fallen for him very heavily. It was like a drug. We couldn't show our feelings for each other in public so the relationship remained totally clandestine.

What can you say about being a mistress, which I was? Weekends were blanks. Holidays worse. I spent them on my own, cycling around the Hampshire and Berkshire country-side, trying not to think about him and failing miserably, desperate to spend even a couple of snatched hours with him, whatever the emotional cost. Months drifted by and it got no better. Stolen lunches in pubs were spent watching who was coming in and I hated it, hated the secrecy, hated the lies, and after a year I told him it had to stop, that it was wrong and we shouldn't be doing it. I was desperately in love but in the end I found the courage to call a halt.

Two nights later he turned up on the doorstep with a case and his coat. 'I've left,' he said.

On our way into the studios, Tony's route takes us past Buckingham Palace and I always check to see whether the Queen is at home. If all you can see is the Union Jack, then she's somewhere else; it's the Royal Standard you want. Only once in all these years have I actually seen it running up the flagpole, which means she's approaching any minute. This morning she's not in residence. As to where she might be, she could be anywhere, but given it's May she's probably in Windsor.

Two years ago, I went to Windsor to report on Her Majesty's eightieth birthday for This Morning. When Jack heard I was going, he immediately asked to come too, so I thought, Why not? After all, it was a bit of living history and therefore educational. So I phoned the school and left a message. (Harry wasn't interested.)

So there we were, Jack, me and the camera crew in the photographers' pen when the Queen emerged for her walkabout. I had ordered a posy of flowers – anything to get her attention – and had warned Jack he'd have to hold them. He was only twelve and was starting to look embarrassed when one of the royal bodyguards – a very tall man who had recognized me – came over, said, 'OK, son,' put his hands under Jack's arms, lifted him over the barrier and set him down. The bodyguard then went back to Her Majesty, indicated this little boy – nobody else was on their side of the barriers – and beckoned Jack over. Thankfully he remembered to give her the flowers, they talked a bit, and then she moved on. While all this was going on, my professional side was giving live commentary – no mention of who the small boy was, or what my relationship to him might have been. I was surrounded by people who knew what was happening but, like them, I had to carry on with the job, although my maternal heart was bursting with pride. Jack took it all in his stride.

'So how was it?' I asked, when he got back.

'Felt strange,' he began. 'I haven't been lifted up like that for ages.'

When I finally winkled out of him what the Queen had said, it was nothing revelatory, but he'd remembered to say, 'Happy birthday, ma'am.' (I'd drilled into him that 'Ma'am rhymes with jam.') After thanking him for the flowers, she'd asked why he wasn't at school. He'd told her he had the day off 'to come and see you', at which she had smiled. It's a day Jack will remember all his life. The Queen looked great, happily strolling around in the sunshine with the Duke beside her, fit as fleas the pair of them. I met Prince Philip earlier this year when I was handing out some Duke of Edinburgh Awards and afterwards I was presented and we had a little chat.

'Did you do the Duke of Edinburgh Awards yourself?' he asked.

'No, sir, we didn't have them at my school and I fear I'm a bit old for them now.'

'Hmm,' he said, looking me up and down. 'You said it.'

I do love a bit of history. When I was in charge of entertainments with CTC, I'd often organize historical trips. Now I set them up for Phillip, Lyn, David and me. We're based in one of the greatest cities in the world yet we hardly see any of it. So, once every four to five weeks we take ourselves off. We've been to Buckingham Palace and the Queen's Mews and the Queen's Private Gallery. We went to Kensington Palace and were given a private tour of Princess Margaret's apartment, which happened to be closed to the public that day. It was utterly fascinating but at the same time rather sad, stripped of all its furniture. The tired-looking kitchen had been designed by Lord Snowdon and reminded me of the aviary he did for London Zoo and the awning for Prince Charles's investiture as Prince of Wales.

Whatever I might think about his kitchen design, however, Lord Snowdon was a wonderful photographer. In one of his most iconic pictures, Princess Margaret is lying in the bath, wearing her tiara, looking beautiful and flirtatious. In it you can see his reflection in the mirror – he's wearing a towelling dressing-gown. So there was this very same bathroom, nothing having changed except for a damp patch and peeling wallpaper. Even more fascinating was her private bathroom – four times the size of the other – complete with an early Jacuzzi, instruction booklet still by the side. A photograph shows how it was originally. Set within a circle of heated towel rails was her dressing-table, covered with a collection of exotic sea shells. Now not even the table remains, while on the wall, where her hairdresser's backwash basin once jutted out, there is only a scar.

Dressed for royal duty, 1987

10. Paradise Lost

That summer, 1986, my father had asked me to go with him on holiday to Majorca and nothing could have been more welcome. I needed distance to get some perspective on the situation with Clive. I couldn't get rid of the image of him standing on the doorstep of my little cottage, in his suede jacket, his bag dumped at his feet and saying, 'I've left,' as if it was a magic trick: 'Da-dah!'

In the end I had let him in, given him a glass of whisky, then sent him packing. Yes, I had been extremely unhappy with the situation, which was why I had called it a day. But at no time had I given him an ultimatum, never said, 'It's her or me.' I simply understood that what we were doing was wrong and it had to stop. I didn't want to hurt anybody and I'd had enough.

The next few weeks were horrible as the war of attrition got under way: the responsibility for the whole situation lay on my shoulders. I was nothing but a flibbertigibbet who, having fucked up this brilliant executive's life, had now changed her mind. And for what? The damage was already done, etc. Over and over I told him it was no good. That we had done wrong and that my decision – difficult as it was – had been made. But every time I saw him all the old feelings came back. I didn't know what to do.

My holiday with Dada came as a great relief. Of course we talked about it. He wasn't judgemental – he hardly had the right to be – but he did say one thing that I have never

185

forgotten: 'When you throw a pebble in the pool the ripples go on and on.'

Over the last few years, my father had more than made up for holidays I'd missed out on when I was little, although Majorca was the first sun-and-sand trip we'd had, the others being all tour-based so that I could see him perform in faraway places. He even flew me to New York for the first night of Alan J. Lerner's last musical, *Dance a Little Closer*; I stayed with Vikki, who was there with the Royal Shakespeare Company.

Our relationship has never been the conventional one of father and daughter. There had been none of the jousting that is usual between parent and child, those times – often painful – when the parent learns to accept that the child is now a grown-up and equal, and the child comes to accept that the parent is not infallible. He couldn't judge me. He had forfeited his right to treat me as a child, and I came into his life as a fully formed (nearly) adult. As a result he was – is – more of a friend, older, sometimes wiser, someone whose judgement I could trust, and I soon found that there was nothing we couldn't discuss. It wasn't just one way. By the same token, he could discuss his emotional experiences with me.

We flew back into Gatwick after an idyllic two weeks in Majorca to find Clive waiting in the arrivals hall. He looked terrible, pale and thin. It turned out that he had spent most of the fortnight talking to my mother – which was how he knew when I was coming back – telling her how much he adored and loved me, and how I'd broken his heart; he'd kept her up till three o'clock in the morning. So then he told my father he was going to take me home. Dada gave me a look, as if to say, 'You don't have to, you know,' but I didn't have the heart to send Clive away.

That night he pushed me again, and I still said no. But somewhere along the line – that night or the night after – no changed into OK. In the end I decided that I had made my bed and now I had to lie in it. He was right. The damage was done. I knew it was not my finest hour and I took no pleasure in the thought that I was getting my happiness at the expense of someone else's. But in the end I'm a fatalistic person. This thing seemed to be happening and it wasn't as if I didn't love him. On the contrary I loved him very dearly, and he was a wonderful man, with that soft, deep, rumbly voice, and I really believed he was special, and that he was going to look after me. I felt secure and safe, and he loved me so much that he was prepared to leave his family for me. He moved his things out of Greg Dyke's spare room and into mine.

One evening, Clive turned up at the cottage shortly after I had got back from the studio. He'd been up in London having lunch with David Frost. No sooner had he dumped his bag and taken off his coat than he went down on one knee, handed me a small box and asked me to marry him. Inside was a ring – a sapphire surrounded by little diamonds – which he'd bought in Hatton Garden that afternoon. It was a true surprise and incredibly romantic. I was overcome. Nobody had ever asked me to marry them before and in a strange way I'd convinced myself it would never happen, so it came as a shock when it did. Even more surprising (and a good sign) was that the ring fitted. I immediately rang my mother and the first thing she said was 'Don't lose it!' Because the sad thing was that nothing had changed. Clive was still married, and in the interests of discretion, no one was allowed to know until everything was legal, so I wore it at home or on a chain round my neck.

Falling in love, marrying the prince and living happily ever after is part of every little girl's childhood dream, but in no fairytale version that I know of does the prince already have children, and it's fair to say that I had never expected it to happen to me. But there I was and, having had a step-parent, I knew it could be a bumpy ride. (At least I'd had a choice in the matter. I could have walked away from Clive, but for his children it was a *fait accompli*.) I was also aware that they would feel resentment towards me and that it wouldn't be pleasant. On my side I had to resist harbouring negative emotions towards them.

Clive's three children were very sweet and confused, wanting to do their best for Daddy while being very loyal to Mum. I spoke to each of them individually and explained that I had been a step-child too, that I didn't want to replace their mother but that I hoped we might be friends. 'And whatever your feelings,' I said, 'you can always talk to me about them, and I will listen and never be cross.' Yet in spite of all my good intentions, I did get cross – silly things like the children not picking up clothes, or coming into the house with sand in their shoes. Because knowing is not the same thing as doing.

The rosy picture I'd painted for myself – that once our relationship was out in the open we'd have more time for each other – was quick to fade. Clive spent weekends seeing his children, who'd be involved in activities, from ponies to orchestra practice and rugby, while I was left on my own. The children also dictated where we would live, not literally, of course, but he had to have easy access both to the studios and to his family. We plumped for Southsea. Neither of us had a previous connection with it and it was by the sea, nice for me and for the children. Southsea is basically the residential part of Portsmouth – in many ways the twin of

Plymouth, two hundred miles to the west – so I felt at home there, and I had always wanted to live by the sea.

Like everything else in Clive's life, house-hunting had to be worked into the diary, and one Saturday morning we set off with three appointments to view. The first two, we didn't even bother going inside: Clive didn't like the street. The third was different. Even from the outside it was handsome. It certainly needed a lick of paint, but it was light and airy with high ceilings and plenty of space for all the kids.

'Right,' Clive said, the moment we stepped out of the front door. 'On the basis that I've found where I want to live, I'm off to play rugby.' That was that. As for actually buying it, I had to do that as his money was still wrapped up in the family house.

Six Hereford Road was a big old Victorian house about ten minutes' walk from the sea front, and I loved it. It was substantial, with seven bedrooms and a dear little garden, which was already nicely stocked, but I could see immediately that I could play with it, plant more and enjoy. Thanks to my mother, a home and a garden are inseparable in my mind, and I get huge pleasure simply from watching things grow. (In due course, I hosted a gardening programme. I'd always had the enthusiasm, but through *That's Gardening* I developed real knowledge.) We moved in just before my thirtieth birthday.

I had time on my hands. Although *Coast to Coast* was on every weekday evening, I wasn't needed in the studio until midday. Clive and I were now living together 'officially' but pin-pointing a date to get married was another matter. It wasn't the wedding itself that presented a problem as much as the honeymoon: finding an entire week clear of appointments and other commitments was proving difficult.

As with all the other ITV franchises, the TVS licence to broadcast extended only until December 1992, and a decision on whether or not to renew it would be made fifteen months before that in order to give any new incumbent sufficient time to effect a smooth transition. Greg Dyke having gone back to LWT, Clive was now TVS's Mr Big and a lot rested on his shoulders. There were union meetings, meetings with other regional executives, meetings with investors, meetings with journalists, meetings with his team, meetings with just about everybody except me.

When Clive left the house at seven in the morning I was asleep, and when I got home at seven thirty in the evening the house would be dark, cold and empty. I took it as my lot: 'This is how it is.'

We were married on 12 November 1988 in Southsea's register office. We came and went in a white Rolls-Royce, and on the way back to Hereford Road – where the reception was being held – I had a sudden idea. 'Could we go via the Esplanade, please?' I asked the driver.

Soon we were heading for the beach.

'What on earth do you think you're doing?' Clive said.

'I want to walk along the front in my wedding dress!'

It was a glorious, blue-skied, cloudless day, and even though it was November I thought it would be a lovely romantic start to our married life, something we could re-member, people standing on the front, saying, 'Look, there's a bride!'

As we stepped out of the car, he fumbled in his pocket for his cigarettes, tapped one out and lit up.

'Aren't you going to walk with me?' I asked.

He took a few puffs and looked about. 'We should get back to the house,' he said at last. 'They'll be wondering where we are.'

Feeling ridiculous I climbed back into the car.

'So where have you been?' people said, as we walked in.

I smiled brightly. 'We went for a walk down by the sea!'

And everyone went, 'Aaaaah! How lovely, how romantic . . .'

We had invited about seventy people – family and old friends: neither of us wanted an office party. On my side there were Mummy and George, Cherry and her babies, Uncle Paul, Auntie Elsie, Michael and Gerald. Vikki came with her Mr Right (or Mr Wright, as he was), and Ben Sumner, my twin from Central. Brian and Jonathan were on tour with a stage version of *Playaway*, so they couldn't make it.

Clive had wandered off as soon as we'd arrived, and by the time I found him, he was sitting in the marquee at the back of the house, with a plate of food and a glass of wine, completely on his own. I was so amazed I borrowed somebody's camera and took a snap.

By this time I had already decorated the house from top to bottom, spending weeks and weeks up a ladder painting while listening to the radio. Sometimes I would still be there when Clive finally came home at one in the morning. Once that was finished I'd taken up ballet and singing – all those things I'd not been able to do when I was a child. Then somebody mentioned pantomime and I thought, Why not?

That Christmas I 'gave my Dandini' – Prince Charming's valet, who does the rounds with the glass slipper – at the Mayflower Theatre in Southampton, with Paul Nicholas as the Prince, and I absolutely loved it. My father had finally got his wish – his daughter was on the stage! Not acting as such – I didn't believe I could act – but performing. And Dada was lovely – so generous and full of praise. His professional endorsement gave me huge pleasure.

191

He'd been on tour when I got married, so had missed the wedding. Another family member who didn't make it was Prampa, my Weston-super-Mare paternal grandfather.

He and Dada's mother – known confusingly as Mamma – had been shadowy figures in my early life. I seem to think they did once come to The Bumbles. I have a vague memory of being made to wash behind my ears, which was totally alien to me. The next time I saw Prampa was at Mamma's funeral. Cherry and I went with Dada to the nursing home where they had both been living for some time. After the burial, Prampa gave me Mamma's wedding ring. They had been together for seventy years.

I was acutely aware that I didn't have the hinterland of grandparents that other people had and I determined to rectify the situation. As Prampa had all but lost his sight, I gave him a Dictaphone so that he could record his memories, recount stories of his life. But I had left it too late: he didn't understand how it worked. 'Ah,' he'd say, when I telephoned. 'I need some more Durex.'

'Durex? Are you sure, Prampa?'

'Yes, Durex. I can't get that thing of yours to work. I think they've run out.'

'Oh, you mean Duracell!'

'Durex.'

'Duracell. What size are they?'

'Size?'

'Double A, Triple A?'

'Eh?'

'Size, Prampa.'

'Durex.'

I suggested he send me one as an example. Good idea. What was my address?

'Six Hereford Road.'

'Sixty-six Hartfield Road?'

'No, Prampa. Six Hereford Road.'

'Right you are. Six Hartfield Road. And where's that?'

'Southsea.'

'Southsea! Good God, I was there during the war. I've got some stories about that I can tell you.'

'Well, that's why I'd love you to record your memories for me.'

'Hmm. So, what's your name, then?'

'Fifi.'

'I know that. I mean the last one.'

'Britton, like yours.'

'Like mine? Good God. Who're you married to, then?'

He was now nearly ninety, and his mind had started to go, but there were some things he didn't forget. Whenever we spoke he would always ask me why Adek – Mummy – never got in touch.

'Maybe it's because you weren't around when she needed you,' I said. I'd thought about prevaricating – after all, he was a very old boy – but in the end I decided I should tell him the truth. 'Unfortunately, Prampa, I think that's the reason.'

My other grandfather, of course, was equally eccentric. I didn't meet him until he was an old man, this tall figure – he was six foot four – sitting in a loincloth in Auntie Elsie's lounge in Ickenham, with the central heating turned up to furnace proportions by Uncle Paul. I was used to eccentric behaviour in the family – my father made his living by dressing up, after all – so his appearance didn't bother me. Far from being frightening, he was positively twinkly and he'd say things to make me laugh. I remember listening to him reciting Keats, Shakespeare and Milton in a wonderful pukka accent, left over from the 1930s. (He completely silenced the curator of Milton's Cottage when we went there later, quoting *Paradise Lost* and *Paradise Regained*. He had never come across anything like it, the curator said, and took him down into the archives.) Even though it's unlikely that, as a child, I understood any of it, I knew I wanted him to like me. I'd heard stories about him all my life and it was like, 'Oh, my God, here he is!' As he sat there, puffing away on his pipe, like the patriarch he was, I gazed at him in awe, marvelling that this was the man to whom all of us sitting around him – apart from Auntie Elsie – owed our existence.

At one point he asked me what I was reading. I mumbled something he didn't hear.

'But you do like reading, Fifi?'

'Yes,' I said.

'So what do you like to read? Do you like murder mysteries, perhaps?'

Whatever I answered, murder mysteries were what he sent. While he was over in England he went to visit his various brothers and sisters (none of whom we ever met), and possibly he'd left personal possessions with them. The first pile I got were Dorothy L. Sayers's Lord Peter Wimsey stories. Then came a few Miss Marples and finally Denis Wheatley. I still have them.

For that first year after our wedding things weren't too bad. There was a stage where we had a nice little social life going, meeting up for supper, going for a drink or playing cards with friends we made together in Southsea. But by the time we had our first anniversary, the franchise business loomed ever more thunderously.

'We haven't met your husband,' people would say, and joke that I'd made him up, that I wasn't really married. It reminded me of when I was little, and school friends would say, 'Where's your dad, then?'

I wasn't living the life I'd expected to live. I had imagined that once we were married we'd be a partnership. But not only was he running this big company on a day-to-day basis, there were longer-term, strategic difficulties. Having been thwarted in its attempts to have programmes taken up nationally, TVS had bought an American production company called MTM – Mary Tyler Moore – and had basically paid too much for it. Huge amounts of money were involved. TVS employed eight hundred people and now their careers and livelihoods were at stake. While I fully appreciate why Clive had to do it, there is no doubt that I was very isolated. The last thing I could do was to confide in anyone at work as I had done in the past – after all, I was now the boss's wife . . .

It wasn't long before I was seriously depressed again. During the week at least I had *Coast to Coast* but I took on other jobs to keep busy. In addition to *That's Gardening*, I had a weekly lunchtime chat show, a mix of *Pebble Mill at One*, *Loose Women* and cut-price *Parkinson* in which we did three interviews in half an hour – my sixth live show in a week. At weekends, however, there was no escape because my husband was either playing rugby or taking the children to rugby. I thought, This is the secret of marriage that no one talks about.

As Clive had three much-loved children I had always accepted that he might not want a second family, but I persuaded him that perhaps we might have just one baby. I had never assumed it would happen straight away: Cherry and Brian had had huge difficulties, and in the end Dada paid for her to have IVF treatment and she had her twins, Christabel and Peter. Two years later Rose arrived quite naturally out of the blue. During the long years of Cherry's anguish I had made a pact with God: if he could give my sister children I would relinquish my own rights.

The first few months came and went. Nothing. Then the next three months, with three more disappointments. As the time went by I realized that my pact with God was coming true. At the same time it was beginning to be a problem at work. While Fred was seen as a decent family man with three children, I was thought to be a career woman who didn't have a maternal bone in her body.

It was my GP who suggested we talk to a fertility specialist who was an expert on intrauterine insemination (IUI). The cause of my failure to conceive naturally was never fully established; we were just one of those couples who had some kind of incompatibility. I was given the same cocktail of drugs and hormones that apply with IVF, the difference being it wasn't done in a test tube. Three times I had such high hopes. And three times my hopes were dashed. My faith in God was sorely tested. What made it worse was that there was nobody I could discuss it with, apart from Mummy and Cherry, but they lived more than sixty miles away.

During this painful time, I did what I could to stay positive. The specialist had stressed the need to keep healthy – walk, cut down the drinking (I didn't smoke), fresh air and a good night's sleep. It was summer and I was sleeping badly, waking up at the first hint of light. Rather than go walking on my own, I'd wait until Clive was awake. 'It's a lovely day,' I'd tell him. 'It's beautiful out there. The sun's warm – let's walk a mile or two . . .'

I remember thinking, Here I am, by the sea, which is what I've always wanted. Come on, feel you're part of it. Feel you're part of this town and this city. Southsea is named after Southsea Castle, built by Henry VIII as part of the country's defences against invaders. It was here that he watched his favourite ship the *Mary Rose* go down, doing battle with the French. This was where Nelson walked before the English fleet set sail for the Mediterranean to fight Napoleon. But I never did feel part of it. I was always an outsider.

Another Christmas, another pantomime – this time in Southsea, playing Fairy Bow Bells in *Dick Whittington*. It couldn't have been easier – the theatre was within walking distance of Hereford Road: two minutes from front door to stage door. The principal boy, Dick Whittington, was played by Lorraine Chase, and the villain, King Rat, by Michael Elphick, very much the sewer rat, covered with black sludge and slime and big heavy builders' boots and generally horrible-looking. Like me, he was playing close to home, and also like me, he'd started life in the theatre backstage – as a fifteen-year-old, he was an apprentice electrician at the Chichester Festival Theatre when it was being built.

My costume was every little girl's dream – white net skirt, velvet jacket and handmade wand. On the first night I heard the clump of Michael's boots coming down the corridor to my dressing room, followed by a knock on the door. 'Got something nice for my fairy,' he said, as he came in, his fist closed. 'She's got to look really good, well-dressed. Hold out your hand.' So I did, and into it dropped two diamanté earrings. There was no wrapping, no box, just the earrings. And I would always put them on for the walk-down – the curtain call. They were my walk-down earrings, and I would always be so embarrassed, do a quick little bob and move away as quickly as possible to the side, but after a few performances Michael said he wanted a word.

'You know what you must do? You've got to go down there, stand tall, take the applause, and *then* walk to the side.'

He was a lovely, lovely man and his death at the age of fifty-five was a tragedy. I still have the earrings he gave me.

Clive continued to work incredibly long hours – when he wasn't with his children he was holed up in some hideous corporate hotel, hammering out yet more deals, anything to ensure TVS retained the franchise. It was no wonder I didn't conceive – we hardly ever saw each other.

The tension was unbearable. One night, after a row, I couldn't sleep and eventually, at around four o'clock in the morning, went downstairs, got out the car and drove to the sea front. The night was clear and cold and I'd taken with me a flask of tea. I sat there so long that I watched one of the ferries go to France and come back again. I felt powerless, tearful with frustration. I was somehow in a back-water unable to get out, just going round and round. It was gone nine by the time I went home. I thought, He'll have missed me by now. He'll be worried. He was still asleep.

TVS's sealed bid was submitted in May 1991 and a few months later, on 16 October, the news came through that it had failed. In 1989 *Coast to Coast* had won the Royal Television Society's award for the Best News Programme of the Year, as it would again the year the bid was rejected. We had been jubilant then. Now it was ashes in our mouths.

Whenever they show compilations of Britton and Schofield's funny bits, what really has us in hysterics is not our manic giggling but the clothes, the fashion horrors from past years. I first met David O'Brien, our fashion stylist, about eleven years ago. I had only recently had Grace and I was still breastfeeding. I'd soon lose the extra weight I'd put on, I thought. It didn't happen. Gradually over the years I got bigger and bigger, until eventually the balloon I had become began to deflate. So poor David (in his twenties when I'd met him) has had to cope with a middle-aged woman whose figure has gone up, down, in, out, sagged, done the full thing. Luckily he has chosen to see my fluctuating size as a challenge rather than a complete bloody nightmare.

As for my style, there was no template for someone like me. On the personal front, I had completely let go of my appearance. Getting through the day was difficult enough; twirling about in front of the mirror was the last thing I'd think of doing. Right from the start David really cared: he knew instinctively that the issue was getting me well mentally, and gently, gently, like the horse whisperer, he got me to look at him without my eyes popping out of my head and my ears flattening against my mane. He got me to accept his view of how I should look. He never took me shopping – that was a step too far. Instead he would bring things in.

On Ready Steady Cook I'd been forced into tents and flapping trousers. David was determined to change all that. We had to become 'fashion fearless', he said. Meanwhile everyone else (the opposition) was a blonde, extensions-wearing, Lycra-skirted, bling ear-ringed stick. He found a range called Nitya and put me in dark tunics with Nehru collars or duster coats with scoop necks, which he'd attack with his shears to take lower, true to his mantra: 'If you've got it, flaunt it.' He'd add soft, narrow-legged trousers and spent a fortune on Gina sandals. (My shoe rack is the envy of anybody who enters my dressing room.) I had a tunic for every day of the week. Some were embroidered, some he got in white, then dyed. He worked on the necklines, scooped, shaped and skimmed. All the while the call volume was going through the roof with larger ladies asking where they could get them.

We did a makeover with a lady who wanted 'the Fern Britton look'. I have to admit to being slightly unnerved. When finished, she looked uncannily like me and I thought, If only we could send you out and I could stay at home . . .

Once Phillip Schofield and I were hitting the spot as a TV couple, invitations to go on other shows began rolling in. I couldn't look as if I'd simply wandered across from This Morning, David said. Something different was required. Our first outing was Celebrity Who Wants to Be a Millionaire? The jacket was from Wallis, the trousers M&S, though the shoes – the highest ever – were from Gina because they combine height, glitz and comfort like nothing else. Not that David is concerned with comfort – another of his mantras is 'Beauty is pain'. If he can put me in Spandex from neck to knee, he's happy because, like all stylists, he adores to get you into super-strength underwear so that there aren't bulges in places they don't want bulges to be. We give most of my outfits names – it makes them easier to identify rather than saying 'that black thing with the buttons down the front'. Laura, for example, is a corset named after the French corsetière whose creation she is and made her first appearance on Soapstar Superstar, which I did with Ben Shephard. Getting me into it involved David and Lyn hauling on the laces like a couple of stevedores but the result was a triumph, even though I could hardly breathe. Once I was suitably encased, the upper layer went on: a simple black dress

29. Mummy and her girls, 1975

30. Surprise! My eighteenth birthday party thrown by Nick, 17 July 1975.

31. My official eighteenth birthday party with Mummy and the family. I'm wearing the famous Milkmaid dress.

32. Four grubby techs celebrate the end of student life: (*Left to right*) Krister Blom, me, Trish Bertram and Michael Townsend. Michael and I had just landed our first job with the Cambridge Theatre Company.

33. Lindsay Duncan (*left*) and Sheila Hancock enjoy the view as Clive Francis demonstrates his skill with a punt on a cast outing. *The Deep Blue Sea* was my first professional job as an ASM.

34. Although not on the acting course, we techs were often co-opted for crowd scenes. Here Amanda, Trish and I enjoy dressing up.

35. My first car, nicknamed Pork Chop. I had just driven from Buckinghamshire to Cornwall, staying in the middle lane all the way.

36. Vikky and Dada in Times Square, New York, where she was working with the Royal Shakespeare Company in the late 1980s.

37. Dada and I may not have had holidays together when I was a child, but he made up for it in later years. This was in Manhattan.

38. Prampa and me on the beach at Weston-super-Mare shortly after I got married.

39. Mummy, me and a very pregnant Cherry, expecting her twins Peter and Christabel in 1986.

41. Which one is the Ugly Sister?

40. Jan Hunt as Prince Charming, and me as 'his' sidekick Dandini in *Cinderella* at the Mayflower Theatre, Southampton, Christmas 1988.

42. Panto time again, but this time in Southsea. Stirling Rodger, me and Michael Elphick doing the 'Time Warp'.

43. Giving my Dandini.

44. An official publicity snap for BBC's *Breakfast Time* in 1983.

45. *Top of the Morning* at GMTV.

46. LNN's Entertainment Presenter. Have microphone, will interview.

47. Six-month-old twins and a broken wrist. I smiled for the camera but inside I was dying.

48. The garden at Little Coppice, which I would leave within a year of this photograph being taken. Grace was four weeks old and the twins, Harry (*left*) and Jack, sitting in front of Clive, were three and a half.

49. My beautiful Mercedes, purchased on impulse. The most extravagant thing I've ever bought, just weeks before Grace was born.

50. Old friends and fellow techs Vikki Heywood, Ben Sumner and I meet up at the christening of Ben's son – my godson – Tom. Grace was only a few months old, hence my mammoth breast-feeding boobs.

51. 1998. Forty-one years old, single and feeling liberated, enjoying sun, sand and sea at Mother Ivey's Bay.

52. With Cherry in St Mark's Square, Venice, Easter 1998. Mummy came too, the three of us celebrating my newly single life.

53. On the *Ready Steady Cook* live tour.

David had picked up in New York topped with a lurex shrug, wrapped and tied and pinned until I felt like a million dollars. He wanted me to sparkle, and sparkle I did. After the show the phones never stopped ringing.

'You do realize don't you,' David said, 'that what we've got here is a data base of potential customers who would buy these clothes. We have our own collection.' I'd never thought of it like that, but he was right. Initially I was like, 'Yeah, yeah, so what?' But with his usual gentle persistence, I was eventually convinced and one day we sat down and talked through what we liked, what worked, what was us. That was when the idea of Fat Birds was born.

The best present ever. Christmas Eve, 1993.

11. Tomato on Legs

On 31 December 1992, TVS bowed out with a New Year's Eve extravaganza, hosted by Fred Dineage, Matthew Kelly and me. In fact Meridian, who would take over officially at midnight, had been in charge in all but name for well over a year. They had been committed to a smooth handover and had wanted to keep the existing on-air faces, which included mine. I hadn't wanted to stay – my feelings towards the people who had cost my husband his job weren't exactly charitable – but I had signed a contract to remain until the end of the franchise, though I had made it clear that I didn't want to stay beyond that.

Clive, however, had cleared his desk as soon as it became obvious that TVS weren't going to be allowed to appeal. Luckily, within days he was asked to set up a news and facilities organization called London News Network. This was a brand-new venture to provide a seven-days-a-week local news service for London, which had never happened before, a joint operation between LWT and Carlton, who were replacing Thames as the providers of Monday-to-Friday programming in the capital.

Mark Sharman, my former producer on *Coast to Coast*, who had gone on to become head of news at TVS, was also taken on by LNN, and it was he who offered me a job on *London Tonight*, rather than Clive who – understandably – was vulnerable to accusations of nepotism.

I explained about Clive and the sensitivity of my position,

but Mark was adamant. 'This is nothing to do with Clive,' he said. 'I want you to come and cover entertainment.'

He was feeling sorry for me, I said.

'With your background? Come off it. There's nobody who can bring to this job what you can.'

One problem: my contract at TVS had another three or four months to run. I grasped the nettle, and made an appointment to see my boss, to try and get them to release me early. No dice. Unbeknown to me, Clive then rang this same guy (whom he knew well having worked with him for all those years) and that night he told me it had been sorted. I was released.

'How did you do that?' I said. 'I tried everything and failed miserably.'

'I told him you'd had an emotional year, and you'd had three miscarriages, which is basically true.'

'But that's *not* true!'

'Come on. You've had a rough time. What's the problem?'

Pleased though I was to be out of TVS, I felt distinctly uncomfortable. Three failed fertility treatments are heartbreaking, but they're not miscarriages.

Although I left TVS shortly afterwards, I returned for one last time, for the emotional bowing-out gala on New Year's Eve.

London being arguably the entertainment capital of the world, entertainment was legitimate news, and Mark was right, it was a dream job for me: any first night in the West End, there I was, microphone in hand, crew at my side. Theatre, film, you name it. Exhibitions, actors being fêted by BAFTA – whatever it was, I'd go and report on it. It was bloody hard work – and for half the money I'd been getting at TVS – but I enjoyed it enormously and I was working round the clock.

We sold our house in Southsea and rented a little flat on the river. It felt good. It felt like a new beginning. Another chapter: living by the Thames in a smart little gaff by Tower Bridge.

LNN were based at LWT's famous building on the South Bank. It was ten years since I'd done my first stint in the BBC newsroom and things had changed radically since then. The most obvious difference was the lack of noise. As a brand-new company, LNN had invested in the newest technology – I had been used to the clatter of electric type-writers. Not only was there no noise, there was no paper, and we were at the mercy of computers that crashed. To an old-timer like me (all of thirty-five), it felt unnatural.

I loved being back on the road with my crew, just the three of us. I loved all that rushing about, being at the centre of things, coming back with my own film, cutting and scripting it, getting the story I wanted to tell. To all intents and purposes I was my own director, piecing together the jigsaw with the help of the editors. You'd tell them what you wanted, they'd tell you what would work. Co-operation at its best. Before going out on a story I would say to my crew, 'This is what's happening, we're meeting him, we want to talk to her, and I want to get this out of it, so can we shoot in this room? Is this location OK? Where's best for you?' Then they would take over and consider the visual side. Although the cameraman would carry a small kit of lights, I would end up humping bits and pieces as well: once a stage manager, always a stage manager. I would always feed my crew. I knew it made a difference. 'Tell you what,' I'd say, if it'd been a long day. 'If you can do another hour of this, we'll sit down and have a proper meal.' They worked so hard for me. Back then we were all young and we were all learning.

Entertainment covered a multitude of sins, including the Harrods sale. Why? Because Tom Jones was opening it, of course. The task was Herculean. I had to get to Tom Jones, fighting my way through his myriad fans (not to mention Mohamed al-Fayed's security guys) and persuade him to say something witty or sexy on camera, get the film back, cut it, voice it and have it on air for midday. I was totally responsible for the 'package'. Once done, I'd hand it to the editor, they'd slam it in the machine and that was it. On. From start to finish, two and a half hours.

First thing in the morning I was crowded into the press pen with photographers, cameramen, journalists – half of London. Eventually along comesTom Jones sharing a horse-drawn Harrods' carriage with al-Fayed himself. I'm surrounded by people shouting, 'Tom, over here!' Once he's in the store, you join the general scrum. But in this, at least, I am no greenhorn. One thing I know for certain is that wherever else the poor man is dragged he will end up in the toy department. So, with a nod and a wink to my bemused crew, that's where we head, while the rest of the press pack follow the pied piper (actually Scottish pipers) in the opposite direction.

So there we are, poised among the toys, and we hear the sound of bagpipes coming towards us. It's worked! Instead of constantly trying to catch up, we're ahead of the game. Now for the *coup de grâce*. Tom Jones's recent hit song was 'Kiss'. Could I get him to kiss me? The poor sod didn't have a chance. But it wasn't me, it was my fetching thigh-high split skirt, and Mohamed himself, who said, 'Give her a kiss,' and he did. He smelt delicious. All that was required then was his voice saying, 'Watch me tonight on *London Tonight*.'

Not only did he do that, but he gave me an interview too. We rushed back, cut it, voiced it, and got it on air for twelve o'clock. It would be re-cut for the afternoon bulletin and screened in full Technicolor glory on *London Tonight* at six.

When we'd moved up to London I had been referred to the Lister Hospital on the Chelsea Embankment for full-on IVF. At our first appointment, 1 March 1993, Dr Marie Wren went through our notes and ran tests on us both. The results came back: no problems.

'Well, let's do it, then,' she said. Within a week we were on the starting grid.

Anyone who has undergone IVF knows how hard it is. I learnt to give myself daily injections, my handbag rattling with syringes and phials of hormones, and a letter saying that I was not a junkie and that I was permitted to have them. At eleven a.m., no matter where I was, I had to find a discreet loo and inject myself. Then there were the regular scans every few days, to see how the egg follicles were developing. Finally, after the go-ahead, there was a massive injection of hormones at midnight to kick-start the release of the eggs. Within only a few hours I was on the operating table having them harvested.

'Well done,' Dr Wren said, when she saw me on the ward afterwards. 'We collected twenty-one, and they're of such good quality, would you consider donating some?' Once it was established that I had enough healthy eggs for myself, she suggested I donate five. So I did, with a form describing myself physically, my likes, my dislikes, my interests and my hobbies, for the prospective mum. It's all utterly confidential and I will never know if anything worked.

Meanwhile Clive did his bit, and we went home to wait, a

nail-biting three days before we'd know if any of the eggs had fertilized. The phone call came late one morning. Yes. We had seven or eight good ones, the best three of which would be implanted. Hours later I was back in the Lister, on the bed, legs up in stirrups. Once I was in place, a TV screen was switched on, linked directly to the lab, where we watched as the three little clusters of cells – the image highly magnified – were transferred from a Petri dish marked with our name to a very fine pipette. Then, to my amazement, instead of waiting several minutes while the pipette was brought up from the basement, or wherever the lab was, the wall opposite slid open, and I found myself staring directly into the lab, while they were staring right up my jacksie. The pipette was passed through the 'wall' and the whole procedure was over within seconds. I had to wait for twenty minutes to let things 'settle' and then I was free to go.

This was now my fourth attempt and I'd become quite fatalistic, used as I was to the crushing disappointment of it not working. I'd already told myself it was the last time, my final shot. I just didn't think I could cope with any more, the hopes raised – held in check – then dashed. Even so it felt strange. For four weeks I'd been in daily contact with the hospital, monitored, scanned, injected. Now I was on my own. In two weeks' time I'd know. Either my period would come, as usual, as it had every month of my life since I was thirteen, or it wouldn't. All medical intervention was over and we could only wait for nature to take its course.

While all this was going on, we'd been moving house. The flat at Tower Bridge had only ever been a stepping-stone, but to where? As LNN was operated jointly by LWT and Carlton, Clive seemed to spend his life driving between

London and Birmingham, while I still needed to get into central London. We had decided to look in my old stamping ground, Buckinghamshire.

Little Coppice, in the village of Penn just outside Beaconsfield, was a repossession, and Clive fell in love with it the moment he opened the front door. As he had to move quickly, I didn't even get to see it until the deal was done. I can't say it was a disappointment – it was a handsome thirties house with a large garden – but whoever had lived there before had been determined to keep themselves private and it was surrounded by thick dark hedges. There was nothing that could remotely be called a view, and consequently I felt very hemmed in. But there were huge pluses. Not only was Penn close to an exit on the M40, it was only about twenty minutes away from Mummy, and Cherry, who had moved into The Bumbles when Mummy had moved in with George.

By the time of the implantation, we were settled in our new house.

I didn't know what being pregnant felt like, so when pains started around the time of my period, and my bosoms felt tender, I was convinced it hadn't worked. But then there was nothing. I was always regular, so gave it a few more days, past when I thought I was due, before I called the Lister.

'So what's happened?' they said. They'd been wondering why I hadn't called.

'Well, nothing,' I said.

'You mean no period?'

'No, nothing.'

'And you haven't done a pregnancy test?'

'Well, no.'

'Then go and do one right now, then ring us back.'

I whipped round to the chemist in Penn, which was next to the doctor's surgery, went home, did it, and Bob's your uncle.

Next stage was a scan, they said, and made me an appointment a few days ahead when they judged they'd be able to see a heartbeat. I still didn't allow myself to feel too excited. It was early days, I kept telling myself, so I carried on with my routine as if nothing had changed, going into work, doing the show, not saying anything to anyone.

The lady in the scanning department moved the sensor slowly over my tummy while staring at her screen.

'Congratulations,' she said. 'You've got two babies here. Take a look.' She angled the screen so that I could see and, sure enough, there they were. I was used to seeing an empty cavity, but this was different: two little dots, separated, each held in some sort of white outline, each with their own little placenta.

I took a sudden breath. I couldn't wait to tell Mummy and Cherry – my sister had had twins so I'd know what to do. Then my heart started pounding and I felt myself going into a flat spin. What about Clive? He'd been prepared to have one more child, but two?

I rang him as soon as I got home. 'I've got news for you,' I said.

There was a pause. Then, 'There's two of them, isn't there?'

'Yes.'

'Fucking hell.'

That night he didn't get back till late. It was April and the nights were already quite light. He went out in the garden and stayed there, smoking cigarette after cigarette, walking around as the dusk closed in, while I lay on the sofa with my feet up thinking about the two little beings inside me.

Eventually he came in. 'All right,' he said. 'I've got my head round it now.' And that was that.

Two days after we got the news, I had a call from Peter McHugh, Clive's best man. He was now at GMTV, which had taken over from TV-am in the shake-out of 1991. He wanted me for the slot that is now called *LK Today*, then *Top of the Morning*, which ran from nine till nine thirty. It would mean getting up at five, but it, too, was based at the LWT building. Was I interested?

I was very interested. The timing couldn't have been better. My job with LNN was very physical, and now that I was pregnant, I would have to give it up sooner rather than later. I explained the circumstances to Peter, and he was fine. So, deal done.

The main breakfast show at GMTV was fronted by Eamonn Holmes and Lorraine Kelly. They went on until nine, then handed over to me for the mums-who've-just-come-in-from-the-school-run slot. I did it on my own. I can't claim it was that innovative, by now the accepted mid-morning mix of fashion, makeup, horoscope, problem page and news stories – *This Morning Lite*, you might say – and I was out by ten.

All in all, everything was panning out brilliantly. Even the journey into work didn't bother me. For the first time I didn't have to get there under my own steam: I had my own driver! When I was at *Breakfast Time* I'd had taxis, but this was so much more civilized. The car was only a Ford Granada, but to me it was a Rolls-Royce. I'd get in, and there would be Tim, and I'd think, This is nice. He'd arrive every morning at six and deposit me back home not long after eleven. Tim had a great sense of humour and we used to sail in and out, and have a good laugh on the way back.

And then something strange happened. I became conscious of a peculiar smell at the new house, so strong that it made me feel quite sick – to the extent that I dreaded getting out of the car. 'I can't live here,' I told Clive, one day when it seemed really bad.

'Give it a year, and if you still can't bear it, we'll move.'

I also couldn't stand the colour of the pink rhododendrons – pregnancy had affected both my sense of vision and smell.

When I was ten or eleven weeks pregnant, Clive and I drove down to spend a weekend with my father in Sussex in a cottage he sometimes rented near Chichester, not far from the theatre. It was tiny but lovely, down a little lane among the fields and I loved going there. That first night I woke up and didn't feel quite right so I went to the loo and found I was bleeding. I grabbed a wad of loo paper, walked very slowly back to our bedroom and tried to wake Clive. He was dead to the world. I ended up shouting at him: 'Wake up, wake up! I'm losing the babies!' But nothing. I walked gingerly downstairs thinking, Don't panic, don't panic. I didn't want to wake my father and worry him. There was no point in having a drama. If I'd lost the babies, I'd lost them. Tears welled in my eyes. I always carry a huge Filofax around with me, which doubles as a diary and an address book, and luckily I still had the number of Mr Golland, the doctor who'd overseen the IUI in Southsea. He had given me his home number in case of emergencies, and this was definitely an emergency, I decided.

When I heard his voice at the other end of the line, I felt an overwhelming surge of emotion. I apologized for waking him, 'But I'm bleeding and I know this is nothing to do with you, but I'm down in Chichester and couldn't think of who else to call and you know my history . . .'

'Don't worry about that,' he said. 'Now, do you remember the pessaries I used to give you, the ones to support the hormones?'

I did.

'Do you have any with you, by any chance?'

'I think I might have.' They had given me the same ones at the Lister for use in the early stages.

'Well, pop one in. If you're losing them there's nothing I or anyone else can do, but it should slow things down. Now go back to bed, try to sleep, and come and see me at the Nuffield first thing in the morning.'

I slept fitfully and was wide awake by the time Clive opened his eyes.

'I had a terrible dream last night,' he said. 'I dreamt someone was losing a baby.'

'Yes, you fuckwit, that was me.'

It was Sunday and Clive had to go over to Winchester to see his children. I understood, so he dropped me off at the hospital on the way. As good as his word, Mr Golland came and talked to me, scanned me, examined me, reassured me. Everything appeared safe, he said. I was to stay where I was, however, until things had calmed down. And I felt, Thank God, I'm in the right hands now. It was wonderful to be looked after and to feel so safe and secure.

A nurse popped her head round the door shortly after midday. I had a visitor, she said. Indeed I had: Dada, complete with a beautiful wicker basket full of Sunday lunch. ('Remember you're eating for three now ...') It was my favourite roast lamb, with china plates and proper knives and forks, a little jug of gravy, another of mint sauce and a glass of wine. His girlfriend, the lovely Jane, had done it, and while I tucked in, he sat and talked and it was really special. He was a good father to me that day. The best. It

213

was like years of kindness compressed into a single hour.

So what had happened? Nobody knows for sure but I'd had three eggs implanted and I like to think that this little bleed was the third. I've told the boys this was their third brother, called Wilf. So they sometimes talk about Wilf, which is rather sweet. I'm not sure whether it's the truth or not, but it's what I prefer to feel.

I didn't know at that stage I was carrying boys. I could have done – but I chose not to. Much better to wait until Christmas Day to open your presents.

Although that was the end of my problems with them, the second half of my pregnancy was blighted by the presence of a fibroid. I had known it was there. Before I met Clive I'd had a well-woman MOT and it was spotted. 'Nothing to worry about now,' the doctor had told me, 'it's only the size of your fingernail, but it could cause problems if you get pregnant.' Fibroids feed on the hormones of pregnancy, and especially since I was carrying two babies, mine didn't improve the situation. The pain was excruciating. Sometimes I'd be doubled up with it and end up in hospital on pethidine.

One day when I was about four and a half months pregnant, I had been taken in with the usual agony and a nurse I didn't know came into my side room. 'You the lady who's having twins?' she said.

'Yes, that's me.'

'Well, looks like you've lost one, dear.' And with that she left the room.

I lay there staring straight ahead, trying to breathe normally. Come on now, I said to myself. Take it on the chin. And I thought, I've brought this on myself. I was worried I couldn't cope with two. I've made it happen. I willed it to happen. And now it has.

I got out of bed as if I was sleep-walking, hoping to find out what this would mean – would it stay in there or miscarry? – when I saw the same nurse coming towards me.

'About the baby who's died . . .' I began hesitantly.

'Oh, no, dear, it wasn't you at all. It was the other lady.'

My emotions had just gone round 180 degrees and now they were sent spiralling back in the other direction. The waves of relief were soon supplanted by a weight in the pit of my stomach as I thought of the poor woman to whom the news had really applied. I never mentioned it to anybody.

Although I was very busy with the new job, sorting out the house and redesigning the garden, I was also incredibly lonely. I'd made friends in Southsea and at TVS, but they were now sixty miles away. I'd sit on the front porch in the evening, hugging my tummy and waiting for Clive to come home.

Carrying two babies inside you is not the same as one. I was vast. I couldn't see my feet, let alone put my shoes on. Walking was agony, sleep nearly impossible. One position that worked was sitting at the kitchen table, a pillow under my tummy and another across my chest so my bump was supported and then I'd flop forward. Or I'd pile up some cushions in the corner made by two walls, sit down and sleep propped up like that, my feet wide apart. I couldn't lie on my back because the twins were pressing so much on some bit of me that I'd feel faint, as if oxygen wasn't getting to my brain. Swimming – the water took the weight – was the only time I felt normal. One day Mummy and Cherry took me out to lunch at a friend's house. I was wearing a bright red, rather smart maternity suit. It was during the final stages and under my huge bump, my legs were quite thin. Cherry said I looked like a tomato on legs.

I carried on doing *Top of the Morning* for as long as I could but, at around seven months, my GP said I should call a halt. I was now back in the hands of the NHS at Wycombe General Hospital. I already knew Bill Tingey, my gynaecologist, as he was a friend of Cherry's and had brought all three of her children into the world. He was known as Tiny Gyny and he was a hoot. In early December, about four weeks before the twins were due, Clive took me into the clinic. All these very pregnant women were sitting there when the great man blew in, wrapped up in a little coat, his muffler round his face, bringing with him a blast of freezing Arctic air from the steppes of Amersham. Then, lowering his scarf, he looked about the room full of vast, bovine women and said, 'Is this the contraceptive clinic?'

Getting into the bath that morning I'd seen blood around my ankles, and as I didn't have a wing mirror to hand, I'd asked Clive where it was coming from.

'You've must have cut yourself shaving,' he said.

'Listen,' I said, 'first I couldn't reach anywhere with a razor and, second, I haven't been shaving.'

It wasn't much but it was enough to get me to Mr Tingey.

'Hmm. I can feel a foot,' he said, as he rummaged about. 'I think we'd better have you in. I'll deliver these babies by lunchtime.'

I'd known it would have to be a Caesarean. At the beginning I'd been all set up for a beautiful home birth: independent midwife, lavender oil, whale music, the lot. Then one day, coming into hospital for the fibroid pain, I'd been whisked into a wheelchair and someone had left my notes on my lap. Naturally I'd started reading them, and the first thing was a letter from Mr Tingey: 'Fern is not going to get the birth she wants,' he had written. Something to do with the way they were lying.

The twins were delivered that lunchtime. After waddling down to the operating suite, I'd been hoisted onto a table like an ironing-board, so narrow I was convinced I'd fall off. Clive was barely recognizable in green scrubs and what looked like a J-cloth on his head.

Then came the epidural. Recovery is better if you're awake, they explained, though you don't actually see what's going on, thanks to a little screen. First, they needed to check that the epidural was working by spraying me with ice-cold water. 'Obviously I can't feel that,' I said. 'You might as well sprinkle me with warm Evian. Why not just jab me with a pair of scissors?'

'Don't you worry,' came back Tiny Gyny's voice. 'You won't feel a thing.'

Then it was, 'Right, we've started', and I was, 'Oh, have you?' So while he and I were having a bit of a chat, he was cutting away. And then there was this feeling as if someone was rummaging around in your bottom drawer.

The next thing I heard was, 'Get me a box!'

'What do you need a box for?' I said, somewhat alarmed. Were they born? Didn't they have anything better to put them in than that?

'It's for me to climb on so I can reach better,' he explained. Then, 'Push! Push!'

'What – me?' I'd thought that was the other kind of birth.

'No, not you.'

I watched as two nurses bent down in front of my little screen; the instruction had been directed at them. They had to push from the top and the side to get the babies to pop up through the incision in my stomach.

Then somebody said, 'It's a boy!' and out came Jack, and I can see his little body now, like a newborn lamb, covered with patches of creamy-white stuff, as if someone had rubbed in some Nivea and forgotten to wipe it off. And he had this wonderful smell of fresh air. Once he'd been whisked off to be weighed and cleaned, it was back to rummaging and 'Push!' and out came Harry, a skinny little thing. Unlike Jack who had given a lusty cry, Harry was mewing like a lamb, which meant he had some kind of respiratory problem, though I didn't appreciate this at the time. He was lifted up and put on my chest and I talked to him gently, saying hello, and welcome.

'Well done, Mum,' said Mr Tingey, kissing my cheek – a lovely moment, and he was the first person ever to call me that. 'Right, that's my work finished. I'm off to the Seychelles.'

Both boys were put in the Special Care Baby Unit, exactly as had happened with Cherry's twins, so I didn't panic. But it was strange to know that I'd had them, yet not have them beside me.

Mummy and Cherry were allowed in to see them and they came and relayed what was happening. Jack was fine, but Harry was having problems with breathing. However, he had weight on his side. They were both a respectable six and a half pounds. Some time that first day, I was taken to them in my wheelchair. Poor Harry was covered in lines and drips and alarms and bing-bongs. He was so weak I wasn't allowed to hold him. At the non-acute end of the ward, Jack was yowling. He was fine and angry and wanted to feed and, as he was in good form, they decided he could be brought up to my ward. Once he was suckling I just wouldn't let go of him – I kept him for hours on end.

As for Harry I would go and see him at midnight. A nurse would come with a wheelchair and take me down to the SCBU ward just to see him. One momentous night I did manage to feed him. He was so weak that it took every ounce of energy out of him, but the contact and the milk settled him, so it was Catch 22. I used to sit by his little incubator in tears, unable even to touch him. One night a tear rolled down my cheek and his little eyes just followed it.

Eventually one evening Sister Sawbee, from SCBU, knocked on my door and pushed in this pram with my two little boys lying side by side. 'I think they need their mummy,' she said. It was the first time they had ever been together. They didn't cry, and neither did I. Well, not much.

I was half in euphoria, half living in the worst fog in the world. We had lots of visitors, including all the grand-parents: Clive's parents up from Wales, Dada on his own, bearing teddies. Clive dropped in every morning before work, and Mummy and Cherry would pop by with nighties and knickers, soap and hairbrushes – all those little extras that husbands don't understand. But basically I was in my own little bubble, just me and my boys.

Then, on Christmas Eve, we went home.

My day off and oh, the joy of not having voices in my ear. All presenters on live TV have what's called open talkback – their earpiece – which provides the two-way connection to the gallery where the director, producer and PA sit. Imagine having a conversation with someone beside you while listening to a telephone call at the same time and trying to concentrate on both. For a newcomer, it's daunting, but quickly your brain learns to separate what the interviewee is telling you from the gallery instructions. This background 'chatter' is happening every single moment during the two hours that we're on air. I've learnt to cut most of it out, except when I'm addressed specifically. Phillip, on the other hand, is extremely good at taking in everything that's going on behind the scenes. He hears what the computer's doing, what the edit suites are doing, what the vision mixer's doing, everything. We have a very good balance.

Every live current-affairs presenter longs to step up to the mark when there's a big news story. Although obviously you don't want terrible things to happen, you want to be in the thick of it when they do.

In the same way that we all remember where we were when the World Trade Center was attacked on 11 September 2001, I will never forget the morning of 7 July 2005. The previous day the country had been jubilant when it heard that London had won the bid for the 2012 Olympics. The news came through just as we came off air, and when the newsreader said, 'And now the Red Arrows are going to fly up the Thames,' Phillip and I rushed up to the studio roof, just in time to see them. It was sensational.

The following morning the papers and news bulletins were full of the pros and cons of the Olympics coming to Britain, and Phillip and I were planning a silly sketch, pretending to limber up for a track event. On our way out to shoot it on the Embankment, we passed the gallery and Lolly, the director, waved us in. 'Sky News is saying that something has happened on the Underground,' he said. 'A big power failure or something.' We watched the monitor as Big Bob Crow – general secretary of the RMT, the transport workers' union – came on saying, 'We don't quite know what's happened.' Then Joe Pasquale, the comedian, arrived. He was our first guest that morning, and, seeing the crowd of people in the gallery, he walked in. Phillip and I greeted him, then left to shoot our mini sketch.

As we were mucking around, we could hear the sirens wailing across London. 'Whatever's happening,' I said, 'I think you and I had better change into black because something's going on and it's not good.' My old-fashioned news training had kicked in.

By the time we had made our way back to the studio, the news had come through that a bus had gone up, and it was like, 'Oh, fuck, this is not good.'

The producer of the day was comparatively inexperienced. She said she wasn't sure whether having Joe Pasquale at the top of the show was a good idea. No, it certainly wasn't. ITN were on air now, so we turned our attention to them: they looked bedded in. It seemed distinctly possible that we might not get on air at all.

'If we do go on,' I said to the producer, 'what we need is to get some people in place, some eye-witnesses, a security expert, whatever you can.' Shortly after that it became apparent that we wouldn't be going on air at all and that ITN would keep going throughout the morning.

By chance, Cherry's daughter, my niece Christabel, and a friend had come to see the show that day, and although they were nine-teen, I said, 'You're staying here with me in the studio, whatever that means. If we're stuck in London tonight, we'll sleep in my dressing room and you'll be fine.'

The first thing was to get hold of both their mums to assure them they were safe. Then it was back into the gallery again, and the ITN broadcast to get a sense of what was going on. The sound of London was very different from any other I have experienced. Apart from the sirens there was an unearthly quiet, with none of that low-grade background hum of activity: building workers, music, pleasure cruisers plying their trade on the river. With the London transport system completely shut down, all you could see were people walking, calmly leaving their office buildings with their rucksacks or briefcases, just making their way without fuss in the direction of home. It might have been Essex, it might have been Surrey, it might have been Buckinghamshire. Quietly, no panic, no problem, just stoically 'Well, we'll get home.' And so did we. Somehow Tony, my driver, found his way round the various roadblocks and the three of us, Christabel, her friend and me, all got safely back.

A week later, Phillip and I were again on the Embankment, this time for the one-minute silence, to pay our respects to those who had lost their lives. Everywhere we looked people were standing on pavements, heads bowed. One city, one thought, one emotion. It made me very proud, particularly for our generation. We don't often stand for contemporaries who have died.

Celebrating Mummy's 70th birthday

12. Mrs Tent

At the end of January 1994, Mummy turned seventy and Cherry and I were determined to give her a real treat. The morning was taken up with beautifying: a facial, a massage and a visit to the hairdresser. Then we took her to lunch, and finally to a very posh dress shop where she could have what she wanted. She chose a lovely black cocktail suit, still looking every inch the film star's wife and putting both her daughters to shame.

The one good thing about living in Penn was being near my family. Once the twins were on the way I realized how lucky I was. How on earth would I have coped in Southsea? I hadn't wanted to get things too organized on the principle that I didn't want to tempt Fate, but there came a moment when it couldn't be put off any longer. Cherry gave me things like old cot sheets and babygrows that were lovely and soft after constant washing, and I valued that feeling of continuity. I remember one wonderful afternoon spent in a specialist baby shop in Maidenhead with Mummy and George where we went mad, buying two beautiful little cots, nice and old-fashioned, and blankets and mobiles – one with little ducks that went round, another with circus animals – and music boxes with strings that the babies would learn to pull. Pride of place went to a brilliantly engineered double pram that folded down to almost the size of an umbrella. I also bought my rocking-chair, which still sits by the Aga in the kitchen. Even though George had a huge estate car, we only just managed to get it all in.

Post-natal depression isn't inevitable, even for someone with a history of depression like me. The incidence ranges from ten to fifteen per cent, and I genuinely didn't expect that I would succumb. Why would I? I'd wanted these babies so much, gone through so much to get them – and Fate had smiled on me. Now I was the proud mother of two gorgeous sons. With hindsight, I don't think the time they spent in SCBU helped – it certainly knocked my confidence – but I wasn't being thrown in at the deep end, as most mothers are from day one, and told to get on with it. I put up a barrier of fear: that one of them wouldn't survive but that I'd have to stay strong for the other, so I was 'I'll take whatever you give me, Universe, I'm ready to absorb any-thing.' You know something terrible is going to happen, so you think, Right, I'll protect myself by thinking that I'm ready for it.

As it turned out, the boys thrived, and it also turned out that I was quite good at looking after them. But quite good wasn't good enough. I had to get it absolutely right. If they weren't fed at five fifteen, I was failing. If I hadn't got their cots made, sheets changed, and the washing wasn't in the machine by eight o'clock in the morning, I was failing. I was clinging to a sheer rock face without understanding where I was going or what to do next. I became terrified of not being on top of things. It wasn't just because there were two of them: I've heard the same from new mothers who have only one little bundle to cope with. If you haven't showered and dressed and had something to eat before they wake, you'll never catch up. So you get up half an hour earlier than you gauge they will, and from then on you're on the run. And I'm still like that: my motor is constantly running, looking for the next thing, the next thing, the next thing to do, to do, to do.

It was now that I started to put on weight. Throughout my life I'd gone up and down, between dress sizes twelve and fourteen – not that size as such was ever that important to me: I would simply feel uncomfortable when clothes got too tight. But in the television world I was considered big rather than slender and was always being told to 'lose half a stone'. As a television man to the core, Clive fell into that category. He had met me when I was a sylph, so it surely couldn't be that difficult to get back to where I was, could it? But now that I was breastfeeding two hungry boys, I was eating for England to get through the day. Milk, whether from a cow or you, contains a vast amount of calories and it has to come from somewhere.

For the first six weeks I had a fantastic maternity nurse called Jean – fantastic in all ways but one. She had a blind spot about breastfeeding, particularly at night when she'd take over at every opportunity, giving them a bottle of milk I'd previously expressed. And when she ran out of that she'd feed them formula without me knowing. What I needed was something rather different: someone to wake up with me, fetch me a cup of tea, perhaps, while I sat there feeding them, having a chat or just replenishing my water jug. (I was constantly thirsty because of the volume of liquid they were taking.) Or perhaps helping by changing a nappy, or putting one of them down when he was done and I was busy with the other. But nobody was listening. I either let her give them bottles, or did the entire thing on my own.

Mummy was my lifeline. Every day she would pop in and either throw the Hoover round the house, stick a shepherd's pie in the oven or sit and talk. There is no one like your own mother at times like this.

When the boys were four months old I had a call from Mark Sharman, my producer at TVS and subsequently at

LNN. He wanted me back at LNN for a show called *After Five*.

'Why would you want to do that?' Clive asked, when I sounded him out.

'Well, I've had a fourteen-year career and it seems foolish to chuck it up. This way I could ease myself back in gently.'

'I've never thought of you as having a career,' he said.

It wasn't long, only half an hour, and all I'd have to do was present it, Mark assured me. 'I'll make it really easy for you, you don't have to be in till two thirty and you can go straight home after the show.' If he wanted me that much, then why not? And the idea of getting out of the house, of dressing in normal clothes, of being offered the odd cup of tea was suddenly very appealing. At home I was a milk machine and felt incredibly isolated. Even from the upstairs windows the hedges blocked everything. You could hear the road, but you couldn't see life going by, and that was what it felt like. Life was going by and I wasn't part of it.

The good news was that Jean had left and I had a new nanny. Super Sue wasn't some flibbertigibbet but a proper person with grown-up children of her own whom I already knew as she had looked after Cherry's twins. She would arrive at one o'clock and just take over. Everything up till then I'd have done myself, which usually included, weather permitting, a walk in the pram and then back for their morning snooze. They'd wake around twelve thirty, I'd feed them again and they'd usually drop straight back to sleep, blissed out with milk – you feel so loving and so loved. At one feed Harry would be on the right breast, the next it would be Jack, and so it went on. From the beginning they were both very different, in the way they looked, the way they sounded. I could always tell which one was crying if I was downstairs and they were up.

LNN's offer didn't run to a car. Tim had been co-opted by Clive who had moved to working full-time for Carlton in Birmingham. But the fact that I'd have to go under my own steam didn't strike me as a problem. The opportunity to get out overrode all other issues. I'd drive to Beaconsfield station and catch the train. Great in theory, but in reality a nightmare, especially coming back at the height of the rush-hour. I'd get the Underground from Waterloo to Marylebone and, with luck, be on the six twenty back to Beaconsfield, standing all the way. It wasn't long before I was running to keep pace with myself, chasing my tail, chasing the clock. There were no margins any more. But being back at work gave me stability. I had a reason to wash my hair, put paint on my face, get out of the house, go and be nice to people, and become that other Fern Britton.

One day I literally fell, tripped over when running to post a birthday card to Alastair Stewart whom I'd worked with at TVS – he'd become a great friend, along with his wife Sally, and was Harry's godfather. As I got up from the pavement I saw, with a strange sense of acceptance, that a bone was sticking out: I'd broken my wrist. I could no longer bath the boys, couldn't push the pram or drive the car. So from then on I had to get a taxi to the station and a taxi home again.

The wrist was a sign that should have told me to slow down, but the only way I could keep the demons at bay was by staying busy. When I got back to the house, Super Sue would leave for the day and I'd be on my own. Looking after the boys was suddenly not enough. I did anything to fill my time rather than have to stare into the chasm of nothingness that surrounded me. Seeing me up stepladders and cleaning out cupboards, my mother would say, 'Oh, for God's sake. Look at you, you're ill,' and I'd say, 'This is my house, now go.' Because once I was on my own I was fine.

It was only a problem when other people were around. I needed sanctuary.

Looking back, I can see I must have been awful to live with. I never stopped tidying, clearing up, everything with an eye on the clock. The necessity to get on top of things was snapping at my heels. Jean had suggested that I be as organized with the boys as I would be about work. I knew how to do that. So I wrote down a detailed schedule and stuck to it rigidly. And if anything went wrong, it was as though a spring in a watch had snapped: everything went flying. The specifics changed as the boys got older, but the principle remained the same. It was back to my days at Central: lists, lists and more lists. Organization was everything. Clive didn't understand how important timing was to the smooth running of the house.

'What time will you be home?'

'I don't know.'

'Well, can you give me some idea?'

'Seven thirty.'

But it wouldn't be seven thirty, it'd be nine. Or I'd phone and say, 'How far away are you?' And he'd say, 'Only twenty minutes,' but in fact he'd still be in Birmingham.

I know I was acting irrationally and some might say obsessively, but the point still needs to be made. Men don't understand basic psychology. Rather than say you're going to be home at seven, tell your wife you're not going to be back till nine, and when you walk in at eight she'll love you!

So there I was one afternoon with a broken wrist trying to paint my toenails – all by myself because I wouldn't let anyone help me – and Mummy, looking at this, decided to take the law into her own hands.

'I've called the doctor,' she said, standing at my bedroom

door, 'and made you an appointment at ten o'clock tomorrow morning, because you're not right.'

'I'm absolutely fine.'

'No, you're not.' She stood there for a minute, looking worried. 'I'd like to stay,' she said, 'but I can't. I've got to go.' And she left. She didn't only have to cope with me: she was caring for George who had recently been diagnosed with Parkinson's.

Naturally I rang the surgery. 'I understand that my mother has just spoken to you. I want to say that this was a misunderstanding and I'm absolutely fine, so perhaps you could cancel the appointment.'

Before I knew it the health visitor was knocking at the door. 'This isn't right,' she said, and handed me a questionnaire: the Edinburgh Test. I'd seen it before. I remember very clearly the answers I had given the first time: 'How often have you thought of suicide? Never; once or twice; occasionally; all the time.' So, what are you going to put down? Tick: 'never'. Are you managing to laugh at things more or less than you did before? And so it goes on. You can cheat and lie your way through all of that, and I did.

Why? Because I knew the pain I was in: it was utterly real, mental and physical. I had been there so often already in my life and I just thought, I don't want to have to look at it again. I don't want to have to face it. I don't want to have to explain it to anybody. So it was easier to lie: everything's hunky-dory and I'm coping fine.

The second time I answered truthfully and, of course, it showed I was suicidal. The answer to 'How many times do you think about killing yourself?' was 'All the time'. I used to fantasize about getting into the car and just driving at a wall. All I had to do was turn the wheel a few degrees . . . It

231

wasn't to kill myself, just to turn off the light, make things stop. It's to stop the noise in your head, the pain in you – you just want it to stop. It's not an indulgence, and it's not attention-seeking, and it's not being needy, all the accusations I'd had thrown at me. It's none of that. If there had been an option saying, 'Do you want to go to sleep for a year?' the answer would have been a resounding 'Yes'.

Sometimes when somebody commits suicide you hear people saying, 'My God, but we only saw him last week and he was laughing away, nothing wrong with him at all.' They don't get it. It's like the dolphin. The dolphin is cursed with this very smiley face, so you think it's happy all the time. Well, perhaps it's not. I, too, am blessed with a smiley, happy face and – in my case – the smilier I am, the unhappier I'm feeling inside. When I'm looking relaxed and in repose people sometimes come up to me and say, 'Cheer up, darling, it may never happen!' It makes me want to kick them in the balls. It's then that I'm at my most contented.

Once I'd been diagnosed as having post-natal depression, I was put on Prozac. My GP – the sweetest man – warned me that it might take a bit of time to kick in but that I would soon feel better. It wouldn't cure me, he said, but it would be 'a bridge over troubled waters'. I'd had what amounted to a breakdown, but nobody had known because I'd become so adept at hiding it. I'd be privately sobbing and if somebody came into the room I could turn round and go, 'Hi, how are you? Let's put the kettle on.' I'd go to the loo and turn the bath taps on and weep and weep so that nobody would hear me. I'd get into the car and drive and give myself dreadful sore throats from screaming. I would take a deep breath and go, 'AAAAAAAAGH,' at the top of my voice. I wanted to hurt my throat. I wanted my voice to sound raddled. I wanted there to be a physical sign of what I was going through.

Clive decided that what I needed was a holiday.

'I don't want to go,' I told my nice doctor. 'It's going to be ghastly.' He understood. He saw that my marriage was falling apart. Nobody else did.

'I don't know what really happened between you and Clive,' a friend said recently. What? I thought I was shouting it loudly: 'HELP, HELP!' I thought it was so physical you could see it. Can you not see this cloud of toxic black poison that surrounds me? Can you not see that it's engulfing me? Can you not see that I'm disappearing behind the vapours of it? Can you not see that I've disappeared?

Nobody could.

We set off for the dreaded holiday in two cars. Clive led the way in his brand-new air-conditioned Jaguar with his daughter from his first marriage and her friend, while I followed in George's estate with the boys and Jean. She was with us to help out: Super Sue had her own life to lead and couldn't just dump everything to come. Jean was driving, my broken wrist rendering me completely useless.

There are holidays from hell that you can laugh about afterwards. Not this one. Everything about it was hideous. Clive had booked some sort of gîte and I still cannot believe how anybody could take money for letting it. There wasn't a loo roll, there wasn't a light-bulb, there wasn't a piece of soap and the cots were a disgrace. Needless to say, there wasn't any food, not even a baguette or carton of milk to start us off.

'I'll go and get something,' Clive said. So he sailed off with his daughter and her friend, leaving Jean and me to sort out the babies. Two hours later they returned, looking cheerful. The local town was a delight. They'd wandered

233

around, seen the sights, found a café and had something to eat. Given that no shops had been open, they'd brought us back a couple of slices of congealed pizza.

I think Clive and the teenage girls probably had a lovely holiday. They would shoot off to some splendid beach or other (we'd hear about it later) while Jean and I tried to find some shade for the two little people who had just learnt to sit up.

I realized that the Prozac must be working when I found that I hadn't cried for a day. Then a day became a week. You start to feel a little bit distanced from the raging grief that's inside you. Slowly you get some perspective on it all.

On paper *After Five* should have been perfect for me: a bit of news, a bit of arts, a bit of music, a bit of human interest, like a scaled-down version of *This Morning*. But the truth was it wasn't working. I have no doubt whatsoever that I was difficult at that time, but for it to work you and the producer of the show have to get on, and the new producer and I just didn't. He didn't understand me and I didn't understand him. We would argue about what was right and what was wrong. Basically we didn't like each other.

One day my agent called. Peter Plant was very ill with cancer and made no bones about the fact that he was sorting out his clients, getting them fabulous contracts before he died. I was lucky enough to be one of them. Knowing I was unhappy at *After Five*, he'd been keeping his ears open for something else. And now he had it. He'd got me an audition, he said, for a brand-new cookery show for the BBC.

'But I hate cooking, Peter, you know I do.'

'You'd just be presenting. You wouldn't have to go near a saucepan.'

'I'm not even a foodie.'

'For me, please.'

I sighed. 'OK, Peter, for you.'

The audition was for a spanking-new half-hour show called *Ready Steady Cook* – beyond that I knew nothing other than that there was an audience, and that although it would go out daily it was not live. For two weeks I would work three days a week, doing three shows a day; they would be stacked up, and I'd have the next week off. The schedule was better than anything I'd ever had before.

The day of the audition I was picked up from home in a nice car and driven to the studios in New Malden, south London. I was then swept straight into my dressing room and kept out of the way until they wanted me. It was an audition in the old-fashioned sense of the word. There were three of us up for the job, one being a very famous lady presenter. She was being seen first. We were kept well apart and I never even passed her in the corridor.

While her audition was going on, a girl came and took me for a coffee.

'Now, tell me about the show,' I said, as we sat down. I knew by now that the audition would be played for real, the whole thing, as if it was a pilot.

So there, in the canteen, she gave me a spot-on picture of the format, the timing, everything, and I got it straight away. I remember thinking, I know exactly how to make this work.

Then it was my turn. I went into the studio and did it, straight off, just like that. It was one big ad-lib. Afterwards the man who had invented it, Peter Bazalgette, came bounding down the stairs from the audience, a broad smile across his face. 'That's exactly the way I saw it on paper,' he said. 'You've done it!'

Even more surprising was how much I'd enjoyed the audition.

I wasn't too hopeful, however: Baz – as he was known – might have liked me, but the word on the streets was that the BBC wanted the slimmer, younger, more glamorous presenter.

In the meantime I continued my daily trek into London. One day a lady of about my age came on the programme. She was a farmer's wife and her husband was with her, a lovely man, ruddy-faced and clearly uncomfortable in a starched Viyella shirt. This lady was dying of breast cancer – in fact, she died two weeks later – and she had come on the show to promote a documentary which was going out that night, a legacy of warmth and love she was leaving her children. We saw a clip I could hardly bear to watch.

'Here you are,' I said, after we'd seen it, 'sitting so wonderfully calm and accepting. We're the same age, you and me, both mothers of young children . . .' I never even finished the sentence – my voice broke, my eyes welled – but she responded by comforting me. In my earpiece Mark Sharman – unusually working on the programme personally – was saying, 'Wrap it up, go to the break.'

So there we were, the wife trying to comfort me while she was being comforted in turn by her stoic husband. Meanwhile I was consumed by the awfulness of my own self-indulgent behaviour. How could I even think of killing myself? I had everything to live for. How dare I be so pathetically selfish?

Once they'd left the set, Mark came down and asked if I was all right. He was a good friend and knew I was in a fragile state. 'When we come back from the break I think you'd better apologize,' he said, so of course I did. What I didn't know was that the switchboard had lit up with people saying, 'I was in tears as well . . .'

Going home that night, coming out of the Underground up the steep escalators at Marylebone station, I tripped and fell heavily on my broken wrist. And by the time I got home I was in tears – the renewed pain, combined with the intense emotion of the day, had sent me spiralling down into the blackness again. I was written off work for a month.

Within a few days of my return, I was called into the office of my immediate boss, the programme editor.

'Are you happy here, Fern?'

'No.'

I agreed to go. They had it all planned, but it was nicely done. I gave them another couple of weeks while they got their presenter of choice in place, Caron Keating. During one of my last programmes Mark Sharman popped in to see me during the break and gave me a hug. 'I've just heard,' he said. 'You've got that new cookery show.'

If it hadn't been for Baz I wouldn't have got it. The BBC had indeed pushed for the younger, sexier presenter. But Baz had fought for me and won. Once I'd got the job I recounted how I owed it all to the way that young girl had briefed me before I went on.

'What was her name, then?'

'I can't remember.'

'But who was she?'

I described her as best I could, but it rang no bells with anyone at the studio. Nobody claimed to know her. I certainly never saw her again and there has since been no explanation of who she might have been. But whoever she was, or wherever she came from, she handed it to me on a plate. To quote St Benedict: 'Beware the stranger at the door. They may be an angel in disguise.'

How do you solve a problem like Clive? I'd hear people say, 'My husband's my best friend . . .' and I was like, 'How does that work?' I felt as if he was in one play with one script while I was in another play with another script and, no matter what scene we were doing, we were never going to be in the right story together. And I didn't know how to get out of it.

I went to see a therapist called Lesley. She helped mainly by listening and not being judgemental, though she did suggest I tried to bridge the ever-widening gap between me and my husband. 'Look, he's working hard, bringing back the bacon, and when he comes home you're in bed.'

'Yes, I'm in bed.'

'Well, why can't you wait up for him and have supper with him and a glass of wine?'

'Because he gets in so late and I'm hungry and tired and I've got to get up in the night because of the babies.'

It was Lesley who first suggested I consider going to Relate, formerly known as the Marriage Guidance Council.

'So, what time can you both do?' the woman asked.

'Well, my husband doesn't get home till seven or eight.'

'I'm afraid we don't do that late an appointment. He'd have to come in during the day.'

'I don't think he'll do that.'

'Well, you either have trouble and want help or not. It's up to you.'

I knew there wasn't a hope in hell that Clive would drop everything to deal with what he saw as my problem, so I began to see this counsellor on my own once or twice a week. It was better than nothing. In the meantime I continued taking Prozac. It isn't something you get hooked on, my doctor explained, it doesn't numb the senses, just alters the part of your brain that allows you to feel happiness and normality. You can't expect to live in a state of constant bliss, but you can expect a constant note of contentment, with dips down and spikes up. But I have only experienced a constant level of lowness, with regular descents into darkness and mild hysteria.

I can't remember now what I wore for the *Ready Steady Cook* audition. Whatever it was, it must have looked OK because otherwise I wouldn't have got the job, whatever Baz might have said. Once we were on air, though, I wore what the stylist decided I would wear. I still remember the shock of that first day when she took me shopping. The person I saw in the mirror was a mother of twins, a bit over-weight, but nothing too serious. She saw someone huge and dressed me from head to toe in tents and flappy, wide-legged trousers. At a stroke, my view of what suited me was utterly confounded. I kept saying, 'But I think it's jeans and a shirt and possibly an apron and just change the apron every day.' My protestations didn't last long. I didn't have the emotional wherewithal to deal with it. My self-esteem was on a level with the floor anyway, and so I thought, OK, this is clearly all I deserve. So what if I'll look like a frump? My confidence was completely destroyed. From being somebody who used to love clothes, high heels and shapely evening dresses, I became Mrs Tent.

Back at work. One of the things I love about This Morning *is that you can talk about and do anything. Once we did a consumer test on vibrators, and had three ladies testing three different brands where the one that came out top was the Rampant Rabbit. The company that supplied it were so delighted that they sent us half a dozen of these things as a thank-you. I rang up and said, 'Look, there are thirty women in this office, not six.' A bit naughty, but within a couple of hours an entire box had arrived. All the girls were delighted because it's not the sort of thing you would necessarily go out and buy for yourself.*

One thing ITV is paranoid about is product placement. You can mention something by name once, but from then on it has to be non-specific. So, having mentioned Rampant Rabbit at the beginning of the programme, you have to find euphemisms. It's no wonder Phillip and I spend our lives trying not to laugh. This business is known as 'compliance'. It's very tough and includes a range of things you can't say or do — not even charities are exempt. You can mention them once, but after that you have to use a generic phrase, 'this cancer charity', 'your charity' and so on. You can't even wear a badge or a flag. The only emblem of that nature that's allowed is a poppy on the run-up to Remembrance Sunday, and that only after a lot of argy-bargy. 'Language' is also subject to censorship. We can say 'vibrator', but not 'dildo', 'breasts' but not 'tits', 'intercourse' but not 'shag'. Not that we would. So what if one of the guests comes out with something unmentionable?

In May 2001 The Vagina Monologues *had just opened at the Ambassadors Theatre in the West End and we had invited one of* the performers – the beautiful blonde model Caprice – to come on and talk about it. So before we start, I explain to her how, because of 'compliance', she can only say 'vagina' once, because it features in the title of the show. If we had been doing a medical item, she could have said it as many times as she liked or mention any other part of the female pudenda. 'Oh, let's have a look at your labia and clitoris, and make sure it's all in working order. And how about your vulva?' All that is permitted, and I love medical items for that reason: after all, we're all women watching (or mainly) so let's get on with it. Of course, we're never rude, and we always smile and laugh anyway, because it's silly and we're British.

So, that morning Caprice comes on to talk about the show: three actresses talking about the female sexual experience drawn from interviews with women from all round the world. Lovely. Naturally I ask her about her own role in the proceedings.

'Well,' she begins, 'the monologue that I'm doing has everyone laughing and is one of the most important.'

'Great,' I say. 'And which one is that?'

'It's called *Reclaiming Cunt*.'

I totally froze, sat there like a rabbit stuck in the headlights, rigid. What was I to say? 'Oops, sorry, Caprice, I should have warned you not to mention the C-word?' Should I have given the poor girl an entire lexicon of unacceptable terms before we kicked off?

The next day a newspaper wrote, 'The presenters appeared not to notice . . .'

When something like this occurs, our general instruction is to move on as if nothing has happened so that people at home will think, Did she really say that? For once there was total silence from the gallery. Not a word in my ear. We all behaved like ostriches.

I never thought that compliance would affect me personally, but I am now aware that it does. It has meant I've had to put something very dear to me on the back-burner. After years of designing my studio clothes, David O'Brien and I had created a 'Fat Birds' collection, which we had hoped to put into production sooner rather than later.

First the name: obviously it's my initials, and David once heard me referred to as 'that Fat Bird off the Telly'. Obviously he doesn't call me that. His name for me is far more genteel: 'Fat Neck' is his term of endearment, while I call him 'Creature'.

'But you can't call it Fat Birds,' thin people say. 'It's abusive.'

'No,' I retort. 'I am a fat bird, and we fat birds, we know we're fat birds, and anyone worth their salt sees that it's humour.' The bird theme we intend to pursue: we had an idea for a range of dresses called 'Plump Pigeon', and slim trousers called 'Sparrow Legs', and there's got to be a 'Robin Redbreast'. Not abusive at all. Affectionate, funny, making you feel this is great and you're having fun. It won't be high fashion but very sexy, very female, comfortable, wearable and washable. Silhouette is everything to me, so whether it's separates or a dress or whatever, the silhouette comes first, then David makes the mechanics work. As for the swirly florals and jazzy patterns that fatter ladies get offered, per-lease.

'It will look fabulous,' the shop assistant says, of the high-waisted dress. 'It draws the attention away from your tummy.' No, it doesn't. It makes me look pregnant! The other day, at a meeting of fashion people, they were telling me about where they thought shapes were going, and I said, 'None of you have been fat, have you?' And they went, 'No.'

I'm seen as flying the flag for larger women – I didn't choose to be in that situation but as I am I may as well make use of it and improve the shopping options available. Designers seem to believe that bigger women have zero visual taste or discrimination. They think you want to wear great big floral tents and wide-legged flappy trousers. No, you don't. You've probably got a very good bosom, very good shoulders, nice bottom, good legs, and why shouldn't you accentuate a bit of that? But thinnies seem to think that fatties need to be covered up. What is it that is so decadent about flesh that

243

they have to keep it hidden? I've never met a man who's frightened of flesh. The problem lies with women and their obsession with being a size zero with no bosoms and no wrinkles. Why do we want to be girls? We're not girls, we're women.

I've never met a man who's been abusive to me or turned off by my generous proportions. Women, yes. A few years ago I was looking for something special so I went into a shop in a local town and was holding something up against me to see if I might squeeze into it, when the owner offered her verdict: 'We don't have anything in your size. Are you thinking of losing half a stone?'

'Always.'

'Still, nice to look, isn't it?'

'No, it's not nice to look, it's nice to spend the money I have burning a hole in my pocket,' I said, and left. I will never go there again.

The average body size in this country is probably about a sixteen, which means there are hundreds and thousands of women out there considerably bigger than that. But the majority of clothing ranges stop at sixteen. And big women are not necessarily skint. The result is that people over that size don't go into shops because they don't want to be treated like pariahs. You're treated as if you're thick, as if the energy that should be in your brain has been redistributed round your body. It's demeaning. If gypsies or black people or lesbians were excluded in this way, there'd be the most enormous outcry, and I still intend to do my bit to change that, to make life just a little more pleasant for ladies with curves.

However, it turns out there are problems with compliance that can't be resolved over a cup of tea, so for the time being Fat Birds will have to wait.

A caravan step is the most comfortable place to be

13. Spooky Nonsense?

From the first show in October 1994, *Ready Steady Cook* was an instant success. The format – which has since been exported to America, Australia and Europe – is simple. Two chefs join forces with two members of the public. These 'contestants' bring with them a shopping bag containing five pounds' worth of groceries. The idea is that the chefs take these ingredients (meat, veg, cheese, whatever) and cook a meal in twenty minutes. The winner is the 'team' that the audience considers has done best. There's a larder of basics (butter, oil, cream, flour) and a selection of spices, but otherwise they cook with what's been brought on.

Certainly in my day the chefs genuinely didn't know what was in the bag. It wasn't totally haphazard, though: the contestant would always have had a conversation with a home economist beforehand; they'd have filled in a form saying what foods they didn't like, what they wanted to cook, what they wanted to learn. Sometimes they'd be steered in another direction, but only if there'd been too much, say, chicken on recently – that kind of thing. The chefs were never involved in these preliminary discussions. They'd just turn up on the day, put on their whites (dipped in tea because real white is too bright for television – or, at least, it was then) and we'd be off.

We had a family of eight or ten chefs, including a couple of women. They were all serious professionals, working in top kitchens. Being on *Ready Steady Cook* was seen as a way of getting their names known, so increasing the popularity of their restaurants. They were like a repertory company. On each day we recorded, we did three shows and there'd be three chefs who'd rotate so they all did two shows. Although it was a half-hour show, each one took an hour because of the recording breaks.

There were three sections: the first was meeting the chefs and the contestants, and inspecting the contents of the bags, after which recording stopped for five minutes – time for the chefs to think what they were going to do and collect what they would need: pans, knives, graters, whatever. Equipment like that was kept behind the scenes – the ovens were turned on before the show began. Meanwhile I'd give the contestants a guided tour of the set, showing them where the bread and the cream were, identifying each herb and doing my bit for health and safety, such as, 'The oven really is hot and the knives really are sharp.'

In spite of these precautions, accidents did happen. There would be the cocky ones who within the first ninety seconds would be pouring with blood having slashed a main artery in their hand with the sharp knife and would be off the set for the next twenty minutes. There were shows where you saw very little of the contestant because they were being attended to by the nurse. At home they were master of their own kitchen, but producing a meal in a studio in twenty minutes isn't the same, and although the chef did most of the work, the contestant was supposed to help rather than hinder.

Then, recording once again under way, I'd say, 'Are you Ready, Steady, Cook!' and start the clock. The following twenty minutes was sacrosanct; there was no editing for any reason.

While chefs and helpers were getting on with it, I'd keep up the chat, asking questions of the chefs ('Why are you chopping the carrot like that? Is there a knack?'), asking contestants about their lives, based on my briefing notes ('I hear you like amateur dramatics'). Most importantly, of course, I had to keep track of what was going on so the audience didn't get lost. My being a total novice had its advantages. I'd say things like 'That looks burnt to me,' and they'd say, 'Not burnt, Fern, caramelized ...' and the audience would laugh, because they were making the same journey as me. New chefs to the programme might say, 'Now, here's how to chop herbs,' and I'd raise my eyes to heaven, turn to the audience and say, 'Oh, we know that, don't we?' And, just like a pantomime, back would come, 'Yes, we know that!'

The chefs were very sweet and very funny. 'The trouble is, Fern,' one once said, 'that you always come over when I'm in a mess. You should try to leave me alone.'

'No. Seeing you in the shit and watching how you get out of it is how we learn,' I explained.

The chefs weren't professional performers, but the most successful definitely had a touch of the showman, and the rivalry was absolutely genuine, to the point of nobbling each other. I've known cases where one chef has gone in before we started and turned off the gas and the water to the other work station just to steal a march on their rival ...

At the beginning I had been someone who thought cooking was boring, but over time that changed. It was like, 'Hang on a minute, here I am with all these seriously good Michelin-starred chefs, why don't I just relax and absorb some of it?' Just like our audience, I found that you needn't spend half a day in a kitchen to end up with something very nice, and that putting different flavours together was really quite fun. I began to enjoy constructing dishes and became much more adventurous, particularly with the

249

children. I found a fantastic book on how to make baby and toddler food, and before long I was doing that and freezing individual portions. Super Sue was soon into it as well, preparing batches of things to make my life easier once I got home.

But it was all a facade, only millimeters thick. I'd arrive back from work to take over from Sue and it would be, 'Everything OK? And the children?'

'Yes, all OK.' 'Jolly good,' I'd say, while thinking, I'll just nip upstairs and kill myself. Because for all my cheery, smiley persona at the studio, nothing had really changed, and I was exhausted.

Sometimes when I got back, I'd just hit the floor. 'I've got to go to bed,' I'd say, and would. But the following morning I'd be up at six and the whole ordeal would start again, putting one foot in front of the other, getting the children washed and fed and slept and up and back to the beginning. One night I was in such a bad way that I went to bed in the spare room fully dressed, thinking it would save me time in the morning. If I could have had breakfast at night I would have done, just to get ahead of myself.

I was in a complete black cloud and I couldn't see my way out of it. And it went on and on and on and I just couldn't feel anything: I couldn't feel excited about work, I couldn't feel grateful for what was happening, I couldn't feel lucky because I had a lovely home and lovely babies. Intellectually I knew I had many blessings to count, so why did I feel just black? People would say, 'Oh, you haven't got a care in the world,' and I'd think, Hmm, if only you knew.

One day I saw that a psychic was coming to the local theatre and booked tickets for Mummy, me and Cherry. As a family we've always been interested in spooky nonsense: Nana was definitely psychic and Mummy's the same. I may not have inherited this family ability, but Cherry definitely has. So there we were, mother and two daughters sitting in the stalls of the local theatre, when this middle-aged Yorkshireman came on stage. The very first person he pointed to, after his don't-be-scared preamble, was my mother, saying, 'The lady there in the middle with glasses on.'

Mummy immediately turned to look behind her. 'No, you,' he said. Then he gave her an extraordinarily detailed – and accurate – message from George's son, the student doctor who had been killed in a car crash. When he had finished with her, he turned his attention to me.

'Do you belong together?'

'Yes,' I said.

'You will have a daughter within the next twelve months.'

After a little frisson of excitement, I did a quick reality check. How? I wasn't going to go through IVF again. From many perspectives it seemed a highly unlikely proposition.

Meanwhile the boys were getting bigger. In the blink of an eye my babies had become toddlers. Another blink and they were walking. Next they were at nursery. Childcare concerns were changing but I was determined that nobody involved should get overtired, so I had a very complicated rota with Mummy and Super Sue, the idea being that nobody would end up with that feeling of week-in-week-out exhaustion.

As for their father, he was working the kind of hours nobody should have to work, and by the time he came home they were in bed. The woman from Relate had eventually found Clive and me a nine p.m. appointment and we went nearly every week for the best part of two years.

251

His gripe was that I had plenty of help – and indeed I had – so why didn't I find time for him?

I knew within hours that I was pregnant. It shouldn't have been possible. All those years of IUI, then IVF, and now Mother Nature . . . When I was three weeks late I bought a pregnancy test.

'Clive, I've got something to show you,' I said. 'Look at this.' I handed him the dipper.

Half an hour later a car came to take me to the airport. I was going to Spain for *The Holiday Programme*, and during the filming I hugged this lovely secret to myself, thinking, And I know it's a daughter, and I'm going to call her Gracie Bluebell. Being away on location is always a time to let your hair down and the crew were all drinking beer and wine but I was going, 'Oh, no, thanks, I'm on antibiotics, I won't have anything to drink.' I was thirty-nine, and this really was the last-chance saloon and I wasn't prepared to take any risks, however slight.

The pregnancy was normal, apart from the fibroid, which did exactly what it had done with the boys. So I'd be juggling *Ready Steady Cook* with going in and out of hospital, where I'd be on pethidine, then going back to do the show, then into hospital again. I didn't let on at work what was going on. If you're an alcoholic or a drug addict, they can sort that out, but if you're ill, Keep Quiet. Once, towards the end of the pregnancy, I slipped on a patch of oil behind one of the counters while we were recording, slamming right onto my microphone power pack, which sits like two metal cigarette cases on a belt in the small of your back. As this happened during the twenty minutes' cooking time we couldn't stop so I just had to pick myself up, have a good laugh and carry on, while feeling like a Wobbly Weeble.

Grace Alice Bluebell Jones was born two days before her due date on 27 April 1997. Everything went like clockwork. It was a Sunday and I'd been in since the Friday when my waters broke. Instead of going into labour, though, nothing had happened. The following morning the midwife suggested, 'Go and have a walk up and down Marlow Hill.' So, up I got, and wandered up and down and around, and when I came back I was breathing heavily.

'Great,' she said, when she heard me. 'You've started!' But I hadn't, I was just out of breath.

At nine o'clock the following morning my new gynaecologist, Miss Sumner, stopped at my bedside. 'Hmm,' she said, looking at my notes. 'I think we're going to have to deliver the baby this afternoon.' Immediately I burst into tears. Until that moment I'd been convinced I could have a normal birth.

'But why are you crying?'

'Because when the boys were born they were taken away from me and I didn't see them.'

'I can assure you that isn't going to happen. Don't worry, everything's fine.'

I spent the early afternoon watching the Belgian Grand Prix on television, which, as I love Formula 1, was a great way to wile away the time before I had to waddle down to the delivery suite. As I clambered onto the ironing-board, I thought, Ah, yes, I know how to do this.

So Grace arrived in the world and was perfect. She came straight up to my room and went straight onto my breast. I wouldn't let her out of my arms, let alone out of my sight.

There was one thing the staff seemed worried about. Her temperature was a bit low, they said, so they brought in an incubator, installed her in it with a couple of extra cardigans and several pairs of socks and I watched as she got redder and redder. But her temperature was still too low, they said. Finally the midwife came in and peered into her little greenhouse.

'Hmm,' she said. 'I think I'd change the thermometer.'

She was right. It was broken! Gracie was absolutely fine.

I wasn't quite so fine. For a while I said nothing: I didn't want to be a nuisance, and I would have gone through any amount of pain to have my darling little girl. Even so . . . As the anaesthetic began to wear off, I felt as though a red hot poker was burning in my stomach. I was in agony. Eventually I rang for the nurse.

'No, you're fine, Mrs Jones,' she said, looking at my notes. 'You've got all the painkillers you need.'

So, OK, get on with this, girl, grit your teeth.

At some point Grace vomited her feed and the lovely nurse wanted to change the sheets, but I literally couldn't move. 'I can't. This is really burning.'

That was when they fetched the anaesthetist. 'Oh, fuck,' he said. 'We didn't write up the notes . . .' It turned out I should have been on serious painkillers, not paracetamol. So it was action stations, and then *aaaaaaah*! Bliss.

I loved those five nights I spent in hospital. Everyone was so kind it made me want to be a midwife, and stay cocooned for ever in that female world. Gracie was always smelling lovely and clean, and it was a beautiful, happy time.

When she was one day old, the boys came to see their new baby sister. Gently and gingerly they held her and we took photos. They were brought by their new nanny. As soon as we'd known another baby was on the way, Clive and I had accepted we'd have to have somebody living in – though she would go home every weekend. Lauren came from Leicestershire and arrived about a month before Grace did. By the time I went into labour she knew the family and the routine. We'd put another two rooms and a bathroom into the loft, so she had her own domain.

When Grace was ten weeks we went to Norfolk. It was my fortieth birthday and we rented a big house for a nice family holiday by the sea with a friend, her husband and their twins – Juliet May, who'd put me in that lilac catsuit when I'd danced for Craig Rich, back in the early eighties. She'd given birth to her pigeon pair just four months after I'd had Jack and Harry.

I still feel bad for Juliet and her family. This was supposed to have been a happy time for all of us, but the atmosphere was terrible. Clive and I had been together for thirteen years, married for nine and I had a ten-week-old baby, but it couldn't go on. And neither could the holiday. We cut it short and came home.

Two weeks later Princess Diana was killed in a car crash in Paris and the world mourned. She should have had some happiness in life – a daughter had she wanted one – but she didn't have the opportunity. Yet she'd had everything going for her, just as people said I had everything going for me. It was a moment of truth. I thought, There's no time to waste. I have to get out. Diana's death gave me the strength to do it.

In the middle of September we had Gracie's christening in Chalfont St Giles, at the parish church where, when I was ten, I would go to evensong on my own, walking back in the dark pretending I was holding a child's hand. Since the birth of the twins I'd been attending services there. I'd been confirmed, and was even on the cleaning rota. My un-happiness did not go unnoticed. There were times when I'd be standing with tears rolling down my face, unable to sing, unable to speak. One Sunday, as they were singing 'Breathe on Me, Breath of God', my tears were falling like Niagara, and this lady saw me. She just came up and passed me a handkerchief. Simple Christian fellowship.

A few days before she was baptized, I pushed Gracie to our local church, St Bartholomew's in Penn. It wasn't locked so I went in and walked down the aisle with the pram. I was completely alone so I could behave in the way I wished to behave, which was to kneel on the floor and virtually prostrate myself in front of the altar. 'Please, God, help me be happy, help me to accept what I've got, help me to feel something in my life. Help me to see Clive differently, help me to save things.'

One day my vision was obscured by black particles. I could see nothing but this black. I finally found the words you don't think you can say: 'I can't do this any longer. I can't live with you any more. I want a divorce.'

At first he didn't take me seriously. I was ill, he said. Everything would be fine. I just had to be patient.

I didn't believe him. 'I'm sorry, Clive, but you're going to have to give me six months' space. I need to get my head together.'

While he was thinking, Six months and she'll have got over this little blip, I was thinking, Six months and that'll be the end, I'll be free. Within two weeks of the christening, Clive had moved out.

The response of just about everyone was the same: I had a five-month-old baby. I must be mad. People would call me up saying, 'You're not well, are you?' And I'd say no, but I'm getting better now that I'm on my own. They didn't believe me and it was tough, but not as tough as what I'd been through before.

About two months before Grace had been born I'd told my GP, Dr McGirr, that I was worried I'd get post-natal depression again. With the boys increasingly independent,

I was getting back on my feet and was terrified of falling into the abyss. He was convinced that this time it would be all right. However, he knew a psychiatrist at the local hospital who specialized in post-natal depression. It might be useful to go and see her, he suggested. 'But you must take Clive along too,' he said, once the appointment had been made.

'Not very likely,' I said. 'You know what he's like.'

'No, you're mishearing me. I said, "You *must* take your husband."'

On the appointed day Clive made it with a squeak to spare.

The woman specializing in post-natal depression was on sabbatical, we were told. We'd be seeing a locum. She began by talking about my childhood. I'd spent years talking about my bloody childhood, which had got me absolutely nowhere, and I said so. She insisted. So the hour dragged by, going over the same old stuff, until finally she said, 'Tell me, Mrs Jones, when you watch television do you think the people on the screen are talking to you?'

'No, I don't.' It seemed a very odd thing to say, so I was half laughing.

'Do you hear voices in your head?'

This was getting ridiculous. 'No, I don't hear voices in my head.'

'When you're out shopping, do you think people are walking along pointing at you and saying your name?'

'Well, yes,' I said. She began to interrupt but I carried on: 'Because they do – they think they know me.'

This woman had no idea that I was on television. She had no notes, nothing, and she wasn't the kind of person who watched *Ready Steady Cook*. She was talking simply to a Mr and Mrs Jones who might have walked in off the street. All she knew was what I'd just told her, a whistle-stop tour of my childhood followed by problems relating to my marriage. Work might have been mentioned, but not what I actually did. I began to see the funny side – because it was totally ridiculous. So I was laughing and saying, 'No, you don't understand. They *do* know who I am, which is why they say my name.'

'Hmm.'

'Come on, Clive, you've got to back me up here! Explain what I'm talking about.'

They both looked at me as if I was off my head.

'Well,' she said, 'I think you're psychotic and you need a lot of help, and until we get the therapy sorted out, I'll get you medicated.'

I sat there utterly bemused. This really was mad.

'Right,' I said. 'Well, first of all, obviously I disagree with that, but also may I just say one thing? My husband already thinks I'm deranged, and now you've told him I am, which I don't think is helping anybody.'

'You do too much thinking for him.'

So even before Grace was born the Fern is Mad campaign was under way. If mad is spending ridiculous amounts of money, then mad I certainly was. I've heard since that women with post-natal depression have bought thousands of pairs of shoes and worn none of them. Anyway, this was pre-natal and I made do with a Mercedes. One day, on my way to Waitrose, I drove straight to the Mercedes garage instead, and bought myself a beautiful red ten-year-old 500SL – think Bobby Ewing in *Dallas* – which I'd previously spotted in the window. I rang Clive from the garage. 'I'm sorry, darling,' I said, 'but I'm running a little late. I've bought myself a car.' It was delivered the following week. We were going to a Relate meeting that evening and I said, 'Hop in.' He didn't mention my new purchase. No 'Oh, this is nice,' or even 'What on earth did you do this for?' He just sat there and told me about all the director generals of the BBC since Lord Reith. Which of us was bonkers?

On being ushered into the consulting room, the woman started as she always did with 'So, how's it been this week?'

'I can tell you how it's been in the last twenty minutes,' I said. 'We drove here in my gorgeous new sports car, which Clive had never set eyes on before. But he never once referred to it. Instead he told me the name of every BBC director general since Lord Reith.'

Clive raised his hands, as if to say, Madwoman – what do you expect?

In the eyes of the world, the car was the clincher. Here was I, about to give birth, and I go and buy a very expensive Mercedes. Once Gracie was born, and word got out that I had asked my husband to leave, this verdict was confirmed. I was clearly barking.

The only person who didn't accept this universal verdict was Dr McGirr. When I told him what had happened with the hospital locum he looked exasperated.

'Tell me truthfully,' I said. 'Am I psychotic?'

'No, you're not.'

Eventually the mental-health unit rang me with an appointment.

'Thank you, but I'm not coming.'

'You've got to come.'

'I'm not coming.'

'You have to.'

'No.'

They would have to section me first. 'I suggest you talk to my GP.' After that I never heard another word.

I might not have been mad, but I was far from fine. I was hanging on to life by my fingernails. Cherry had been diagnosed with bowel cancer only a few months before. She'd been extremely ill, had been operated on, followed by months of chemotherapy. George's Parkinson's was making him increasingly frail, so Mummy had far too much on her plate for a woman in her mid-seventies: George ill, Cherry ill, and me up the wall. Luckily at home I had continuity in the shape of Lauren, our nanny. Coming from a broken home herself, she understood the situation, and although only in her early twenties, Lauren was a wonderful ally and I could not have survived without her. Over the two and a half years she was with us, she saw our marriage fall apart in front of her eyes, which for a young girl must have been hard to take on board, but she was always very supportive of me and a real godsend.

Although Clive had 'left', he'd come back at weekends to see the children and stick his dirty laundry in the basket while he was at it, and I'd think, Well, if this is your way of wooing me back . . .

All the time I was getting fatter and fatter, eating what the boys left, eating what Gracie left, eating another doughnut for extra energy, and when the babies had gone to bed, opening a bottle of wine. Self-medication. It was as if I was building up the castle walls, shoring up my defences. Clive wanted me back as I had been when he'd first met me. I was his possession, something to be wrapped up and put in a trunk in the attic. He was happy I was there, but not too bothered about keeping me polished and cherished. As a friend said to me about her husband, 'Over the years I have tended his fire, lit it and kept it glowing while he's let my embers grow cold.'

As far as the boys and Clive's colleagues were concerned, he was working in London. But at the sound of the key in the lock on a Friday night, my heart would sink. It didn't help that my family adored him. I tried to explain, as objectively as I could, that – nice as he might be – it didn't work with me.

'Look, Mummy, I'm not expecting you to understand why this has happened. All I ask is that you accept it.'

Although there is no doubt I was depressed, when people described me as 'depressive' I would jump down their throats – the implication being that I was liable to depress other people, as if it was somehow infectious. But, no, you can't catch it, though I do admit that over the past ten years my friends had peeled away as I'd become a bore. Whenever anyone rang to see how I was, I would give them the entire catalogue.

That year I let nature take its course. I hunkered down, tended the garden, told stories to the children, went for walks, went to work – taking the new baby and Lauren with me, leaving Super Sue in charge at home with Mummy as a brilliant back-up – and gradually the darkness seemed to lift. I breastfed Grace for about fifteen months so at weekends, when Clive took the boys to his flat in London, it would just be me and her, as Lauren, too, went home. With Grace I relived the joy of babies. The way they smell, the way they put their little hands round the back of your neck, the way they look straight into your eyes, the way you're the one they run to when they're a bit scared, the way you can make them go to sleep, the way they make you laugh, the way you can make them laugh, the way they light up your life. When the boys were away I would go into their empty room and kiss their pillows, because they smelt of them.

I enjoyed the tranquillity, the solitude of my own bed. It was so healing to be in my own space, without the permanent sense of failure – of not being a proper wife, or a proper mother, or a proper daughter, or a proper sister.

There were times when I faltered. I'd be doing fine, then something would happen to send me plunging into the depths again. In July 1998 a variation was introduced into *Ready Steady Cook* where, instead of ordinary members of the public, two celebrities would bring the bag of goodies. It was while we were recording a block of these that my mother discovered a lump on her jaw. It was serious.

'If I were you,' the consultant told her, 'I'd think of this as only the beginning.' They were going to operate quickly. Not since her stroke all those years before had my mother ever had anything wrong with her. She was incredibly fit, with the energy of somebody half her age, and when I'd been under the table, she'd never turned me away. Now the one time that she needed me, I failed her because I couldn't be there. The recording dates for *Celebrity Ready Steady Cook* were fixed. If I pulled out, it would cost tens of thousands of pounds. I went with Cherry and Mummy as far as the operating theatre but then I had to go straight to work. It wasn't as if there was anything I could do while she was in theatre, and she had Cherry with her, but I remember standing in my dressing room, hanging my head and sobbing my eyes out. By now I knew how to cry without ruining my makeup. I'd bend my head at right-angles to the floor so the tears would fall straight onto the carpet. Then, at the knock on the door, and the voice saying, 'Five minutes, Fern', I could pull myself together, go on and do the shows. 'And will you please welcome ... Fern Britton!' A part of me was always detached, seeing this other person, being sparky and funny. But on the way home it would all come out. I'd open the window in the back of the car and let the tears run down my face.

Before starting the first show that evening I'd had a call

from Cherry, saying that all had gone well and Mummy was in Recovery. Just before the second show, however, there was another call. Something had gone wrong. She was back in theatre and they'd had to open her up again.

When I was little and Nana died, I didn't realize she'd had cancer until I was older. By the time our beloved uncle Pete passed away, when I was eighteen, I understood it had something to do with a lifetime of smoking. Cherry's diagnosis had come as a bolt from the blue. She was only in her mid-forties and the mother of three young children, a non-smoking, fit and beautiful young woman. And now my mother.

I asked Alan, my driver, to go straight to the hospital, but on the way there I had an idea. Whenever I'd come round from an anaesthetic, I'd always felt cold and shivery and unable to stop shaking, and I thought Mummy could do with a hot-water bottle. I asked him to go via the house so that I could get one. When I got to the hospital, Mummy was on her side in the bed, with a long bandage around the right side of her jaw and face. I tucked the bottle under the sheets and gave her a kiss. It was the one thing I could do for her. In the end all was well, the tumour was benign, but the guilt I felt for not being there when she needed me weighed heavily.

One day, an assistant producer on *Ready Steady Cook*, a girl called Cat, sidled up to me, looking distinctly cat's-got-the-cream.

'Phil Vickery fancies you,' she said.

'Oh, really?' I said. 'Which one's he?'

'You know, the one you call the osteopath.'

Phil Vickery had joined the team about a year after me. But, odd as it might seem, I had never really noticed him, because when you're in the depths of despair, just getting from A to B and coping is all you can do. It's as if you're on tramlines. You don't veer off the track. When I'd get into work I'd say, 'So, who are the chefs today?' There were always three, including the obvious ones, like Antony Worrall Thompson, with whom it's fair to say I had a difficult relationship. (He thought it hilarious to throw squid at me, for example.) And Ainsley, of course. But others I didn't recognize by name. When the answer was 'Phil Vickery', I'd say, 'Which one's he?' And they'd go, 'You know, the good-looking one.' Then I'd hear the vague ringing of bells. 'Oh, you mean the one who looks like an osteopath?' Because he always rolled up the sleeves of his jacket in a very neat, medical kind of way. And they'd go, 'Yeah, that's him.'

So I thought, Hmm. I'll have a closer look next time.

I knew Phil had been married and was divorced and that he lived in a beautiful little house in Somerset and was working all hours of the day and night at the Castle Hotel, Taunton, where he was head chef. In the afternoons, when he'd finished cooking the lunches, he'd take his dog Max out across the fields, and he might pick wild garlic, if it was the season, for dinner that night. Then he'd put his feet up, have a twenty-minute kip and get himself back to work. And that was his day. We'd been sitting in Makeup one morning when he'd told me about it. And I thought, What a lovely life that sounds. Busy, certainly, but a nice peaceful life. He had a couple of girlfriends hanging around – one in particular, a researcher on our production team – but as for his fancying me, it didn't seem very likely. It wasn't as if anything had ever sparked between us. As far as I was concerned he was just one of the chefs. But of course I was amused and flattered – I mean, who wouldn't be? He was a

54. At the Castle Hotel, Taunton on New Year's Eve 1998, one of the happiest days of my life. That night Phil cooked dinner for hundreds, then we exchanged platinum rings that we still wear.

55. Visiting 'The Street' during the nationwide *Ready Steady Cook* tour in 1999.

56. In the kitchen of the Green House, pregnant with Winnie on my forty-fourth birthday, July 2001.

57. My girls: newborn Winnie and four-year-old Grace. August 2001.

58. Totally surprised by Michael Aspel and his Big Red Book . . .

59. . . . *This is Your Life,* January 2002.

60. Phillip Schofield and me having a laugh at the British Soap Awards in 2004.

61. On the other side of the sofa, Phillip and I guesting on the Paul O'Grady Show, 2004.

62. My wonderful family, 2003.

63. Like mother, like daughter: Winnie and Mr Holly, 2002.

64. At the Royal Television Society Awards in 2006. Harry (*left*) and Jack were allowed to stay up late on a school night to watch their dad collect a gold medal.

65. Mummy with all her grandchildren, Christmas 2006. (*Clockwise from bottom left*) Rose, Grace, Peter, Winnie (almost hidden), Christabel, Harry, Jack.

66. The farmhouse, Phil, the girls and the hens.

67. Dada, Winnie and Snowy.

68. Marvellous 'granny make-up' Lyn with me as the Queen, one of her brilliant creations, for the Christmas edition of *That's What I Call Television*, 2006.

69. With Zandra Rhodes in her gloriously colourful and eclectic studio.

70. *This Morning* team snap in Rajasthan: Julie Dawn Cole, me, Kate Groome and Shu Richmond, raising money for Women for Women, 2006.

71. Our film crew at the finishing line after our 400 km bum-numbing cycling from Agra to Jaipur. They nurtured us all the way.

72. My fiftieth birthday party, July 2007. A wonderful evening on every level, not least to have all my family together. (*Left to right*) Brian, Cherry, Mummy, Phil, Peter, Jasper, Tink, Dada, Jane, Me, Grace, Harry, Rose, Winnie and Jack.

73. With Phil on my fabulous fiftieth.

74. Egypt 2007. Mummy has always loved travelling, though she drew a line at riding the camel. That was left to me and Gracie.

75. In Basra with the troops, December 2007. Great lads and girls.

76. Dolly Parton. A woman's woman and a real star. As for her figure . . . check out that tiny waist.

77. Our lives in their hands: (*left to right*) make-up queen Lyn Evans, Fat Birds magician David O'Brien, and ringmaster (Executive Producer) Anya Francis. Colleagues and true friends.

78. Phillip and me off duty at an awards ceremony. Still sober . . .

79. The British Comedy Awards 2007 with Jonathan Ross, me and a bear. All three of us made the news the following day.

80-4. 23 May 2008: Phil and I renew our wedding vows in front of my beautiful family, my blessing. A day to remember. A day just for us.

young, good-looking guy, younger than me certainly – but I can't say it was any more than that. I had reached a point of equilibrium in my life. It had finally dawned on me that I was happy on my own. I had belatedly realized that I didn't need a partner to validate who I was. And did I want to inflict someone on the children? No. I wanted to be free to love these three gifts from God without having to concern myself with anybody else.

Ready Steady Cook had become a phenomenon. We'd started as a quiet little show that had had no pre-press or razzmatazz, then people found it, and gradually began to feel they were part of a little club, and the little club of people who watched it grew and grew. On the rare occasions I'd go out to a restaurant, somebody'd always emerge from the kitchen with a bag containing two potatoes and a tin of tomatoes, saying, 'See what you can do with that in twenty minutes, Fern.' We were up against Channel 4's hugely popular *Countdown*, very definitely king of that slot, but it wasn't long before there was clear blue water between us.

To celebrate the five-hundredth edition of *Ready Steady Cook*, a party was organized one evening at London Zoo. I've always loved a good party and this was one of the best. Everyone got extremely pissed but for some reason I was only drinking water that night. Just the dancing was enough to make me feel as high as a kite. I was free – I could fling myself about and generally strut my stuff. I'm sure I behaved like a total nitwit but enjoyed every last minute of it. Phil Vickery was there, along with everyone else, and he'd had a bevy or three, which was unusual as he didn't normally drink. When I went to get yet another glass of water – I was wringing wet I'd been dancing so much – he was standing at the bar surveying the action. 'So, come on, then,' I said. 'What about it? Aren't you going to ask me to dance?'

'I might in a minute.'

So I was there, jiggling around, waiting for my water, and I kept on at him. 'Please. Come and have a dance.'

'I might in a minute.'

Then suddenly he turned to me, put his hands on my shoulders and looked deeply into my eyes. 'I think the world of you,' he said. And I thought, What? 'And I'd like to spend the night with you.' I was suddenly completely plugged in.

'Pardon?'

'And I mean all night.'

'Oh,' I said. 'Well, how do you kiss, then?'

'I don't know.'

'Well, you'd better come outside, because I've had ten years of shit and I'm not doing it any more.'

So out we went, round the back of one of the animal enclosures – I can't remember what they were, monkeys, or zebras, I think, but I wasn't really looking – and we had a bit of a kiss, and he went, 'How's that?'

And I went, 'OK.'

'Does it need workshopping?'

'Might do,' I said.

Then we went back to the party, and that was that. I got into the car and drove home and never heard another word from him. Not another word.

It's Friday morning. My day for a lie-in, but not for too long as I've a lot to do. Phil's taking me to Dublin for the weekend, just the two of us. I've been there before but only for work so it'll be lovely to just wander and explore. We're meeting up with a friend who he used to work with in Somerset. He's a hotel manager, or general manager or whatever it's called. Richard is half American and half English, but the American side predominates. Everyone is 'sir' or 'ma'am'. Nothing to do with his work – though no doubt it helps – but just how they do it in North Carolina or one of those southern states. He now runs some of the biggest and most luxurious hotels in America, and he's adorable, with a great sense of humour. And he and his wife Melissa are flying into Dublin for a week's holiday. They're setting off on their jaunt around the Republic tomorrow morning, so we'll have drinks and dinner with them tonight – a nice grown-up time without any kids – meet up for breakfast, then it'll just be Phil and me.

As for the children, the boys are going with their dad, and Phil's parents are coming up from Kent to look after Denver and the girls. Before they get here, I've got to put the place in order. I need to clean out the hens, clean out the hamster, make sure there's enough food in the fridge, write down directions to the riding stables for the girls' lesson in the morning. Most important, I have to sort out our bedroom. We haven't got a spare room at the moment because what was the spare room is my office.

They say, 'You don't marry a person, you marry a family.' Usually this is intended as a caution, but in Phil's case I was very lucky. His brothers are fantastic – one a doctor, one a blacksmith –

while Bob and Tess Vickery are the most brilliant in-laws anyone could wish for. Bob is a retired Post Office engineer, known by the kids as Mad Grandad Bob, who has built a brilliant model railway around his garden, the kind you can sit on and ride. Tess is beautiful, tall and slim. She used to have red hair but now it's a lovely strawberry blonde. She came originally from the north where her parents ran a shop like Arkwright's in Open All Hours, where they sold everything from liquorice to Daz, mousetraps to Lucozade. She was the oldest in her family, and the next to arrive were twin sisters, so Tess would be either upstairs looking after the little girls, or downstairs in the shop sitting on a pile of something, watching the stream of customers, and then, as she got older, weighing things. She's a great teller of funny, happy stories, and a great cook, which is where Phil got it from. She's been a very good mum and now she's a very good grandmother, and both she and Bob have entirely absorbed my children into their family. It can't have been easy, but they've done it, and all the kids adore them.

It'll be a busy weekend. They'll have to let the hens out in the morning, and put them back at night to keep one step ahead of Mr Fox. There'll be eggs to collect, but otherwise that's it, in terms of hen management. The biggest problem is Denver. He has done something drastic to one of his ligaments – a footballer's injury – and he's being operated on this morning. Phil has taken him to the vet's and he's incredibly tense. Gun dogs like Denver, and his predecessor Max, take years to train. Max died of cancer about six years ago and Phil was devastated, having trained him up himself from a puppy. When Denver comes back he'll have his leg in a plaster cast and will be feeling extremely sorry for himself, but at least the girls will be on hand to give him lots of cuddles.

Now that the children are older, it's much easier to leave them. When they were babies I would write out yards of lists. At five past nine they must have this, and at ten thirty-seven they must have that. But grandmothers are grandmothers, and once they wave you off, it's up to them. I have no doubt they indulge the kids as much as I would if I were in their place. Bob and Tess had their own three sons, and now they have six true grandchildren and three step-grandchildren as well, so they're more than up to it, and I know I couldn't be leaving my girls in better hands.

Me and my 'osteopath'

14. Boy, Oh, Boy

Summer 1998, and my first holiday as a free woman: just me, the kids and Lauren. So, I thought, I can do what I want to do and go where I want to go. Grace was now fifteen months old and the boys were four and a half – the perfect age for a proper bucket-and-spade holiday, and where else but Cornwall? It was then I remembered the caravan that Craig Rich, the weather man in Plymouth, had lent me all those years ago. I had never forgotten the place, the wild walks, the sunsets, the protected sandy beach. There would be no traffic to worry about, no constant getting in and out of the car. At first I couldn't remember the name of the site, and then it came to me: Mother Ivey's Bay. I got the number through Directory Enquiries, spoke to a lady and explained my situation. Amazingly she managed to find me a caravan for the last two weeks in July. I was incredibly lucky because everything there gets booked up very quickly in the school holidays.

In the meantime I'd been asked to do a glamorous photo shoot for, of all things, *Family Circle* magazine. I'd recently done an interview where they'd asked me about clothes, and I'd said that clothes didn't interest me much, but I relished the idea of being photographed naked, *à la* Rubens, draped in gauziness. So that's what they wanted to do. It would be flagged as my fortieth birthday, although actually I was just coming up to forty-one. It wasn't gauze in the end, but a nice piece of *faux* fur.

★

As for my non-dancing admirer, a couple of weeks later when we were back at work, he'd arrived at the studio looking as if he was about to get the sack. What did he think I'd do? March up to the head prefect and say, 'How disgraceful?' In fact, the London Zoo declaration might never have happened. There were no little looks, no nothing. He didn't entirely ignore me and, with everyone else on the team, I was invited to the opening of his new brasserie in Taunton. Naturally I wanted to go, so I persuaded an old friend, Peter Windsor – a kind man recovering from a romantic break-up – to come with me. I didn't mention a word to Peter about why I was so keen to flog halfway across England, and a good thing too – because who should be there laying claim to Mr Vickery but the researcher I'd thought was history. The good news was that I found myself amused rather than jealous. Even so I thought, Count me out. Here is a complicated man who's not into following things through.

A few weeks later, just before the series finished, I happened to mention that I was taking the children on holiday to Cornwall.

'Well, if you're coming down the M5, why not break your journey in Taunton?' Phil suggested. It wasn't a bad idea. From Penn to Padstow is a long drive, even without three children under five, so a stop halfway would be very welcome. He would sort out the accommodation, he said, adding, 'And perhaps we could have dinner together?'

'Lovely.'

I set off after lunch. All day I'd been getting calls on the phone: 'Chef says he'll meet you for dinner about seven o'clock.'

'Lovely, thank you very much.'

'Chef says he can't make it till nine o'clock.'

'OK that's fine.'

'Chef says it's more likely to be nine thirty.'

By then I was thinking that Chef can fucking well fuck off. In the meantime we had arrived in Taunton, settled into our extremely well-appointed room and I'd ordered room service for Lauren and the kids, but Harry wasn't well. His forehead was burning and he was running a temperature of well over a hundred. By now an experienced mother of toddlers, I knew that these things come and go but, even so, it's better to be safe than sorry and I asked the concierge to call a doctor. Harry was fine. Calpol and bed. I was just watching the news when the phone rang. Who else but my hot date.

'I've finished now,' Phil said. 'Do you fancy something to eat?'

Frankly I didn't. After all the business with Harry I hadn't even thought about food for me. But I'd come all this way, so OK.

Down I went and Phil set us both up with a gin and tonic and we sat down in a quiet corner of the bar. We were talking general stuff, when suddenly he leant over. 'I meant what I said, you know, at the party.' This was now about three months post London Zoo.

'Really?' I said. 'That's interesting.'

'So, do you think . . .?'

'Well,' I said. I mean, busy man, busy schedule. 'Have you got five minutes?' How the conversation (or anything else) would have continued I have no idea because at this point the girlfriend-researcher appeared from nowhere. Having heard that I was Taunton-bound (I later discovered), she had jumped on a train and arrived just that second. So instead of a *diner à deux*, it was *diner à trois*, which was, of course, delightful. In fact she was very nice but it was watching Phil's discomfort that gave me the greatest pleasure. I amused myself by giving him sardonic glances and heaping praise on the food, with 'Oh, this is lovely,' and 'Really?' and 'Do tell me more.' All very gratifying. The meal over, I waved a cheery goodbye and headed upstairs thinking, Boy, Oh, Boy, Is He In A Mess. And to think I'd only stopped off to break my journey . . .

The next morning I went to settle up. I was quite prepared to pay for our rooms but I'd understood from Phil that dinner was on him. When the bill arrived, I stared at it in disbelief. Accommodation fine, but all three dinners? I paid.

Lauren and the kids were already in the car waiting for me, and we were just leaving when I saw a figure sprinting across the car park in our direction. I stopped.

'So you're going?' he said.

'You,' I said, 'have got to sort yourself out.' Then off we drove to Cornwall.

A few days later it was my forty-first birthday, which he knew because I'd told him. He might not have had the precise address and postcode of where I'd be, but I was leaving enough clues. Not a card, nothing.

The irritating thing was that I was definitely interested now, but I wasn't about to play games. I was too old for that and I couldn't be bothered.

I was at home the whole of August but we were back in the studio on Friday, 2 September. All three children were with Clive that weekend because Grace was now weaned, so she no longer needed me around to breastfeed her. I made sure the house was tidy and I made sure that I was tidy, then cancelled the BBC driver and told Production I'd drive myself into the studio.

Phil was one of the three chefs that day, and during a recording break he was talking to the floor manager. 'So, Lisa,' he said, 'got any plans tonight?'

'Going home to the kids, that's all. What about you? Anything lined up?'

'Nothing,' Phil said.

So I'm there, thinking, Please somebody ask me what I'm doing. They didn't. So I had to announce, 'Well, I'm not doing anything either, empty house, nobody home this weekend.'

We finished the show, and everybody had a drink – as you do – and just as I was leaving Phil happened to walk past and I remembered Shakespeare's classic line: 'There is a tide in the affairs of men which taken at the flood leads on to victory.' For 'victory', read 'Vickery'. It was now or never.

'Get in the car,' I said, without even looking at him. 'Get in the car.'

So he followed me out to the car park. Meanwhile the whole gang of girls he would usually catch the train with were piling into a taxi, going, 'Come on, Phil!'

I had the boot open and was putting my bags inside.

'It's OK,' he called to them. 'I'm just talking to Fern.' Then, turning to me, he said, 'What?'

'Just get in the car,' I muttered, and carried on being busy.

'Look, it's OK,' he called again. 'Fern's giving me a lift.' And in the wing mirror I watched as the taxi pulled away.

Then he opened the passenger door and got in, and so did I. He hadn't a clue where I was taking him or what was happening. But on the way we were laughing and chatting and by the time we arrived at the house we were firm friends.

The next morning, while I waited for the kettle to boil for our first cup of tea, I scooped up his clothes and threw them into the washing-machine. I had a hairdressing appointment, which I couldn't change, and I thought, He can't go anywhere if his clothes are all wet. By the time I got back he was sitting in the armchair watching sport on television wearing nothing but a T-shirt and an expression of terror. He'd been waiting there for two hours, thinking, My God, her husband might walk in at any minute, and when he heard my key in the lock he was convinced his number was up.

I stood in the doorway and looked at this miraculous sight. 'Well, well,' I said, addressing the world in general. 'There appears to be a naked man in my house ...' Then added, 'Actually, this afternoon is our village fête, and I always go – it's one of those things. Would you like to come?'

'Yeah, OK,' he said, and as I wandered out to the kitchen to get us another cup of tea, I thought, This is nice.

So he came to the village fête and, of course, all my family were there: Mummy and Cherry and Brian and their kids. They vaguely recognized my companion, but I didn't give them chapter and verse, though they definitely gave him the once-over.

That evening I had been invited to dinner by a girlfriend, Kim Goody, a singer and actress I'd known since TVS, so I called to ask if I might bring someone along. She lived in Blackheath, all of two hours' drive away, so we went in the Mercedes, roof off, Bert Bacharach on the CD, singing along to all those wonderful songs, under a beautiful big harvest moon.

Kim had no idea who to expect. Not being a daytime-telly watcher, she had no idea who Phil was or what he did. All she did know was that we were very new and that I was happy. And if I was happy she was happy. So she said, 'Why not come and chat to me while I cook?' And Phil was wonderful, he didn't say a word, just let her get on with it. Then, dinner over, we sailed off into the night.

The next day was Sunday and, what else but shopping at

Waitrose, followed by a late breakfast. 'That was silly,' he said, as I put down the coffee pot. 'I should have done croissants.'

'Don't worry,' I said. 'I did look, but they didn't have any.'

'No, I mean I could have made you croissants.'

Hmm, I thought. This is a new chapter.

Phil was due back in Taunton the following day, so that afternoon I drove to Beaconsfield, put him on the train and sent him home to Somerset.

Within two days we were absolutely helpless about each other. Helpless. Then two days after that the newspapers had it on the front page.

I don't know how they found out. Of course, somebody might have seen us at the fête and decided it was worth a phone call, but apart from my family, I'd only told two people – the first being Clive. I'd called him on the Monday morning. Although we had been separated for nearly a year, we were still married and I wanted him to know about Phil before the children met him, which would only be a matter of days. He seemed fine about it, but half an hour later he rang back and it was a very different story. I had to get out of the house. Now. He was going to change the locks, he was coming back to live there, and he was going to have custody of the children. He planned to be working from home so he needed everything cleared out, including the garage, which he'd be using as an office. Oh, and he was going to sue me for adultery, he said.

I said, 'See you in court.'

I don't know what happened between the two phone calls. I always knew that the house wouldn't be mine for ever, but I knew now I'd have to find somewhere else sooner rather than later. What was clear was that I had obviously hurt him a great deal.

The only other person I'd told was my producer, Mary Ramsey. 'I'm telling you this, Mary, because I've got a feeling that it's going to be out soon enough, so I'd rather you knew first.' She looked at me quizzically. I took a breath. 'I've fallen in love with Phil Vickery, and he's in love with me.'

Her jaw dropped. Then she pushed her glasses up her nose, and said, 'Fantastic!'

That night I was at home watching *Newsnight*. Phil had just called to say he was on his way from Taunton and I was tucked up in bed feeling warm and happy. He had told me not to wait up.

'And now,' said Jeremy Paxman, wrapping up the programme in the traditional way, 'for tomorrow's papers.' And there it was, across the screen, in full embarrassing Technicolor: a picture of me under a classic *Sun* headline: 'Ready, Beddy, Cook'. I pulled the sheet up to my chin and laughed.

Meanwhile Phil had stopped at a motorway service station to get some petrol just as the first editions were being delivered. When I went down to open the front door, he handed me our very own souvenir copy, his face wreathed in smiles.

It had all happened so quickly I hadn't given a thought as to what other people would think, but that night I was recording another celebrity version of the show and was nervous at what the reaction of the audience would be. I needn't have been. The moment I walked on there were cheers and a huge round of applause and a woman shouted, 'Good on you, girl!' For once my smile was utterly and completely genuine. So that's what it's going to be like, I thought. And it has been: from that moment on, people have only ever been pleased for us, glad for us, happy for us, and I am forever grateful. Thankfully we were both unentangled: Phil's marriage was long since over. Mine too, if not on paper. This new state of happiness and rightness felt a bit like putting on new shoes. You know they're going to mould to you very soon, but for a while you think, Can this be us? And it's lovely.

Of course, to be 'outed' by the *Sun* could have been incredibly embarrassing. In one sense it made life easier: it relieved me of any need to explain. The downside was that we were now media property. Within less than twenty-four hours, reporters and photographers were coming up the drive. Nor was it only me. They found Phil's ex-wife, and when we realized what was happening, Phil called his parents to warn them. They were completely taken aback, though his father's reaction when Phil told him was extremely positive. 'You lucky sod,' he said.

Meanwhile I was under siege. My agent arranged to put out a press release, hoping that would keep them at bay.

'This is ridiculous,' Phil said, when I called him to agree the text. 'You shouldn't have to put up with it. I'm coming to get you.' Of course, a picture of the two of us together was exactly what they wanted. Then I had an idea.

The drive at Little Coppice had a bridleway next to it, which went up to some other houses. 'Whatever you do, don't come up the drive,' I said. 'Continue on about a hundred yards and you'll see a footpath on the right. I'll be waiting.'

By now it was Friday so Clive came and collected the children for the weekend, as he always did. Then, taking a small suitcase and wearing a mac and headscarf as disguise, I left by the kitchen door, crossed the garden and went via the back gate onto this path, which was overgrown with nettles and brambles and hardly ever used. It had recently been raining and was thick with mud. It joined the lane outside the house of Pauline Quirke and her husband Steve Sheen, which had electric gates, CCTV and the rest of it. The last thing I wanted was for her to see me on the camera looking like a refugee encamped outside her house. Suddenly there was a whirring and a clanking and the gates began to open. Pauline in a limo.

'Hello, Fern. What you doing here?' she said, jumping out.

'It's a long story.'

'I've been reading about it. So what's happening?'

'The press are out the front so Phil's coming to get me.'

'Do you want to wait inside?'

'That's very kind, Pauline, but, no, he'll be here any minute.'

She drove off. Later Phil told me that they'd met coming up the lane, and she'd jumped out again, told him where I was and not to worry about 'the bastards'. From that moment on, Phil and I were really just together.

In the end the threatened change of locks never happened, but I'd got the message. I quickly found a house in Great Kingshill about five miles away. It was important that Jack and Harry stayed close to their school and their friends. I took nothing with me. Apart from an empty wardrobe, you wouldn't have known I'd gone. I made up the beds, changed the *Mail* back to the *Guardian*, cancelled the milk, paid the household bills, then sailed off into my new life with never a backward glance.

The Green House had been the first one that came through the letterbox. Phil and I had been to see it together and liked it straight away. It was a converted bungalow: five tiny bedrooms, close to the boys' school, what was there not to like? We saw it in the dark so didn't know it was on the main road but we got used to it. It had a dear little garden, which was important to me. My garden at Little Coppice had been the one thing that was hard to give up.

Phil and I never had the darling-will-you-share-your-life-with-me conversation. Overnight he went from being a single man with no children to stepfather of three under five. As his sous-chef said to him, 'It's like open the packet, add hot water, instant family.' He turned out to be a complete natural. He didn't push himself on the kids, but they quickly got used to him being there. They were so little that we didn't need to explain anything – though I made sure we kept them fully informed about what was happening in a way they could understand. The boys would wander in and say things like, 'Phil, do you like the Teletubbies?' Grace had no real memory of things being any different and she adored him from the start.

There were those who saw all that was happening as yet more proof that I was mad, and I continued to be attacked. Clive was a decent man. I should never have broken up the marriage. I was headstrong. It was simply a case of 'the grass is greener'.

I refused to feel guilty. I had spent two years going to Relate and years before that trying on my own to make my marriage work, and I'd done with grieving. A marriage should be a partnership and a friendship, not an endurance test, and I decided that I'd endured for too long. So I had made a decision and got myself out of my unhappiness. Are children really going to benefit from having parents who irritate each other within three seconds of meeting? Are they going to enjoy having parents who barely exchange a smile? And how will a child form a healthy relationship for themselves if they don't have a blueprint at home?

In March 1999, Mother's Day fell on one of Clive's weekends. He wasn't prepared to do a swap but agreed to drop off the children for a couple of hours on Sunday morning as long as I got them back to Little Coppice by midday. There were 'folk' coming to lunch, he explained. For some months Jack and Harry had been mentioning a boy called Thomas and his mummy who seemed to spend a lot of time with Clive. Consequently I decided to deliver them a little after twelve to see if I could get a glimpse of the mysterious 'folk' coming for lunch.

'That's Thomas's car,' the boys announced, as I pulled up in the drive of my former home.

Clive came out to meet us, closing the front door behind him.

'Didn't you say you had something you wanted to show me, Jack?' I quickly invented. The little chap nodded vigorously. 'So, may I come in, then?'

Clive could hardly say no.

It was an odd feeling, going into the house I'd made into a home, and I shivered as I moved out of the sunlight into the dark of the hall. Standing in the shadows beside the stairs was a boy of seven or eight.

'Hello, Thomas,' Clive said.

'Hello, Thomas,' I said, and Clive looked startled, so I decided to take a closer look at Thomas.

There are moments in life when your heart pounds so loudly in your chest that you think you will die, and this was one of them: I know this boy, I thought. I followed Jack upstairs to his bedroom and walked to the window. I'd created that garden. When I'd first seen it, it was mainly down to grass and the borders were narrow and mean. I'd dug them all out and planted a classic English herbaceous border. The box balls, now four feet high, had been smaller than footballs then. It was now at the height of its spring flowering. And there, at the far end, inspecting the daffodils

– how many hundreds had I planted? – were people I recognized: an older couple and a woman my age. Thomas's mother and her parents. In seconds I'd taken it all in. At the same time, Clive opened the boys' bedroom door.

'Er – would you like to say hello to Vikki since you're here?'

'Vikki?' I said, turning to him. 'Vikki who?'

'Heywood.'

'Oh, I don't think that's appropriate, do you?'

Vikki Heywood, whom I'd known for the best part of twenty-five years. The person I always thought of as a good friend.

When I got home I howled, while Phil did his best to calm me down, but I was beside myself. Why did it hit me so hard? I was the one who had left, not Clive, and he had every right now to see whoever he wanted. But Vikki? Her marriage had broken up some time before and, as old friends do, we'd talked about it, and also about me and Clive. In many ways they were much better suited than he and I had ever been. They were both *Guardian* readers, both 'intellectuals'. But why hadn't he told me? I'd have been happy for them. Did I see it as a betrayal? Or was it simply that it was Mother's Day? Or was it that great, unanswerable question: how long has this been going on?

I decided to write to her. I thought back to all the times she had been good to me: looking after me in Cambridge, driving me to Holkham in Norfolk in her little orange Beetle, huddled against the promenade wall in our duffel coats, looking out at the wild sea, eating sandy sandwiches and drinking tomato soup out of a Thermos, talking about life and boyfriends. Then later, riding on Bodmin Moor, riding on Rotten Row. I had problems with Clive, I wrote, and he had problems with me, but I didn't want there to be a problem between us. Our letters crossed in the post, with Vikki saying much the same things.

The funny thing was that she had worked not far from him in St Martin's Lane in the West End, and I remembered now how she'd told me he'd asked her to lunch in the boardroom and, I'd thought, Wouldn't it be great if they hit it off? What really upset me, I think, was that she and I went back so far. My college friends were the last set of people who had known me before my life with Clive. And now even they were lost to me.

I've noticed that when I'm kicked in the balls in my private life, my career gets an unexpected boost. Immediately after the car accident I had been approached to do BBC news. Now, at this emotional low point, something good was about to happen.

In 1988, a few months before Clive and I were married, TVS – with three other television companies – had been invited to make a pilot for a magazine show to run for two hours between ten thirty and twelve thirty every weekday morning. Our version was called *Home Today* and I was put with a really nice guy called Andy Craig. With so much riding on it, and where you're in direct competition with other people doing the same thing, you need to have interesting people who are good at talking on the pilot. We managed to get Jilly Cooper and her husband Leo, and Jack Tinker, the legendary *Daily Mail* theatre critic, and a 'new boy' called Dale Winton, so it was a fun show. It was a long time since I had been so exhilarated by what I was doing. Finally, I thought, I had found my niche.

It was not to be. The contract went to Granada, a husband-and-wife team called Richard Madeley and Judy Finnegan. Although unknown in the south, they were famous in Granadaland, having practically met and fallen in love on air, on the equivalent programme to *Coast to Coast*. Although Granada was Manchester-based, *This Morning*, as their show was called, was broadcast live from Albert Dock in Liverpool where a fantastic new studio had been specially built. The inaugural broadcast went out on 3 October 1988, and over the next ten years the programme became a huge success, both as a format but also a personal triumph for Richard and Judy, as they were soon known.

In 1996, after eight years in Albert Dock, *This Morning* transferred to London – to the same studio it's now in – Richard and Judy's view being that Liverpool was too far away to attract really big celebrities. Then two years later they decided four days a week was quite enough – after ten years non-stop they were understandably knackered, so Fridays were given to a rotating series of established presenters, including Caron Keating.

When TVS's *Home Today* had failed to make the grade, I had been very despondent. I'd felt this was my chance, and I'd lost it, that it was never going to be my show. I might be built for it, but it was never going to happen because it was someone else's.

Somebody somewhere must have kept a copy of that original pilot, and in the mid-nineties Andy Craig and I were asked to fill in for a week in Liverpool. Then, when Judy had her hysterectomy in 1998, I joined Richard on the sofa in London. So, in 1999 when they were casting around for a permanent Friday replacement, perhaps it wasn't entirely surprising that my name came up. Nonetheless, when my agent called I couldn't believe it was actually happening. Even though I'd never stopped working, *This Morning* had always been in my head. At home I'd have it on in the background, just like everyone else, because I absolutely loved it.

My co-presenter on the Friday gig was John Leslie, ten years younger than me, incredibly tall with a lovely Scots accent, and we got on immediately. He was an old *This Morning* hand, having been with them since 1994 as entertainment correspondent when he left *Blue Peter*. I couldn't have been happier. The pressure was off because it wasn't my show, so I could go and enjoy it every Friday, really enjoy it. The great plus was that I could continue to do *Ready Steady Cook*, and there would be only one morning a week when I wouldn't be there to see the children off to school.

I had been working on *Ready Steady Cook* since its inception and, as always in these long-running shows, it's crucial not to let things slide. Over time variations had been introduced: as well as celebrity guests, there'd been the gourmet bag, then the budget bag. We would have themed date-specific programmes involving food, such as pumpkins and Hallowe'en. To cover their backs, however, Production had stopped naming the occasion: the cooks would come in wearing masks, and there'd be skeletons dangling off the ceiling, but I wasn't to mention Hallowe'en. Then there was Bonfire Night: we'd have firemen in talking about the dangers of bonfires, while Health and Safety had agreed we could light some indoor fireworks – but I wasn't allowed to end the show by saying, 'Have a nice Bonfire Night.' Why not? Because it might not go out before Bonfire Night. This ridiculous situation even extended to Christmas-themed shows. I tried to explain to the new producer that this had never been a problem before, that the whole point was to air them in the run-up to whatever day it was. I was overruled.

The last straw was St Valentine's Day 2000. To have the whole place festooned in balloons, with hearts everywhere, and not to mention the V-word was ludicrous. That was it for me. I'd had six good years, including a fun roadshow and it was time to move on.

I decided I owed an explanation to the guy whose idea it had been, and who'd fought on my behalf. 'I'm so sorry, Baz,' I said, 'but I can't work with this producer any longer. Thank you for all of it, but I think it's time to let someone else have a go.' We parted amicably.

If I hadn't had my Fridays on *This Morning*, I wouldn't have been able to give it up because not only did I now have the mortgage on the Green House to pay but George had finally had to go into a nursing home. I was happy to foot the bill. He had been very ill for several years with Parkinson's disease, recently compounded by a diagnosis of prostate cancer. Mummy had nursed him at home for as long as she could, but she was destroying herself in the process. The least I could do was to pay for his care. She had looked after him supremely well, and to see them together was incredibly poignant. He was ten years older than her, and knowing that the struggle was coming to the end, he would constantly tell her how much she meant to him. It's one thing looking after small children – every day they become more independent – but when you're a carer there is none of that to look forward to. Mummy would never complain. At her most tired she would simply detail what she had to do. There were twenty-three procedures between getting up and getting George dressed, checking this and checking that, checking his feet before swinging him out of bed and taking him to the loo, all of those things. Every couple of months George would go into the local cottage hospital, to give her a break, and this had made it possible for her to go on as long as she had. But now he needed more help than she could provide.

It was another challenging time. Not only was I down to working one day a week but Phil had been sacked from his job at the Castle Hotel. He had been there since 1990 when he took over from Gary Rhodes. He had done stints on *Ready Steady Cook* since the early days, and would also do stints on *This Morning*. Phil is a natural communicator as well as being a great cook, and it had always been considered beneficial to the Castle that he had this public profile. Since he and I had become involved, however, although he would still do a five-day week, he was only there when he had to be, and it hadn't gone down well.

There's no doubt that it had become very complicated: trying to keep Kit Chapman, the owner, happy while spending as much time as he could with me. Phil had worked his socks off for years and years. He had left school at fifteen and been involved in the restaurant business ever since – the hours they do are ridiculous. I was concerned for him, not least the amount of driving he was doing. Much as I loved having him at home, I'd worry that he wasn't at work, and wouldn't hesitate to say so.

'Don't worry, Fern,' he'd say. 'I've given so much that I'm allowed to have this bit of time off.' But then Phil hit a wall. Not literally, but psychologically. He had overdone it and he rang me one day from Taunton in tears.

'This is ridiculous,' I said. At my insistence he went to the doctor who, thankfully, insisted he had two or three months off.

Of course, I was delighted at the outcome. But when I asked if he had it in writing, he said it hadn't occurred to him to ask. I know how these things work, and although he didn't want to do it, I made him go back and get a medical certificate. 'You have to set up a paper trail,' I said. So then he had his couple of months off, which was exactly what he needed and, just as this was about to end, he was invited back to see Kit.

We drove down together in my little red Mercedes, roof off, sun shining, and I sat outside in the car park while Phil had his meeting.

'Well, that's it,' he said, as he got back into the car. 'I've left.'

'What?' I said, aghast. We had discussed all sorts of possibilities in terms of the future, but not this.

'Kit just said, "We think it's best if you move on."'

They'd had it all prepared. From underneath the blotter the big boss had fished out a piece of paper, already printed. 'Just sign here,' Kit had said, 'and you're finished.'

Thank goodness Phil had kept his hands firmly in his pockets, because subsequently he brought a case for unfair dismissal, won, and was awarded damages for breach of contract. But it was horrible while it lasted, his reputation smeared by the whole tribunal thing. But it had its positive side: in terms of his and my relationship I felt there was a balance. He had pulled me through the worst of my troubles, and it was good that I could help him through the worst of his. We'd seen each other at our lowest, at our most paranoid, at our most vicious and unkind and vulnerable. We absolutely clung to each other, and – although it all worked out in the end – it wasn't obvious that it would while it was happening. Phil picked himself up, set up an office in the little spare room upstairs and invented a food company called the Food Bureau with his friend Steven Poole, and they began developing recipes for food producers and supermarkets. He was still doing *Ready Steady Cook*, and soon he was being commissioned to write a book. It wasn't long before we were thanking Kit Chapman.

Stuff in the papers reminds me of a funny story about Carole Caplin. I am always going off with things nobody else wants. The hens are an obvious example. I come from a background where you don't just chuck things away. You never know when something might come in useful. But, as the saying goes, 'One man's gift is another man's burden,' and when Carole Caplin came on the programme I had no idea what would happen.

It was just after her involvement with Cherie Blair, when she was trying to launch a career as a life coach, so she was with us to talk about eating well and looking good. I've always been a bit suspicious about de-tox dieticians, in fact I put them in Room 101, when I was on that, together with flowers bought from garage forecourts. I'm always very interested, but as soon as they start to waffle on, you think, 'This is rubbish'. Anyway, the interview was fine, and off she went. The next day, I'd just finished the morning's programme and was in the daily debrief when one of the researchers put her head round the green-room door. 'Carole Caplin's here with a whole load of groceries for you,' she said.

'Pardon?'

She repeated what she'd just said.

'Look, I really don't want to see her, and what do you mean by groceries?'

'You know, bags and bags of shopping. What shall I tell her to do with them?'

'Oh, I don't know. Just say I'm in a meeting.'

When we went back to the studio, there it was, about ten bags of seeds, buckwheat pasta, healthy spaghetti, big glass tubes to keep *it in, yoghurts, live fruit drinks, everything you could think of, all virtually inedible (in my book) health-food stuff, all pro-yoghurty, non-animal and soya-heavy. There must have been more than a hundred pounds' worth.*

Among all this stuff was a bag of hemp seeds, saying very clearly on the packet, 'Do not grow but sprinkle on your breakfast cereal.' Now, as many people will know, hemp is basically cannabis seed. I like gardening, and I like bringing on seeds, so I decided on a studio challenge. There were about eight of us, and we got little plastic cups from the water dispenser and shared out the seeds, and the competition was to grow them. I took mine home and planted them in the conservatory at the Green House. And throughout the summer when Phil and I were away with the kids in Cornwall, my mum would come in and water them. I'd explained why I was doing it. Whenever we spoke I'd ask her how they were coming along and she'd say, yes, they were doing very well. But I hadn't realized quite how well.

We got back from Cornwall to find these nine-foot giants. Just like the plants in the film Saving Grace *(filmed in Port Isaac, just up the coast from us in Padstow). Well, there was nothing to do but harvest the stuff − because there was the competition to think of. Before we picked the leaves, we took pictures of these things that were now the size of medium-sized trees. Harvested then dried, I took a sackful into work, feeling convinced that nobody else's haul could be quite so impressive. I was right. Because when I went, 'Look what I've got!' they all went, 'We didn't do it!'*

So there I was with this great big bag of cannabis, feeling stupid. I took it home, wrapped it up in newspaper, put it at the bottom of the dustbin and that was the end of that. I sometimes wonder what would have happened if a policeman had dropped by. If they'd arrested me at least I'd be able to say, 'Well, Carole Caplin gave me the seeds . . .'

A very private wedding

15. Something Borrowed

I sold my red Mercedes and Phil sold his car. We pooled the money, raised a bit more and built a conservatory, because now that Phil was using the little spare room as an office, we needed a bit more space downstairs. We were planning our future together.

Looking at it now, it's extraordinary how quickly we made the commitment to each other. Both of us had said we would never get married again, and we used to drive past weddings shouting, 'Don't do it!' because we were happy as we were, and with the negative experiences we'd had, we didn't want to tempt Fate.

Fairly early on Phil had talked about starting a family. He loved my three, but this was something he needed for himself, and I, of all people, understood that.

'I'm sorry,' I'd said, 'but I can't do that unless I'm married, and I can't get married because I'm still married to someone else.' That didn't mean I didn't want a divorce, but there were complications and it took time. So we had to wait and wait.

I don't think it was anything religious on my part. I'm just much too old-fashioned and simply felt it was the wrong way round. If you can't commit to each other, how can you commit to a child? Yes, we were living together, but my view was – and still is – that it's better for a child to arrive in the world knowing that the wedding has happened. I was also not entirely convinced that I had the courage to go through it all again: first the business of the fibroid, and then the cloud of depression. But, given my history and my age, the chances anyway were slim. So in the end I thought, Let's give it a whirl. It was the least I could do. Phil had already given me so much, and he needed a child of his own and it would be wonderful. It would work or it wouldn't.

Yet I continued to be nervous. Could I really cope with another child at my age? Would it complicate matters? But if I don't, I thought, I'll always regret not trying. Phil had made it clear that if it didn't happen that was fine as well. So I thought, Let's just get on with it.

But not yet.

Time passed and even the boys began asking, 'Are you going to get M?' Even at the ripe old age of six, they understood this was a delicate subject.

In the end, the divorce came through earlier than I had expected. When we decided on a date we didn't tell anyone. We met the registrar and booked it about a month ahead. I explained that there would be nobody there and could we please keep it confidential. We wanted this for ourselves, not for the world, and certainly not for the press. He said, 'No problem.' The banns were posted but slightly round the corner out of sight.

Somebody must have seen something because, within a week, my agent had a phone call from a newspaper. 'He said that they know you're getting married on May the twenty-fourth and they know it's twelve o'clock. Is this true?'

I lied: 'No.' I was determined that this was something we would do on our own. No family, not even the children.

'He says they've seen the invitations.' I knew then that they were flying a kite because there were no invitations, not least because there were no guests.

On the day – and it was 24 May – we got up, got the boys off to school, and Super Sue arrived to look after Gracie. It wasn't a usual working day for her, which was why she said, 'I can't remember now why you asked me to come today.'

'Because Phil and I are getting married . . .'

'Yes, I know that, but . . .'

'We're getting married *today*!'

Instantly she was in a total fluster, insisting I had to do things properly. Something borrowed would be her bracelet. In fact, I'd already thought along those lines. The something blue was a Porsche we'd hired for two days.

So off we went, me in a long lilac-y skirt and a creamy cardigan, Phil in his favourite crumpled-linen jacket.

A couple of girls from the office upstairs were brought in as witnesses. As for the registrar he was fantastic. He was his own one-man show, everything from confetti-thrower to photographer. Every couple of minutes he'd do a bit of ceremony, then say, 'Shall I take a picture of this?' So there were all these empty seats behind us and this woman in a cream-coloured cardigan with tears sparkling in her eyes. I barely managed to get the lines out. Then, after thanking the girls and asking them not to say anything, we drove off in our lovely blue Porsche to one of the most stylish restaurants in England. I would love to say it was one of the great culinary experiences in my life but it wasn't, and I felt like stuffing its two Michelin stars up its superior bum. When my fish turned up it was raw. The waiter agreed, and took it back. By the time we left I had a headache as bad as any I've ever had in my life. Our mobiles had naturally been switched off, and once they were back on again, work started ringing. They were worried they hadn't been able to reach either of us, they said. Had anything happened? Well, yes, actually. We just got married.

Instead of turning off for Great Kingshill, we drove straight to Little Chalfont, down the lane I used to walk

297

along from the station on my way home from college, and pulled up in the drive of Three Trees.

'Gosh, you look posh,' Mummy said, when she opened the door. 'What have you been up to?' Then she caught sight of the Porsche and put two and two together. 'You've just got married!'

'You don't mind, do you?' I said, giving her a hug.

'Not a bit of it. I'm delighted. Much the best way to do it – just like Dada and me.'

Finally it was home to the children. Super Sue had told them what we were up to and we arrived to a snowstorm of confetti, and banners saying, 'Congratulations, Mummy and Phil!' which they'd been busy painting since they'd got back from school.

Our wedding night was equally unconventional. My head was thumping so much that I went to bed, while Phil lay next to me and watched *Match of the Day*. As for the reception, we had an afternoon tea party six months later, at Cliveden, a National Trust house, part of which is run as a hotel, about fifteen miles away. I bought a new dress for the occasion – not a bridal dress, but I did have a bouquet, which I threw over my head in the traditional fashion. It was caught by the girlfriend of one of Phil's former chefs. As so many children were there, we hired an entertainer called Peter Pinner, who was brilliant, which meant that the parents could have a quaff and a chat without worrying what their offspring were doing.

When we look at the pictures of that afternoon now – as a family – Harry, Jack and Gracie feature prominently, as you would expect. Winnie is less visible, though as she's quick to point out she is there 'in Mummy's tummy'! And indeed she is, albeit very, very tiny.

I know exactly when and where our daughter was

conceived. We always say it was late-night shopping just before closing time. It was a beautiful wintry weekend in late November, and Phil and I had gone to Bath to do a bit of Christmas shopping. The shops were all lit and sparkly in the dark and we sat outside a café next to one of those big outdoor heaters drinking hot chocolate, and stayed in a hotel tucked away behind the Circus where the chef was a friend of Phil's and it was all absolutely lovely.

Before she was conceived I didn't dare think about the issues a late pregnancy would bring in its wake. It was 'Let's see first if it works.' As everybody knows, the older the mother, the greater the chance of having a Down's syndrome baby. Even when I'd had the boys seven years earlier, aged thirty-six, I was considered an 'elderly primagravida'. The most reliable procedure is amniocentesis where cells are taken from the amniotic fluid that surrounds the baby in the womb. It is decidedly invasive, however, and far from risk-free. I had talked it over with my then GP and he'd said, 'Supposing one of the twins has Down's and the other doesn't? What do you do then?' The idea of attempting to abort one baby while saving the other was too macabre to consider so I decided to go ahead blindfold, and thank the Lord they are perfect. By the time I had Grace a non-invasive test had been developed called a nuchal scan, which gives you betting odds. This was entirely non-invasive so there were no reasons not to have it. Although they can't give you a definitive 'all clear', the consultant said that, in his view, all looked fine. As indeed it was.

For Winnie I had the same fantastic obstetrician who'd delivered Grace, and Phil and I discussed the whole thing with her and decided to have a full amniocentesis this time round. Our thinking was that if we had a child with Down's we could cope with it. But if a child was born with multiple physical problems, it would be unfair not only to the new-born baby but to the other three children. 'If that was the case, then we would have to take a deep breath and say we wouldn't want to continue,' I explained to Miss Sumner, and she said, 'I think you're absolutely right.' So we had the amniocentesis and everything was perfect, thank God. As for the rights and wrongs of amniocentesis generally, the important thing is to consider the consequences. You've got to make the decision in your mind about what you will do if it proves positive *before* you have the test, otherwise you're going in blind, which isn't right.

The next hurdle was the fibroid. In the non-pregnant state it might be tiny but during pregnancy it grows in parallel with the foetus. Mine happened to be on the outside of my womb, which proved additionally unhelpful. It kicked in at around five months and from then on the pain, as ever, could be excruciating. This time was by far the worst, and I ended up going into hospital almost once a week, staying for a couple of nights. There would be no warning of the attacks – they could happen in the middle of the night or the middle of the day. I could be making sandwiches for the boys' packed lunch or brushing my teeth. I could be fine for three days, and then if I walked up the stairs, halfway to the top I'd be on all fours throwing up because the pain was so intense.

One morning I was on my own getting the children ready for school. I'd left my purse upstairs and began to walk up. I got halfway, then had to cling to the banisters in agony. The boys brought me the phone and I rang the school to explain that they couldn't come in; their teacher came to collect them. I then rang my GP, but he didn't answer, so I tried Mummy. At that moment, by pure happenstance, the midwife turned up. I managed to crawl to the door and let her in. The moment she saw me it was, 'Right, I'll call an ambulance and we'll get you to hospital' – although in the end that wasn't necessary, as within a few minutes Mummy had arrived and drove me there.

So then I lay and waited for the pethidine to work its wonders, and within twenty minutes the pain had gone and they'd left me to sleep. Another day I went in – similar story as before. But when I eventually woke up, they said, 'That's it.' I'd reached my limit. I either stopped having those episodes or I'd have to have the baby now. Although there were still three and a half weeks to go, they were confident it would be OK. In the meantime they'd keep me in to see if it settled. Two days went by. Then, on the second evening, on my way to the bathroom I saw that they'd parked one of the little cots outside my side room, and thought, Hello. Next morning I nipped to the shower and when I got back the cot was inside. Minutes later Miss Sumner came in.

'OK,' she said. 'It's all set. We'll do it at half past eleven.'

I rang Phil. 'Right, mate,' I said. 'Get your arse over here . . .'

'I've had an idea,' he said, when he came in. 'If this is a little girl, we'll call her Winifred Theresa.' (If it was a boy we'd already decided on Wilfred – the boys' third brother would finally arrive.) On the drive over he had remembered that both our grandmothers were called Winifred (Nana had been christened Winifred Beryl) and Theresa was after his mum. I added Violet because all we girls have flower names. And so it was that Winifred Theresa Violet was born on 10 August 2001 and she was perfect.

Looking back, it's strange to think that although I'm the mother of four children I have never experienced labour – but the fibroid was so excruciating that I've probably had my share of pain. It had reached a state of total calcification, according to Miss Sumner. In my drugged brain I think she said it was like a pumice stone and I should leave well alone. 'And if it causes you problems afterwards, we'll sort it out.' I trusted that lady and I've never had a twinge since.

Like my other three, Winnie was born at Wycombe General Hospital. Apart from terrible food – Phil used to bring me in Chinese takeaways – the maternity unit is fantastic, but they could always do with the odd bit of extra equipment. So we asked the head of midwifery if there was something they really needed. 'An additional heart monitor,' she said. They had only one full-sized monitor for thirty-five beds, she explained, plus two small mobile ones. We didn't promise anything but said we'd see what we could do. Apart from anything else we hadn't a clue how much it would cost but it was certainly more than we could afford in the normal run of things.

OK! magazine had suggested we celebrated Winnie's arrival with a series of photographs. We wouldn't normally have said yes, but if we could use the money to benefit somebody else, as well as providing a nest-egg for the new addition to the family, the idea made sense, especially as we would have a beautiful set of photographs into the bargain.

So, less than a year after we had celebrated our marriage, we were back at Cliveden. There was a bit of an interview, then the shoot and that was it. Wycombe General got their heart monitor, Winnie has a bit put by for a rainy day and we have some fabulous pictures.

Six weeks before Winnie was due, it had been announced that Richard and Judy had signed a deal with Channel 4. The news had come as a total bombshell and sent everyone in the daytime-TV world reeling. Richard and Judy were an institution. I remember closing my eyes and thinking, Well, that's it, then. This is the one programme I'm built for but it looks like I've missed the boat. Being heavily pregnant, there was just no way.

My boss, Grant Mansfield, asked me if I would consider doing it. *This Morning* was off until September; they could keep it warm for a few weeks using John Leslie and a stand-in, he said, and then I could take over.

'But I'm having a Caesarean,' I explained. 'She's due on 3 September, the day *This Morning* is back on air.'

'That's all right,' he said. 'You'll be absolutely fine. It happened to my wife.'

'So when did she go back to work?'

'Er – after a year.'

'Exactly. And this is my fourth and I'm forty-four, so I know what I'm talking about.'

I didn't get het up. I just thought, Well, the baby's come at the right time, and she's far more important. You're given what you're given and I was really happy about that. Meanwhile the boss kept saying, 'Blah, blah, blah,' and I remember telling him, 'Look, it's just not my time.'

So *This Morning* returned with Coleen Nolan, of the Nolan Sisters, and Twiggy. As I watched the first edition my heart sank. It was like watching an old friend who'd dressed up in an ill-fitting party frock, with an unflattering hairdo and bad makeup. The new production team just didn't understand the show.

Coleen has since gone on to be a big success on *Loose Women* and I admire what she's achieved, but at the time neither presenter had a track record of live TV autocue or of interviewing. They were performers not journalists, and there is a huge difference. The idea that you just sit there and chat with the guests is very far from the truth.

I wasn't the only one who had seen it wasn't working.

I was getting desperate phone calls before Winnie was a month old.

'You've got to come to a meeting.'

'And flog across London with a newborn baby?'

In the end I took the train in from Beaconsfield and had tea with some of the guys at the Landmark Hotel, right by Marylebone station, with Winnie sitting on the floor beside me in her little bucket seat.

'You've got to come back, Fern.'

'I'm not ready.'

They agreed to give me a bit of time. By now Twiggy had gone and Coleen was doing it with John Leslie, my regular Friday partner. The idea was that they would continue to hold the fort until I felt up to it, though they were talking weeks rather than months. Eventually I agreed, but as I was still in that happy muddle of post-natal euphoria I can't remember much about it. Suffice to say that by the time Winnie was ten weeks old I was on air every day, and baby came too.

As for childcare, Super Sue and Mummy were soon back in harness. After a long struggle, George had died eight months previously and focusing on her new granddaughter helped Mummy through a difficult time. This was also when Karen came on board and, of course, Tony my driver. In spite of my amazing support group, though, I was barely keeping my head above water. At night I'd be lucky if I got more than an hour and a half's sleep at a stretch. At six thirty, Tony would lift Winnie's bucket seat in beside me and I'd just have to hope that the movement of the car would keep her happy while I read my briefing notes, but it was all I could do to keep awake. Once we reached the studio, she'd be in my dressing room in her own little cot. We had a good routine going. A lady called Jan, the green-room hostess, would keep an eye on her when I was on air, but otherwise Winnie would come with me wherever I went. We'd go into Lyn to get my hair and makeup done, then I'd give Winnie a feed and put her down for a couple of hours while I did the show. She'd usually wake around midday, which meant she had half an hour of watching whatever was going on, until I came off at twelve thirty when I'd feed her again. Sometimes, if she wouldn't settle, she'd have a quick slurp during a commercial break. Inevitably there'd be the odd crisis, when I'd be doing an interview and have the PA asking me questions on talkback, such as 'Have you got the Calpol?' and I'd nod violently or go, 'Hmm,' with feeling. I didn't refer to her on air; the only time Winnie became part of the programme was if guests had met her by chance while they were waiting in the green room. Then they'd come on to the sofa and say, 'Oh, my God, I've just seen your baby!'

It helped, of course, that I was working with John Leslie. He was always so full of enthusiasm, like a great big soppy Labrador, and, God knows, he needed to be. After Richard and Judy left, the ratings took a pummelling. The show needed to come back really strong after a shock like that, to reassure the audience that it was business as usual. The opposite had happened, and I would sit at home watching and just think, We're on a life-support machine, we're never going to survive this. One of the drivers had a fantastic maxim: 'Success has many fathers, but failure is a bastard.' No one was prepared to take responsibility. It was a mess.

Once John and I got together, we forged a very good partnership. Together we brought the programme back from the brink, struggled through a year and worked very hard. Gradually it started to build again. People changed in the production team. Once we were clearly going to be OK,

John decided to take a break. The whole business – particularly those early weeks when he was clinging to the wreckage – had exhausted him, and he decided to drop Fridays. I completely understood, and they brought in Phillip Schofield to partner me.

We were just going into our second year together, this time a good clean run, *This Morning* with Fern and John, when the shit hit the fan. Ulrika Jonsson had just published her autobiography and, without naming names, had accused a male television presenter of sexually assaulting her a few years earlier. Needless to say the tabloids went wild, searching for this anonymous presenter. One morning, John and I were sitting together, while I was feeding Winnie, and he had his arm round me, as he often did in a brotherly kind of way.

'They think it's me,' he said suddenly.

'What are you talking about?'

'They think I'm the rapist. You know, Ulrika.'

It seemed so unlikely – John was a funny, bouncy person whom I thought of as a little brother – but he sounded so serious that instead of saying, 'Don't be so ridiculous,' I took it at face value. I knew he'd been out with Ulrika at some point, but he'd had a number of high-profile girlfriends, including a very young Catherine Zeta-Jones.

'Look, John, do you think there has been any situation where you've been with a woman and you felt your intentions might have been misconstrued?'

'No.'

'Perhaps you used a bit too much force – after all, you're a big guy and you might not think of it as force.'

'No.'

He wasn't a secretive kind of person. He would come and visit me at the Green House and we'd talk about his various girlfriends. He was a young man having fun, and why not? I remember one particular afternoon when he dropped in just as I was going to pick up the children from school. 'I'll come with you,' he said. It was drizzling and all I had to offer was a bright orange anorak whose sleeves barely reached his elbows. And he walked down the road with me pushing the pram, and we went into the playground, all the mums going, 'Oooh, it's John Leslie!' When Grace came out he picked her up as if she weighed nothing, then whirled her round and round till she was shrieking with pleasure. When the boys appeared we set off to walk back to the house, this time John pushing Winnie, Jack and Harry chatting nineteen-to-the-dozen, and Gracie skipping round us.

Back at the house, while I busied myself with vegetables for his favourite meal of roast chicken, John was on his hands and knees being shown the various things the twins had made with Lego, then their *Star Wars* stuff, not to mention Spiderman and Superman.

'You know what, boys?' I heard him say. 'If you took some photos, you could send them in to *Blue Peter* and they might send you a badge.' Anyone less like a rapist it would be hard to imagine.

Then one morning Matthew Wright, on his Channel 5 programme, was talking about the Ulrika Jonsson alleged rape and – apparently accidentally – let slip that everyone was saying it was John Leslie.

The Wright Show went out at the same time as *This Morning*, so as John and I were on air we knew nothing until, walking out of the studio doors back to our dressing rooms, we were met by Shu Richmond, the programme editor. 'Matthew Wright has just named you,' she said. John stopped in his tracks and his face drained. We went straight to the green room and by the time we'd sat down everyone was there, his agent, the head of the ITV press office – a lovely woman called Zoe MacIntyre – and finally a couple of lawyers. Meanwhile Shu and I were totally bemused – 'For fuck's sake, what's going on?' Later we learnt that it was an open secret: Matthew Wright hadn't been exaggerating. Everyone in the media had heard the rumours.

As nobody seemed to be saying anything sensible, I suggested that someone phone Ulrika's management. 'At least get her to say if it is John or it isn't. She's got to have the balls to say it one way or the other.' So a phone call was made and a statement did finally appear, but one that did absolutely nothing to clarify the situation, rather the reverse: 'I will never reveal who it is, nor am I prepared to talk about it any further,' she said.

Whatever the truth of the situation, at the time her response struck me as cowardly. I went to my dressing room and brought back a couple of beers, and handed them to John. His agent didn't help, going, 'Lot of use you are running around like chickens with your heads cut off,' while proposing no course of action. Shu and I were trying to draft a press statement – in John's name – along the lines of 'I utterly refute these allegations blah blah, I won't say any more, it's in the hands of lawyers.'

It was never sent. The lawyers, meanwhile, were very downbeat: 'John, you understand you may be going to court.' I saw the shock on his face. He was thrown to the dogs.

I still see him from time to time and occasionally we speak. Over the next weeks and even months, I became the public face of support, someone who would fight the good fight. Whenever the story got ratcheted up, I was the one they would seek out for comment. I never changed my tune: 'I don't know what's happening but my thoughts are with John, and his family, and the John I know is a good guy.'

That was in 2003, but the trial by media of John Leslie continues to this day. All I can say is that the John they describe is not the John I knew.

Over the years I have interviewed many women who have been sexually abused, finding themselves in a situation where they are unable to say no because of fears for their own safety or that of their children. My job is to give them space to tell their story in the way they want to tell it, and not to say, 'A similar thing happened to me,' though it was many years before I understood that I had actually been raped.

It happened when I was living in Cambridge in the little flat above the lighting shop, not long after my twenty-first birthday. Like everyone else in Cambridge I had a bike, and one day I was on my way somewhere and two little dogs ran across my path into the road — Schnauzers or something like that — and they were obviously lost. I stopped, managed to get hold of them and took them into the police station, which I knew was round the corner. The duty sergeant took my name and address, I handed over the little dogs and that was that. A day or two later I dropped in to see what had happened to them.

'A gentleman came to collect them. He would like to thank you personally and asked for your phone number.'

Not having a phone at home, I gave them the one in the office and a couple of days later got a call from the grateful owner, who seemed very nice. He was taking a sports team he coached into Cambridge that day, he said. They'd be having something to eat after the game, and would I like to join them? I said yes. Great. He'd pick me up, he said, as he wasn't sure when they'd be finishing.

When the doorbell rang I peered out of the window and there was this minibus and all these guys hanging out, and they were absolutely charming. We trooped off to this slightly cheesy place and there was a glass of wine, chicken and chips, music and a bit of a dance-floor. So even though it was early in the evening I had a bop with a couple of them and then went home.

The next day, or the day after, this guy phoned me at work again. Would I like to have dinner with him? So I thought, Why not? You're allowed to go on dates with people who are pleasant and nice. You don't have to fancy them. So I said, yes, that would be lovely. Again he said he'd come and pick me up. So, I got home from work, had a shower, swapped my jeans for a dress, and had just finished doing my makeup when the doorbell rang. I pushed the buzzer and let him in. He was carrying two bottles of champagne.

'Ooh, how lovely,' I said, slightly surprised. 'I'll just put them in the fridge.' I pointed him in the direction of the lounge, then went into the kitchen and popped them in the fridge. By the time I'd closed its door, come out of the kitchen and gone round the corner into the lounge, he was on the floor doing press-ups wearing nothing but orange Y-fronts. My first thought was that it was a joke, but within seconds my ha-ha turned into, oh, God.

I didn't have a phone, mobiles hadn't been invented, and before I knew what was happening he was up on his feet and trying to kiss me, pushing me against the wall, then down onto the floor. I was absolutely terrified, and thought, I'm done for, what do I do?

As he pinned me down, I turned my head away and said, 'No!' and then, 'But what about dinner?' He took no notice and simply carried on. Initially I kept turning my head to avoid his mouth. In a strange way I thought, As long as my head isn't involved, it won't touch me. He was a big man and very fit and I decided the safest thing to do was just let it happen, neither struggle nor co-operate, stay limp and get it over with as soon as possible.

When he'd finished he was all smiles. He got up, went to the kitchen, fetched the champagne and opened it. And I was sitting there, with my back to the wall, too frightened to move, clutching

my knees and thinking, *What can I do? Nobody knows he's here.
There's nobody around to shout for. How can I make him go?* I
didn't want to antagonize him. I felt I was safe for a few minutes,
but then . . .

'Where's the bedroom?' he said suddenly. It was a tiny flat, so
finding it wasn't difficult. He came over, pulled me to my feet
and hauled me there, and so it went on, all night. I would lie there,
wondering if he was asleep, wondering if I could just run out into
the street — but where would I go? This was my home. In the
morning he got up, got dressed and left.

It was a long time before I told anyone. I knew I had put myself
in a very dangerous position. I had invited this stranger into the flat
so it was my fault that it had happened. I had agreed to a dinner
date, I had let him do what he did. I had even drunk the champagne because he'd said, 'Come on, drink.' I wasn't strong enough,
old enough, mature enough or brave enough, to say, 'You, fuck off.'
And it was a long, long time before I told anyone. Did I report it
to the police? No. Because I didn't have bruises and he didn't hit
me. What is this conspiracy of silence? Even if it hadn't resulted
in a conviction, the police would have had a record. Where is he
now? Did he do it to others? It's too late to dwell on it now. I
blotted it out, and got on with my life.

Me and Mr Phillip, 'at home'

16. Brown Paper and String

In the spring of 2002, when Winnie was nine months old, we found our new home. The Green House had done us well, but with four children and Phil running his business from there – not to mention Max his Labrador – there were just too many feet and we were bursting at the seams. That was why, for the first time in my life, I bought a copy of *Country Life*. I hadn't really expected to find anything in it – far too grand for people like us, or so I thought. It was simply afternoon dream time.

'But I know that house,' I said aloud, and stopped flicking through the pages of stately mansions at the picture of a 'period farmhouse in Buckinghamshire'. 'It's just down the road!'

Phil was in Italy, working on a range of recipes for an Italian sauce company, but I called him the moment I saw the ad. 'You're not going to believe this,' I told him, 'but I think I've found it. You've got to get home!'

'Don't you think you ought to look at it first?'

'I don't want to see it without you.'

'At least from the outside . . .'

'I know it from the outside! I'll make an appointment for the afternoon you get back.'

We came down the drive, parked, the estate agent opened the front door and we stepped inside: a corridor led away to a staircase flooded with light. We looked at each other, and we knew. We just knew. There was a lot of work to be done, but the basics were all there. Phil had always wanted a farmhouse with some land, and as for the barn . . . It was his dream – and it was no distance from the children's schools. In October 2002 we moved in.

Life with three school-age children and a brand-new baby is not easy, with or without a time-consuming job. Home-work has to be helped with, grazes cleaned and plasters dispensed, rows defused and toys put away; a baby needs feeding, winding, changing and playing with. And all that's fine, until something you aren't expecting trickles into the frame and sits there, like a football from next door's garden. It may not be important, but it needs to be dealt with.

One evening it was getting on for my bedtime. Every-thing had been done between me, Mummy and Phil. We had organized school shoes, lunch boxes, book bags, home-work, got it all sorted out and everyone into bed – bath, teeth, everything done. It was then about nine o'clock, my bedtime. I was just thinking about the awards ceremony I had to attend the next day when one of the boys came downstairs.

'Mum?'

'Mm?'

'Mum, don't forget it's Evacuee Day tomorrow.'

'It's what?'

'Evacuee Day. We've got to go to school in clothes that the evacuee children would have gone on the train to the countryside from London in, and, oh, yes, our lunch box can't be anything modern or plastic.'

So, after you've discounted killing yourself, killing your children or napalming the school, you do it. My mother, who happened still to be there, was brilliant and became my in-house period consultant.

'What about shorts?' she said. 'All boys wore short

trousers back then. They must have something in that line that would do.' They had, and before you could say Neville Chamberlain it began to come together. We found some long socks – ordinary school shoes were fine – and their Welsh granny was a dab hand with knitting needles and had made them some lovely jumpers – really nice ones that the boys loved wearing. So I laid everything out on their bedroom floor, arranged like a body so they could see what to put on. Next, lunch boxes.

'They won't do at all,' my mother said helpfully, as I tore off a couple of bananas.

'Why on earth not?'

'Because we didn't have them in the war. Didn't see a banana for years and years. '

'Well, I haven't got anything else.' And in they went.

'Not that either,' she said, as I started buttering a slice from a Mother's Pride loaf. 'Sliced bread only arrived in the fifties.' Luckily there was a whole loaf in the freezer that, suitably defrosted, I managed to saw into doorsteps of a suitable thickness. As for wrapping them, clingfilm was out. 'Brown paper and string,' Mummy advised. Of course.

'And what about their gas masks?' she added. 'They'd have taken their gas-mask boxes with them.'

A period detail too far, I decided. 'Mummy, it's ten o'clock and I've got to be up at five thirty.'

'Well, all you've got to do is –'

'No, no, no!'

Finally luggage labels. I managed to find some, wrote their names on them, and tied them through the necks of their jumpers. When it was all done, I felt exceptionally virtuous, the perfect mother. So, I went to bed, got up early next morning as usual, got Winnie up, put her in the car, opened my envelope containing script and briefing notes and started to read. Funnily enough one of the things on the schedule was another item on sex toys, although these happened to be the non-vibrating version; they were beautiful, almost like sculptures made of crystal. As per usual, there was a legal briefing on what we could and could not say about these works of art that happened to have a dual function. We also, of course, had to be very careful how we handled them, both from the fragility and the erotic perspectives.

The programme came to an end without a catastrophe of any nature and I then had to dash across London for the *Daily Mail*-sponsored Unsung Heroes of the NHS Awards, which has categories like Community Doctor of the Year. The timing was very tight so I got into the car with Winnie and Tony whizzed us across London to the hotel where it was to be held – I had to be there at two o'clock. It was now three minutes to two, so out of the car, unbuckle Winnie, up the steps to the hotel and into Reception.

'Can you tell me where the awards ceremony is, please?'

'Certainly. You go up the stairs and round the corner and down the corridor . . .' I didn't hear the end as I was already charging up the stairs, Winnie jammed under my arm, round the corner, down the corridor, see double doors in front of me, bang through them into a room full of people, every single one of whom turned round to stare at the whirlwind that'd just arrived, while the man on the stage at the far end said, 'Ah, and here she is now.'

The Scottish TV presenter and journalist Lynn Faulds Wood was standing right beside the door. I knew her from way back, so quickly pushed Winnie into her outstretched arms, then walked towards the stage, trying to make myself slow down. And as I turned to face the audience, beaming of course, I suddenly realized that, with all the faff about the bloody Evacuees Day, I had completely forgotten to prepare for this. I looked out at this sea of faces and spotted Esther Rantzen, Linda Lee Potter, Claire Rayner, Des Lynam and I was, like, 'Shit, shit, shit.' I began to blather about the NHS generally. But then there was nothing in my head at all except a great big void. My problem was that I couldn't remember which prize I was giving or to whom, and what they had actually done or where they came from. I hoped I'd remember in mid-blather, but nothing. Finally when I realized this wasn't working, I smiled again at the audience and said, 'Would you excuse me for a moment?' And, in as stately a manner as possible, I walked to the prompt corner – or, rather, the corner of the stage where the organizer was sitting.

'I'm really terribly sorry,' I whispered, 'but I've mislaid my piece of paper telling me what prize this is and who's getting it.'

'Don't worry,' he said, and handed me a duplicate. So, relief. I walked back to the microphone, took a deep breath, looked down at the piece of paper, opened my mouth and stopped. I couldn't make out a single word. No glasses. Without my glasses I can't see anything nearer than a yard.

Once more, I smiled, apologized to the audience and walked back to the side of the stage, borrowed this chap's glasses and put them on, then went back to the microphone.

'And the winner is Mrs X of X Hospital who does X.' Huge round of applause, thoroughly deserved, though the poor woman didn't deserve me. Naturally I overcompensated like mad, hugging her, kissing her, pumping her hand, smiling for the photographs and generally making myself look even more ridiculous than I had already, if that was possible. I'd never done anything quite so unprofessional in my entire life. I couldn't get off that stage fast enough. I declined lunch, using Winnie as an excuse, rescued my little daughter from Lynn Faulds Wood and we made our escape. I was shaking, absolutely shaking. That was the last time I would ever be asked to anything like that.

Lovely Tony was waiting for me in the car. I strapped Winnie into her seat, strapped myself in, and thought, I might just have got away with it. I'll call home to make sure everything there's OK.

Super Sue answered. 'Only me,' I said. 'Everything OK?'

'You do know it wasn't Evacuee Day today, don't you?'

The boys had got the date wrong, and I was so befuddled I hadn't checked the letter. So I'd sent them to school, dressed in their 1939 Dennis the Menace outfits, and the assembled multitude of parents and children had been in hysterics. That was my worst day as a working mother.

Doing the odd Friday together is one thing, working as a proper double act is an entirely different kettle of fish. Drastic situations require drastic remedies, and every afternoon for about a week following John's departure, Phillip Schofield and I sat on the floor in my dressing room drinking whisky I'd smuggled in. We told each other everything we could think of about ourselves – things you wouldn't dream of telling someone you'd only just met – but which we thought were important, and it worked. We got it sorted between us very quickly, liked each other hugely and forged a really quick friendship. Now we never discuss how we're going to run an interview, it just works with telepathy. Naturally there are days when we're exhausted or we've been working together too much and can get quite annoyed with each other, but there's always this fantastic communication. We're like a pair of bats: we don't fly into each other. John was very much more free-range and I was the one who was focused.

He and Phillip were very different, and it took some adjusting.

I had done five days a week with John for a year and for the next twelve months I did five days a week with Phillip. At some point I stopped breastfeeding Winnie, which made things easier on a practical level as I didn't have to bring her into the studio. Even so I was permanently exhausted, so tired I didn't know where to put myself and it drove me nearly insane. There was only one way out. I would have to give up the show. It was just going round and round in my head: 'I can't do it — I can't do it on so little sleep.' People must think, What's the silly cow complaining about? She only does two hours a day — which in one way is true. But I'd get up at five thirty and work solidly in the car till we got to the studio, then prepare myself before we went on air, with trails and videotapes, then the show. Afterwards there would be half an hour of debrief on how that day's programme had gone, briefing on the next day and further ahead, then off to find Tony and the Merc.

I should have used the time in the car to catch up on 'office work' and phone calls — that was the intention — but all too often I'd drift off. Because once I got home, that was it. The moment Winnie saw me she'd come running. Then Grace would get back from school, and finally the boys. Then there'd be all the muddle of supper and dinner and homework, baths and bed. And by the time I'd finished all that it was nine o'clock and I had to go to bed in order to function the following day.

My *This Morning* contract was coming to an end and, brilliant though Phillip's and my relationship was, I felt utterly drained. Breastfeeding Winnie, the whole John Leslie business, forging a new relationship with Phillip, everything had taken its toll. And in 2004 I made it known that I

wouldn't be renewing my contract. I still loved the pro-
gramme, loved working with Phillip, but I couldn't go on.
And I said, 'I can't do this any more, I'm very sorry, but
I can't.'

ITV's attitude was, surely we can work something out.
What about going part-time? I said that I loved the show so
much I didn't think I could relinquish it to somebody else
part-time and it wouldn't be right for the continuity of the
programme. Then one day Phillip came into my dressing
room, shut the door and just stood there, arms folded.
'You're stupid,' he said. 'You've got to do it. Apart from
anything else I can't do it without you. It would be like
Morecambe without Wise.'

We came to a compromise. I would do it for three days a
week. And then, when Winnie started school, I'd go up to
four.

In the spring of 2005, I saw an advert in a newspaper with a
photograph of Dr Robert Winston, the fertility specialist and
pioneer of IVF. It was a spoof First World War Kitchener
poster, with his finger pointing and the caption said, 'Lord
Winston Needs You.' And I thought, Needs me? What on
earth for? A sponsored bike ride up the Nile, women only,
in aid of a charity called Women for Women. Winnie had
just settled into nursery school and, for the first time in years,
I had a whole day to myself – or, at least, six hours of one.
This will be something for me, I thought. I can go away
in a safe situation with other women, where I don't have
to wake up when it's dark, and the only responsibility I'll
have is for myself.

ITV could have been difficult but weren't. I took it as
unpaid holiday, but if I was prepared to let *This Morning* be
involved, they said, not only would they sponsor me, but

they'd give me a small fee for reporting back and provide someone to help me train. It was an offer I could not refuse.

Julie Dawn Cole – the original Veruca Salt in *Willie Wonka & the Chocolate Factory* – and I are exactly the same age, but there the similarities end. As soon became clear, we had a very different level of fitness. Her role was to motivate me and be my cycle buddy. Whether you're running the marathon (which she does regularly), cycling, swimming or whatever it might be, the trick is simply to do it, she explained. Every Friday she'd drive up from Surrey and we'd do a little bit of running, a little bit of weights, a little bit of everything. Some of it was filmed, most of it wasn't. She always maintained that I would eventually get there. It doesn't matter how little you start with, she said, every bit you do is money in the bank. But don't push yourself, don't injure yourself, don't do any of that.

I've always enjoyed cycling. When I was a child, my bike gave me freedom from George and Mummy; at St Dominick it was a Godsend when I lost my driving licence. I took my bike to Sherfield-on-Loddon when I moved there and began seeing Clive. During those lonely weekends I cycled all round the area. To the north was Stratfield Saye, the home of the dukes of Wellington. To the west were Silchester and the Roman amphitheatre, all that's left of one of the most important Roman towns in England, called Calleva Atrebatum. The amphitheatre alone could hold four thousand people, who would come to watch sports and gladiators.

But by the time we moved back to Buckinghamshire I'd lost the habit. I have no idea what happened to my old bike so the first thing I did was get a new one from Halfords, a hybrid, which means it's both a road bike and an off-road bike, really useful. The first thing to get my head round was the gears. Even though it was not expensive it was a great deal more sophisticated than the one I'd had before. The aim is to get up hills while keeping your feet moving at the same pace, with the same amount of resistance, no matter what the gradient might be. It's called cadence. To achieve this you change gear by gently clicking down levers on your handlebars. There are three positions on the left handlebar, and eight on the right, which, in various combinations, give you the full range of twenty-four.

By now I was very definitely a large woman, who didn't appear to do any exercise. People didn't expect me to do something like this because they didn't expect me to be fit, didn't expect me to be supple, didn't expect me to have the stamina. So not only was it a personal challenge but also gave the lie to the idea that larger people are destined to be stuck in front of a telly. And not only fatties but older viewers who'd had knee troubles or a hip replacement but weren't sure they were up to it. My training and my ride helped people like them as well as me, and later we would hear that they'd done a ride themselves. Taking on a physical challenge like that has a knock-on effect: once you understand what you can do with your body and what you can achieve, it gives you enormous courage mentally.

Of course there was a downside to its being so public. I'd be cycling along and motorists would go, 'Oi, Fern!' and it would be, 'Beep! Beep! Beep!' and they'd always drive too close. That first summer I was knocked off into a big scratchy hedge. Although I managed to save my face (a bit of vanity!), I was badly scratched all up my legs. And whenever I passed a pub, I really ran the gauntlet, waving and smiling to the cheering of the drunks outside. You have to take a deep breath when you expose yourself in this way, no matter who you are.

As November approached, anxiety set in. I can't do it, I thought.

'What are you worried about?' Peter Cohen, a life-coach and friend of mine said.

'I'm worried about letting people down. I'm worried about getting some kind of stomach upset and shitting in my pants as I'm riding along. I'm worried about falling off. I'm worried about being bitten by the flies. I'm worried about –'

'Stop right there. Suppose you let everybody else worry about those things. Why don't you get on your bike and look at the scenery as you pedal along and actually enjoy it?'

Ah, yes, never thought of that . . .

As an introduction to long-distance cycling the Nile trip was brilliant. Although it was four hundred kilometres in total, we returned to our boat on the Nile each night after a day's cycling – all very civilized with proper cabins and showers.

We were certainly an odd sight: a hundred Lycra-clad women of every shape and size. The competitive ones were always at the front, while the ones at the back fell into the older and weightier category. I was somewhere in the middle.

The cycling challenge was to complete the distance in five days. The day was divided into four or five legs, with stops for water and food. At first everything felt alien and even frightening, like the first day at a new school when you're not quite sure about anything and you imagine everyone else knows more than you. The Lycra shorts proved essential: they are padded and lined because you don't wear knickers – the seams would rub – but unless you were incredibly lucky you'd get nappy rash from all the sweating. Every morning you'd Vaseline yourself up, all around your undercarriage.

Although bicycles were provided, you took your own helmet, gloves and saddle – the one you had been training on for months. We had a full-scale support team of bike technicians, caterers and medical staff, who drove along behind us in the Rest Bus. We were completely safe. If you had a puncture or felt ill, people would always stop with you so that you were never left on your own.

At one stage the nice lady doctor suggested I hitch a lift on the first-aid wagon – the 'Rest Bus'. You can spoil a day's riding if you get too tired, and she wanted me to set an example and do one leg riding in the bus. If I did it, she explained, ladies who were really in need of a break wouldn't see it as a defeat. But I couldn't. For me it was a point of honour. While I know there is no shame in accepting help, this was my personal challenge and I didn't need it. As I told her, 'I'm nobody's role model and I'm not getting on that fucking bus!'

As we were basically following the Nile the going was reasonably flat, or that was the perceived wisdom. The reality was rather different. The ride up to the Valley of the Kings was quite peculiar. You have the optical illusion that you're on a flat road, but in fact it's rather steep. I actually thought I had a puncture because the bike just didn't seem to want to go. You think, This is flat, why can't I cycle it? We all felt the same. Once we got there it was, 'I don't understand!' and our legs were like jelly. But coming down from the Valley of the Kings that night was fantastic, virtually freewheeling all the way back into Luxor. Two hours of sheer exhilaration.

Among the cyclists was a journalist who wanted to interview me. I said, thank you but no. Yes, I was doing bits for *This Morning*, but I was basically there as Mrs Vickery. Needless to say, she wrote about me anyway. How I had arrived with a retinue of TV people – a team of flunkeys – how I had my own camera crew, my own trainer. Yes, I did bring a camera crew and Julie did come along, but she was doing it for herself, not training me.

Every day we'd set up a satellite link and I'd do a piece back into the studio. The timing worked well: just as we stopped for our lunch, *This Morning* was going on air, so I'd say where we were, complain about my sore bottom, and so on. Although naturally I couldn't see what was happening back at the studio, I had talkback so I could hear everything in my earpiece as usual.

'We've got somebody here you might like to say hello to,' Phillip said.

'Hello, darling . . .'

It was my Phil, and I burst into tears.

So, in her article, this journalist wrote how appallingly sentimental I was, and how pathetic to burst into tears at the sound of your husband's voice. She said how boring we all were talking about the training we'd done when she'd just spent a couple of days pedalling round the park and was perfectly fine.

I decided to write to her after it was published, something along the lines of 'You really missed the point. It's very sad that you didn't feel the camaraderie and fun and friendship of a group of women.' And there *was* a wonderful camaraderie between us. You'd find you were going the same pace that day as someone you didn't know and you'd strike up a conversation, talking about bits that were hurting, or things you were missing or what you'd like to eat when you got home, dreaming of frothy baths and candles, or our families, and our reasons for doing the ride.

The whole trip lasted ten days. And, in spite of the sweaty thighs, I had a ball. The children were an entertainment in themselves. The moment we arrived in a village, they'd emerge laughing and joking, though a small boy's joke is not necessarily a grown woman's. The best trick was to get a bamboo stick and shove it through your spokes so you'd fall off. One boy managed to get his willy out and wee over my friend as she rode past.

It has always helped that Phillip and I get school holidays off, including half-terms. (The show continues but hosted by other people.) This was nothing to do with me: an extraordinary deal had been negotiated by Richard and Judy all those years before when they had school-age children. Not only did they leave the show intact but the school-hols legacy is fantastic. It means I can spend the summer with the kids, which, since the famous time when I left Phil standing in the Castle car park, has always meant Cornwall.

Since my first visit to Mother Ivey's Bay, when I stayed in Craig Rich's caravan, things had changed. Back in the early eighties it was just a field on the edge of the cliff with his little towing caravan sitting on it. When I turned up with the kids sixteen years later it was to find a fully fledged caravan park lined with low stone walls topped with tuffets of little pink flowers called thrift. I'd been lucky with the caravan I'd rented that first year – it was a cancellation and right at the front. We all jumped out of the car and ran over to the gate that opens onto the coastal path, then down to the beach. We had the best holiday imaginable: the children had taken to the world of sandcastles, rock pools and body surfing as if they'd been born to it. As for me, I was in heaven. Here I was, with my family, doing what I wanted, without any of the attendant tensions, disagreements or aggressive silences, all those things that happen when a relationship has come to an end. This was it,

I decided. Why go anywhere else when you have found Paradise?

Twelve months later, when Phil and I were already an item, I told him I was planning to spend the summer at a caravan park. I didn't for a moment expect he would want to have anything to do with it. His response was, 'Can I come?' Before we knew it he'd bought himself an inflatable boat and built a great big barbecue outside the caravan and at night would go off fishing with his new-found local friends.

A couple of years later we bought one of the caravans; it had three little bedrooms and slept six. It wasn't directly overlooking the sea, but not far away, and from the lounge area you got a glimpse. In total I've spent ten summers at Mother Ivey's, and the last five we were there for the full six weeks. And so the years have gone by, the children getting bigger and more independent, meeting up with their mates. What was so brilliant was that they were totally safe. We'd open the door in the morning, and the boys would go off to the little shop and collect the newspapers, milk and bread for the day, then they'd be off, tearing around with their mates, happy as sandboys.

We'd hire bikes from Padstow, to be delivered the day after we arrived. The summer of 2005, because I was in training, I had to do ten miles a day to keep up. Jack would nearly always come with me, Harry sometimes, though we agreed it was too dangerous for the girls. I had a couple of loops I would do and, as the summer progressed and my legs got stronger, I'd put in a few extra hills.

As for the children, it's the kind of idyll that is fast disappearing. It's very important to me that mine should have a proper knowledge of childhood, the boredom as well as the fun, of having to fill their own time, learning to keep themselves amused – with, of course, speedboat rides, though not all are speedboat junkies as I was and still am. In Mother Ivey's Bay, nothing more powerful than a canoe is allowed; for speed we have to go to Padstow, out of the Camel estuary to the bar and back again.

For a breakfast treat we'd drive out to Treyarnon youth hostel for coffee and sausage sandwiches. Perched on the cliffs it looks down on a natural swimming-pool, which, by one of those extraordinary coincidences, Phil's dad helped to 'build' when he was stationed at St Eval a mile or two inland for his national service. Looking out over the glorious coastline, the sea glinting in the distance, surfers basking like seals waiting for the ultimate wave, who could want more?

Of course, the adults at Mother Ivey's knew who Phil and I were, but no one was ever intrusive or difficult. We were just a family, like everybody else. And so it remained, until July 2005 when somebody – I don't know who or why – took photographs of me in my bikini, then handed them to the press. Article after article was written about how fat I was and how dare I flaunt my flesh in public? I wasn't flaunting anything. I was a woman of forty-eight, for fuck's sake, who had given birth to four children and I was on holiday.

I made as light of it as I could, but it stung. Saddest of all, although our Cornish friends continued to be very protective, my little private heaven was now contaminated.

The strange thing, I realize now, is that being seen as fat has never been a hindrance in my career. In many ways it set me apart from all the rest, those young women who started at the same time as me and who followed the usual formula of thin equals sexy, equals good. But I am lucky. In television, the way you look – and how old you look – still matters, but only if you're a woman. Female presenters get dropped (and attacked in the media) for the shadow of a double chin or a ripple of cellulite, whereas deeply unattractive men with appalling dress sense, bad teeth and combovers are worshipped for their gravitas. So they should be, but so too should their female equivalents. Think of the presenters and newsreaders whom we don't see any more: Moira Stewart, Julia Somerville, Kate Adie, Angela Rippon, Mavis Nicholson, Selina Scott – every one of them a class act.

I will never forget how the men on Breakfast Time *treated Selina. Phil says that men are always threatened by successful, intelligent women. Being beautiful as well only makes it worse; the only way they could handle Selina was to disparage her. I remember Frank Bough once saying, 'I bet she even rides a bike with her legs together.'*

Looking back at Breakfast Time *– my worst experience in television by a long chalk – I realize I was my own worst enemy. My excuse is that I was very young and totally inexperienced. I allowed myself to be walked over until my self-esteem was squished to nothing. Having started life as an ASM, where you just got on with it and never made a squeak of complaint, I didn't have the tools or confidence to stand up for myself. It took me a very long* *time to get over it — I was still boring people with it ten years later. It was a high-powered American TV executive — a friend of Clive's — who eventually woke me up. 'But Fern,' he said. 'You are not that girl any more.'*

So what advice would I give somebody like me who's starting out now? Forget you're a woman, forget they're men. We're all just people — and fairly insecure. Don't stand any nonsense and always be charming. Don't lose your sense of what is really important, and don't get involved with willy-waving — the posturing and bull-shitting that male journalists in particular are prone to, at least in the newsrooms I've spent time in. (Best would be to work in a job where women have the upper hand, like This Morning *where nearly everyone involved is a woman.)*

You will be told to get your hair cut and go blonde, get a stylist, lose weight. If you want to lose weight, lose it for yourself; if you don't, don't. But don't *give up your individuality and become yet another Lollipop head. As for how to treat the bosses, play by your rules, not theirs. Unsettle them. They're used to females who need cosseting and five hours in makeup, and it's easy to get carried away with the car, the chauffeur, the clothes from Bond Street, the jewellery borrowed from Boodles, the flowers. Don't be seduced by any of it. It's all bullshit. I would far rather have a text message, personally keyed in, than a bouquet sent by some man who's told somebody else to order it. For me the greatest achievements each day are not to run out of loo paper, to have clean hair and the children fed.*

But, for now at least, women are treated differently and there are clear lines of demarcation. You start out as a Dolly Bird or Scoreboard Bimbo (some weathergirls fall into this category), then you move onto Bubbly Presenter when somebody gives you a show to co-host with an established male presenter. Then you might have a moment when you have your own series, your Big Vehicle. Then there's a period when the newspapers attack you because you've become pregnant or mumsy, guilty of failing to disguise a post-pregnancy stomach; next you're caught having Botox. Then – if you're lucky – you're enshrined as a Veteran Presenter. Finally it's 'Oh, my god, I remember So-and-so, I thought she was dead.'

Through great good luck – and even perhaps because I haven't conformed to the norm – I am a skittle still standing. But I am not one of those brilliant women who have an Ordnance Survey map of their career or their lives. I cope simply by not thinking about it. I just get up, get through the day and go to bed ready for tomorrow.

Fabulous fifty, fabulous Phil, fabulous family

17: A Weight Off My Mind

In May 2006 I began training for the next Women for Women challenge. This time we were going to Rajasthan in India, and I went to my GP for a check up. Ever since I'd had Winnie I'd been making a concerted effort to improve my fitness and lose weight, but no matter how much I cycled (ten miles three times a week, fifty miles at weekends), no matter how healthily I ate, the pounds were still going on.

When I was younger I'd had polycystic ovaries and that might be the cause of the weight gain, or it might be that the drugs I'd had for the IVF had in some way changed my metabolism. Until the birth of my children, I had stayed much the same weight. Since then – pregnancy following pregnancy – I had steadily put it on, not helped by comfort eating that went hand in hand with my post-natal depression, followed in quick succession by the breakdown of my marriage and subsequent painful divorce. Then I fell in love with Phil and he loved me just as I was.

I always knew that by having a fourth baby I'd kiss goodbye to ever getting my figure back.

'Don't forget I'm knocking on,' I warned Phil. 'And it'll put the kibosh on the fantasy of regaining a flat tummy. My body's going to go.' A third Caesarean, I told him, might be one too many.

'What happens in a Caesarean?'

The colour drained from his face when I told him.

'And you'd do that for me?'

'Of course I will, as long as you never mention the wobbly tummy.'

'I love it,' he said.

As for my children, they've never known me thin. The girls love my 'flobby bits' and my 'bra lard' as they call the lumps that hang out at the top of my bra, while the boys – well, although they are too gentlemanly to mention it, I know that they both have an admiration for larger bosoms. I am glad that they have first-hand experience of what a proper woman's body looks like.

But as the pounds piled on I became more and more aware of the dangers to my health – the increased risk of cardiovascular disease and diabetes. My GP would regularly check my sugar levels and my cholesterol levels, indicators of diabetes, heart disease or stroke, and they were always fine. But now, in early summer 2006, suddenly they weren't. She asked me to go and see her.

'We really have to do something about your weight,' she began. We discussed my options, as we had many times in the past, but this time our conversation turned to gastric banding, a surgical procedure that constricts the stomach so that you feel you've had enough after only a few mouthfuls.

Of course I had heard of it. I had also thought about it. With her help I had tried everything else, so this was the logical next step. I was coming up for forty-nine and if I didn't do it now, then it would be too late if I wanted to get back to the shape I really was. It was nothing to do with plastic surgery, nothing to do with vanity but was an entirely medical procedure, she said. Nor was it a cure-all; I would have to eat very carefully and keep up my cycling (no problem!). She told me she knew exactly the right guy, and before I knew it I had an appointment with a surgeon. Although it's available on the NHS, in my case timing would be crucial. It would need to be done while *This Morning* was off air, and give me enough time to recover before the trip to India.

It was a huge step for me and I decided to tell nobody apart from Phil, who obviously I'd discussed it with, and four close friends. I wanted to take it slowly so that the weight loss would be gradual.

I was booked into hospital on 18 July 2006 for a day and a night.

All you could see following the operation were five small incisions in my midriff. During the procedure a hollow band – later inflated with saline solution – is placed around the top of your stomach so that it looks like a bottom-heavy figure of eight, giving you the capacity of about an egg-cupful of food and liquid. Not only do you feel full, but if you overeat you will be sick, or worse, you may dislodge it, causing complications. Ironically wine and chocolate are the two thing that slip down nicely and I have heard of people who liquidize other high calorie foods in order to satisfy their cravings. Naturally this renders the band useless.

For the immediate recovery period Phil made me wonderful things – I had everything that everyone else was eating but whizzed up in a soup with a bit more gravy. In fact the dietician liked it all so much, she asked if he would write a recipe book for patients to include in the twelve-month support package.

After a few weeks your tummy gets used to being constrained, and the egg cup size may gently stretch, allowing more food to go in. When this happens the saline needs to be topped up to tighten the band. It's an ongoing process which I have had done on several occasions following the original operation, 2 ml at first, and then 0.5 ml each time. The surgeon inserts a long needle into the port of the band to fill it to the required level. Although your stomach is numbed by a local anaesthetic, it is not for the faint-hearted.

While your body is learning to function with less food, it's essential that key vitamins and mineral levels are maintained. As part of the package you are assigned a dietician who I saw regularly, and over those first few months she focused on building up my stamina as I continued my cycle training. I stuck to the rules rigidly, increasing my level of exercise as I decreased my food intake, while ensuring the key levels of nutrients were maintained. And so I began to lose weight at approximately 1lb a week, sometimes more, sometimes less. Two years later and my Body Mass Index was normal.

Three months after the operation I went to Rajasthan for my second outing with Women for Women, and this time we took along a whole *This Morning* team: Julie, Shu (by now my executive producer), Kate the PA, who gives us our timings in our ear, and two viewers who, like me, just wanted to do something for themselves. They had never cycled before but took up the challenge of a lifetime: another five days doing 400 km. Our route took us from Agra to Jaipur, across the ravishing Indian countryside. For a couple of nights we stayed in places billed as 'palaces' but which I would describe as ruins, where the plumbing was eighteenth century at best, where the lavatories wouldn't flush and if you turned the tap on you'd be lucky if there was a dribble of cold water for thirty seconds, but as soon as the guy came with the evening's gin and tonic nobody cared.

When we weren't in a hotel we'd be in splendid Raj-style tents, complete with two truckle beds and Indian rugs laid out on the sand. Ablutions were carried out in an en-suite bathroom which you reached through a flap at the back of the tent. There was even a white china loo. Extreme caution needed to be exercised while you perched, as it was inclined to fall over, not being attached to anything, but just covering a hole in the ground. The shower was a water butt, complete with jug and ladle, which you also used to 'flush' the loo. The worst aspect was the lack of laundry facilities for our clothes, particularly our cycling shorts. You'd do what you could in terms of washing, but the bugs would grow and we all came home with thrush and nappy rash. When you've been cycling for three days, doing ten to twelve hours at a time, everything in your undercarriage gets very swollen and very sore. I was known for always having a big pot of Vaseline in my bag so would be regularly flagged down by my desperate team members. Starting at daybreak and stopping only when night fell, we did between 40 and 120 kilometres a day depending on the terrain and the weather. We were cycling on roads that no western tourist usually sees, totally unsurfaced and scary to ride. Punctures were a constant hazard: one day I got four. It was a non-stop obstacle course, everyone doing their best to avoid potholes and poo and goats and sheep and wild dogs and, in villages, children and open sewers. You stopped for lunch when you saw the tent. The team of wonderful men that accompanied us would have prepared hot dishes, tins of ice-cold drink, cups of tea and we'd eat then lie on our backs, feet up in the air and massage each other. I lived on Nurofen Plus. I'd have two before I started, two at lunchtime, and two before I went to bed.

On the last night, the cycling finally over, we took a five-hour train ride from Jaipur to Delhi. It was gone midnight by the time we drew into the station but the platforms were still crowded, whole families huddled up sleeping wherever there was space.

For ten days we'd been fantasizing about proper beds and

proper showers but when we reached our hotel it was awful. Some of the younger girls just went to the bar. I looked round at my team and said, 'Right. Now's the moment we find ourselves a really nice hotel.'

And that was how I spent my fee: two nights in this gorgeous hotel called the Oberoi. We arrived at about 3.00 a.m. and it was total heaven: electric lights, flunkies in uniforms, beautifully scented ladies smelling of lotus blossom in Indian dress on each floor. When I got to my room, I found the biggest double bed you've ever seen and a note on the pillow saying 'Welcome to the Oberoi, if you don't like these pillows we can offer you various alternatives'. I got in the bath, sinking into a cushion of bubbles, while leaving my door open so the girls could come in and out. Once they'd got themselves settled, room service was called, and gin and tonics arrived. Finally, just before dawn, everyone returned to their rooms and we slept the whole day with the odd break for a massage. It was worth every penny.

I went to see my surgeon as soon as I got back. All was well, he said, and the weight loss continued. I knew it would take a long time, we had agreed that I should do it as gradually as possible. I ate everything, drank everything, that I did before – but no more man-sized portions. A pound a week doesn't sound a lot but it adds up, and the moment came when I realized I could walk into a clothes shop confident there might be something that would fit. It was then that I became determined that, one way or another, Fat Birds would go ahead. I wanted to offer this same feeling to somebody's wife who, after years of loneliness and panic, can go to her husband's annual dinner dance and sit at a table with the young secretaries, who are all thin and beautiful, without the humiliation of looking like a sack. I wanted them to know that there is an alternative to huge, tent-like clothes that won't cost a fortune and will make you feel good. Just like every other woman, I love wearing beautiful things which is why I have such a large collection of shoes and earrings. When you are large, shoes and earrings are the only things guaranteed to fit.

As the pounds fell off, I began to think about why I had continued to put on weight after meeting Phil. Eating is an emotional issue. You overeat because you're unhappy so, logically, when the unhappiness disappears, so too should the need to stuff yourself. In my case that didn't happen. I think it was to do with my fear of depression, of finding myself once again in that black, bottomless pit. Since I met Phil I have been happier than I have ever been in my life, but I have also been fatter, so if happy equates to fat, then why risk losing one with the other? I would much rather be fat and happy than thin and depressed, and perhaps that's how my subconscious dealt with it. On a purely physical level, I felt I needed the strength the extra weight seemed to offer, to be some sort of warrior, able to fend off marauders and to protect my family.

Of course there have been times when I have been frustrated and times when I felt like a frump. Dolled up, I could usually manage to feel positive, but it's a different story when you're on holiday and your shorts creep up your legs, your thighs rub together and your bosoms are flopping about.

I was definitely dolled up on 14 July 2007, for my fiftieth birthday party, held three days early because the actual day fell on a Tuesday. In my family we have always celebrated birthdays, particularly the 'big' ones. For my mother's eight-ieth I took her to Venice where we stayed in the Danielli, one of the most glamorous hotels in the world. I was determined to push the boat out and it was a real treat. My fortieth, however, is something best forgotten. Grace was only ten weeks old and we were in Norfolk. In the morning we played golf and in the evening went to see Joe Brown – the high spot of the day, he was completely brilliant – with fish and chips afterwards. I remember thinking, When I'm fifty I'll do it better than this. And I certainly did. I started planning it when I was forty-eight and it took me two years to save up.

The theme – naturally – was the 1950s. Our guests – which is to say family and closest friends – were asked to come dressed in fifties glam. We had a huge marquee in the garden, lined with white silk and a black ceiling sprinkled with stars, and the tables were silver and pink. We had ten tables of ten, with the one in the middle for children so that parents could easily keep an eye on them, and they all behaved wonderfully. The food was fifties-themed: avocado and prawns, followed by steak and chips (the steak came from our farmer friend Polly) and to end the meal, banana split: bananas, ice-cream, cream and chocolate sauce. My actual birthday cake was tiers of iced cup cakes, a childhood favourite.

While Phil looked dashing in a white tuxedo, I wore a dress that David designed and made for me: full-length, off-the-shoulder black jersey. Apart from looking glamorous (obviously) I wanted something that I could dance in and feel comfortable, and it was so wonderful standing there, the two of us, watching all our friends and family, looking equally glamorous, walking up the red carpet that ran from the front field which we used as a car park.

I had persuaded my brother-in-law, Brian Cant, along with his *Playaway* partner Jonathan Cohen, to 'open the show' and once the main course was over, I went up to the microphone and waited for the hubbub to die down.

'Put your hand up, anyone who remembers *Playaway*.'

A forest of adult hands rose in the air.

'Well, here to entertain you, is Brian Cant and Jonathan Cohen.'

And at that Brian and Jonathan leapt onto the little stage, Jonathan sat at the piano and the moment Brian shouted, 'Give me a P!' the marquee erupted to the slightly odd sound of grown men and women singing the *Playaway* theme song. Brian and Jonathan were utterly brilliant, as they always are.

Their 'set' being over, this was the natural time to start the dancing. Clearly the little stage couldn't get more than three couples on it. Time for my second surprise.

The cake had been there from the beginning, at the back to one side. As Phil and I walked towards it, clapping broke out. Cake cut, we did a little twirl and everybody laughed.

'Ladies and Gentlemen,' I said. 'Let the dancing commence.'

On cue the 'wall' of white silk behind us slid back to reveal a fifties nightclub, complete with black and white chequerboard floor and a sixteen-piece dance band. The gasp was audible, and I have never seen so many people rise as one and head onto the floor as the band started to play Van Morrison's 'Moondance'. It was impossible to hear them and not want to dance.

After an hour, the band took a quick break, and our guests returned to their tables for coffee. Surprise number three. Unbeknownst to anyone, among the guests was one of our great undiscovered comedy talents, Johnny Cowling, who we first saw in Cornwall. Suddenly this anonymous man who hadn't given away who he was, or what he did, stood up and gave us an hour of pure genius. The people on his table, who throughout the evening had been attempting to ply him with drink, were amazed. He was brilliant, a true entertainer who could make anybody laugh, including Winnie.. He is also a sweetheart; he missed his mum's birthday to come up to us.

At the end of the night, as the band packed up, I was still dancing, swaying away on one too many cocktails. Suddenly Phil was beside me. 'Everyone's gone now,' he said. 'I've come to take you to bed.' As I looked around I realized we were completely alone and that the sky was lightening. Gently, Phil took me upstairs and put me to bed. And how I slept. For three hours I was dead to the world but at six I woke. The house was completely still. The sun was up. I wrapped myself in a shawl, unlocked the back door, crossed the grass wet with dew until I reached the red carpet, then walked back into the tent, found a couple of left over cup cakes and had those for my breakfast then danced on my own one last time. Everything had been perfect, completely perfect. I padded back to the house and put the kettle on. Within an hour there must have been fifty people in the kitchen and in the garden having bacon sandwiches and pot after pot of tea. Friends and family who had stayed locally and, like me, didn't want it to end. Over the next few days, people called and wrote saying how magical it had been: 'The best party of our lives.'

That summer, there had been considerable debate in the media about whether Prince Harry should go to serve in Iraq with his regiment. The publicity was such that, in the end, it became impossible and it was decided that he would not go. (Later, once all the brouhaha had calmed down, he did go to Afghanistan.) Around that time I did an edition

344

of *Blankety Blank*. As is often the case on TV shows, there's an awful lot of hanging around, and Joe Pasquale and I were talking about the whole issue. He told me how just before Christmas in 2006 he had gone to Basra, in southern Iraq, to entertain the troops with Katherine Jenkins. He met some of the boys who'd been hunkered down in Basra city, living in foxholes on minimum rations.

'Honestly Fern, you wouldn't believe it,' he told me. 'When I asked what they'd been doing, they said, "we've just been lying in the dust for a week, and we've come out to get a shower and get some food." So I said, "So, you've got a few days off now, then?". "No. We're going back out tonight."'

What really struck him, he said, was how appreciative they'd been, all these young guys saying 'Thanks for coming, Joe, thanks for making us laugh.'

And I remembered how it had been like that when I'd visited 'my' ships in Plymouth over twenty years earlier.

At our next briefing meeting on *This Morning*, I raised it as an idea. Our viewers were the parents and sweethearts of these servicemen, I said. Phillip Schofield was not convinced. 'It's a war zone,' he said. 'You're mad.'

'That's fine,' I said. 'I'll just go on my own.'

Amazingly the MoD said yes. My Phil was fine with it – if the MoD thought it was OK, it was OK by him – while my Mum was thrilled and did her best to get me to take her too, but at eighty-four – however experienced with ack-ack – it was never on. The MoD's key proviso was that it should remain completely secret so the dates were planned around that. I would sign off on 29 November 2007 as usual and be back in the studio the following week. We took off from RAF Brize Norton in a wide-bodied jet, used to transport troops from their various bases abroad and back to Britain.

It was just a glorified bus, and I lost count of how many times we landed and took off again, picking people up and dropping them off. I couldn't get over how young most of them were. Those who were headed for the middle east were already in desert fatigues, carrying only their rucksacks and body armour. We had also been issued with helmets and body armour, though a greater deal lighter than standard issue. My personal kit consisted of spare knickers, suncream and a hairbrush. Our final stop was an unidentified Allied airbase close to Iraq. This was desert without the romance: everything was dusty and the colour of sand. In the early hours of the following morning, we made the flight into Basra – completely different from the one coming in: the Hercules is a dedicated troop- and vehicle-carrier. Seats were metal-framed and canvas-slung and flipped up like stadium seats, positioned on the outer walls of the fuselage looking in, with a double row, back-to-back down the middle of the plane. The floor was an obstacle course of fixing points and shackles. I'd been on a Hercules before, when I was with TVS filming with the Falcons, the RAF parachutists, and although they may look like old workhorses they are highly manoeuvrable planes. As we prepared for landing the pilot began to weave around to avoid being hit by rocket fire. I'd been invited into the cockpit and was sitting directly behind the pilot and co-pilot. It was pitch dark, and you could see the oil fires burning on the horizon. There was no gentle approach. One minute you're high, the next you're in a nosedive heading straight to the ground. We left by the loading ramp at the rear of the plane and by the time we'd got away from the tarmac the Hercules had already disappeared.

The usual tour of duty in Iraq is four months and I was both impressed and humbled by what I saw and the soldiers

I met, including the young women who are now frontline troop commanders. While the tank corps remains men only – they have to be able to batten down and live there for days at a time – the drivers of armoured vehicles that I met were all women.

The COB (Contingency Operating Base) is entirely under canvas from the sleeping block to the cookhouse, gymnasium and church – a proper tented village, including a hospital with operating theatres, X-ray, MRI scanner, physiotherapy, and fracture clinic. Hygiene is a big issue throughout the COB, and I was incredibly impressed at the overall cleanliness of everything, with anti-bacterial handwash available everywhere. If our British hospitals were run with such military efficiency, MRSA would soon be a thing of the past. In spite of the comparatively short time I was there – three days and two nights – I developed a clear sense of how our young soldiers live. I wasn't allowed to see the work they were doing outside the wire, but the lives they were leading within the camp. Much more importantly, I hope I was able to convey this to their families at home in the four films that were broadcast once we had returned. When your son or daughter or sweetheart is on the other side of the globe, in the most dangerous of situations, it helps enormously to visualize how they live, see where the telephones are, where they email from, where they sleep. Within the highly structured framework of the camp, individual space becomes very important and the girls' sleeping quarters in particular felt very personal, with chintzy covers on their beds or fluffy fairy lights and everything smelling delicious.

The reality of their situation was never far away, however. On the first night I was fast asleep when the siren went off. This is a regular occurrence. Inside every tent are 'walls' of breeze blocks a few feet high to stop rockets inflicting

347

serious damage. Having been carefully drilled on what to do, I'd left my helmet and body armour on the floor in such a way that I could crawl straight into it. If you can't reach your armour in time, you must lie with your hands on your ears to protect them from the blast and your elbows by your sides, to stop any flying debris entering your major organs. I counted for a minute then started to laugh – imagining the thousands of people in this enormous compound, doing exactly the same thing at the same moment.

Another rocket attack came the following evening. This time we were outside, me and my director Verina – my Basra buddy – waiting in the dark for a lift to the welfare centre for the social occasion of the week, the barbecue. As we were already wearing our helmets and armour, we flung ourselves to the ground behind the safety wall. Another visitor – not anyone we knew – emerged from his sleeping container and stepped straight over us.

'Oh that's nothing,' he said. 'You shouldn't be down there, it's miles away.'

But as Gracie very wisely said when I told her: 'You don't hear the one that hits you.'

Later that evening, after I had recounted this story to the head of the camp, he told me one of his own. Not so long ago they'd had a couple of SAS men, who were used to being under fire, in the cookhouse when the siren went off. Everybody went down except these two, who continued to drink their coffee and eat their bacon and eggs. The commanding officer got up, went over and said, 'You think you're so fucking cool, you're too fucking cool to be on my camp so get your fucking arses out of here or lie down.' They lay down. As Mummy drummed into me when I was little, when you're in the army discipline is everything: if you're given an order you obey it.

I've always had this feeling I'd end up as a farmer's wife. In 1988, when I was working in Southampton, I did a weekend course called An Introduction to Livestock Farming — I have a certificate to prove it. I'm qualified in the following subjects: tractor driving, pig husbandry, cattle husbandry, sheep husbandry, and husband husbandry. (That last one is wishful thinking.) We stayed in the students' accommodation and they fed us beautifully on gorgeous slabs of yellow cheese, fresh meat and salads. The first night we didn't get to bed till gone midnight after watching the piggies farrow. Then it was up at four for the milking followed by a fun-filled day castrating sheep, bottle-feeding the lambs and taking a cow's temperature up its bottom. One way and another we didn't get much sleep. But who cares when you wake to a landscape that hasn't changed since Tess Durbeyfield first set eyes on Angel Clare? The Dorset fields lay cosseted in mist like swan's down and then, out of the mist, across the dewy meadows came the cows called by Bach's 'Sheep May Safely Graze'. The music soothed them, our tutor explained, and they gave a better yield. And now here I am, the mother of piggies.

Two Christmases ago, I gave Phil a surprise present, a Land-rover.

'I'm terribly sorry,' I said when Phil saw there was nothing for him under the tree, 'but I haven't had any time to get you anything, I'll sort it out afterwards.'

I bought it from Chris Faulkner who lives in the village and he offered to bring it up himself 'Bang on 8.30 Christmas morning'. So while I opened my presents, poor Phil had nothing. Then at 8.25

349

I said, 'Oh, sorry darling, I did just get you this one tiny thing,' and handed him a little package: it was the keys. Then I said, 'Why don't you look out of the window ...' and he did, and there was the Landrover bumping down the drive. Makeup Lyn's husband, Mike, who's in the motor trade, had got the number plates made up for me: HP1 XMAS.

Phil said it was the biggest excitement he'd had in a long time. All it needed was suspenders and stockings and it would fulfil all his dreams.

A day to remember

18: The Not-So-Fat Lady Sings

During the spring of 2008 a week never seemed to pass without some magazine headline heralding 'Fern's Secret Diet or similar.' It was now eighteen months since I'd had the operation, and the media were becoming increasingly focused on my weight loss, however I was very careful not to make claims for any particular regime. I kept to my line – which was true – that it was due to eating less and exercising more. But I was worried. I was increasingly being held up as a beacon of self-restraint which made me feel uncomfortable. Yet what was I to say? Why should my private health issues be made public? Still, I was convinced that the media knew and that they were only waiting for the right moment, which came in May 2008 when I did a series of interviews for Ryvita.

I had been involved with Ryvita for four years and, during that time, they had come up with a series of ridiculous and very funny adverts in which I totally take the piss out of my size. It was all tremendous fun. I had been a Ryvita fan long before they asked me to work with them, and I continued to eat Ryvita after my operation. In May 2008, the company's nutritionists had put together a Ryvita bikini fit challenge which roughly said that if you swapped your breakfast toast and the bread in your sandwiches at lunchtime for two slices of Ryvita, you could lose perhaps six pounds in a couple of weeks, which might help with your bikini body. Naturally, the last thing I wanted was for people to think, 'Oh that's how she did it,' so I made sure that

I never said anything in any interview that might imply that I had. Yet when the magazines came out there they were, bandying numbers around, claiming I'd lost this or that by doing this, that or the other, none of which I'd said, none of which were true.

Why does the press continue to see women in terms of these meaningless figures? 'I've lost half a stone and I can get into size 10 jeans.' Does that make you a nicer person? Everything is presented in a way that implies you will be more attractive to men, more 'beddable'. But those people who are most obsessed with their weight, their beauty regime, their hair, what they wear in bed – those women are often single. Because God forbid that anyone should make their cheeks pink and their eyes glisten by having sex with them! They're like women who get all dressed up for the swimming pool, but never go near the water for fear it'll make their mascara run. Men don't want that. Men want someone who's not constantly looking in the mirror, who is not high maintenance. They want a woman who is prepared to roll on the floor with laughter, kick her shoes off and have a shag if she feels like it. What continues to mystify me is that these magazines – and the women's sections of newspapers – are read by women, written by women, and yet they seem to hate the people they're writing for. I have never wanted to become an icon for large women, I have never even thought of myself in those terms, but then I am not sizist. I don't judge anybody by their size, big or small. I hate the way that women are categorized and pilloried: too fat, too thin, wrong size bosoms, wrong size hips, and as for cellulite ... I just wish we could be content with what we have been given. It's a waste of our precious lives to dislike ourselves. There is nothing wrong with aspiration, but what is this obsession with being 'perfect'? Nobody's perfect. At least I am past the age where that really matters, but it really upsets me when they use a snatched photograph of a gorgeous female celebrity, and a magazine circles a knee and says 'Baggy Knee'. I mean, pack it in. You can't jibe at someone for their race or their religion, but you can about their body. It's the last bit of bullying that is not against the law. Over the years I have been regularly held up for ridicule. I remember one TV reviewer wrote, 'She looks like she's got a couple of dwarfs up her jacket'. The quality of my work – good or bad – was never mentioned.

In early June 2008, following the revelation that I had had a gastric band, the press turned their obsession with women and size – and their cameras – on me. Over the following months, my family and I experienced first-hand what it means to be hounded by paparazzi. They are there when you wake up in the morning, there behind you in their unmarked vans, tapping into your messages, peering into your windows with their long lenses, making ordinary life – going to the supermarket, taking the kids to school, taking the dog for a walk – impossible. As for what they were writing, it was both vindictive and largely untrue.

I'm glad it's now out in the open. But by nature I am a private person, and this was an intensely private decision. When I think what it could have been like if I had made an announcement: holidays dogged by paparazzi desperate to snap me licking an ice lolly, or tucking into a bag of chips. There'd have been pictures of my boobs, my legs, my stomach, my arms. The 'experts' would have had their callipers out, 'measuring' how I was doing. There would have been fingers wagged – too slow, too quick. So I'm grateful to have avoided that. I've had two whole years to quietly get on with it on my own, to do it properly and to do it well.

What the press could not have known was how, in the end, the experience gave me more than it took away. At the same time as newspapers and magazines were claiming that I had become a hate figure to the British public, emails and messages of support – both from viewers and people I'd met as guests over the years – were flooding in to *This Morning*. Before this happened I'd genuinely had no idea that there was so much goodwill out there for me, and I am more grateful for it than any of those good people will know. It has reminded me of far more difficult times, times that I also lived through, times I survived. Twice I almost lost everything, but I'm still here. I have come out the other side of this without the depression returning, with my health – and my weight – better than ever. I'm also grateful for the way in which my children have coped. Like me, they have learned from my experience, and now are only too aware that what they read in the newspapers is not necessarily true. For a little person it's hard to read that your Mummy is a liar. As Winnie said to me one day, 'I know the papers have been horrible to you. They've been horrible to me too. They said I was six and I was only five.' I hope that's the worst she'll ever get.

The way the boys dealt with the constant knocks on the door, not to mention their shell-shocked mother, showed a maturity and inner strength that astonishes me. As for Phil – without him I couldn't have coped. My love for my husband is deeper still, and my joy in my children immense. By one of those strange coincidences, just a week before the dam of vitriol burst, Phil and I enjoyed one of the most moving and strengthening days of our life together, the renewal of our wedding vows made eight years earlier. And when in years to come we look back at 2008, this is what we will remember. The rest is chaff.

When you get married and have children, the last thing on your mind is divorce, and being a step-parent is never easy. Phil has known the twins since they were four and Grace since she was seventeen months old and he genuinely loves them. It's a testament to his commitment that they call him Dad. At the same time they continue to have a very good relationship with their father. The amazing thing is that they each bring the kids something different: Clive is at heart an intellectual, whereas Phil is practical and creative. It's not only media and politics versus food and farming, all three of them come to Phil about everyday things. I often hear him say, 'Well, in life boys, what happens is this . . .' and 'When you get your car and your money . . .' He also has a gentler side and a spiritual belief which Clive does not. When they were younger, they would come back after a weekend with their father and say, 'There is no God, there's nothing when you're dead, that's what Dad says,' and that hurt me, because I have a faith. And I would say, 'Dad may not believe in God, but God believes in Dad.'

I was confirmed about ten years ago when things in my life were at a nadir, so I am Christian. I'm not a very good churchgoer, however. I have been better in the past, but at the moment life is so fraught that I can't even fart in peace. Phil was brought up in a Catholic family and had Catholicism thrown at him for years and years, so for the time being he's had his fill of organized religion, but that's not to say he doesn't have faith.

I would never want to put the kids in a difficult position, so when I told them about our plans, I explained that the ceremony was planned for the day before we went away for half-term. 'I don't want you to feel that you have to come.'

'Why wouldn't we want to? Anyway, we'll get a day off!'

Everyone thinks their own children are special, but as a parent I know you can only do so much. In the end, they are who they are. I have to accept that now that the boys are in their early teens, they're already on their way to being men, but thoughtful sensitive young men. As for my girls, Grace has an old head on young shoulders. Sometimes Phil says, 'Remember, Grace, I'm not your real Dad,' and she'll sigh, raise her eyebrows and say, 'Dad, we've been through all that . . .' Winnie, at six years old, has total self-possession and self-awareness of where she is in the family – front of stage conducting the rest of us.

Phil is a good man, very steadfast and very loyal and I love him more and more. His little treat to himself is a proper cappuccino on a Saturday morning. It wouldn't necessarily be my thing, but when he's there at the café in Beaconsfield, he sends me a text, saying 'I'm here, where are you?' What woman could resist that?

And so the day of our little ceremony dawned. We did the whole thing properly. Bridesmaids dresses for the girls (matching) in pink and white, and suits for the boys. Everything from the British Home Stores website, including my dress. I found a nice little number under the category 'older bridesmaid', colour 'champagne'. The only drawback was bare arms, so one afternoon I stopped at a little bridal shop I'd noticed locally and asked if they had anything in the way of a lacy shrug. Usually they came with the dress, the woman said, but she rummaged around in an old box and found one, several seasons old. As it was a bit dusty, she said, I could have it at half price. My whole outfit came to under £200.

The order of service is headed Thanksgiving for Marriage.

Gracie would be doing a reading: The Art of Marriage – read at our first ceremony by the registrar (of course) – while the vicar would be reading from St Paul's Letter to the Corinthians. Then the music: Andy Williams' 'Can't Take My Eyes off You' to walk down the aisle to, and 'Say A Little Prayer' by Dionne Warwick on the way back.

The weather in the days leading up to the Big Day had been off and on, but Friday 23 May was warm and sunny with clouds scudding freely across an English sky. It was a busy morning at the house. I creamed up my feet because they get dry like an old lizard, and I painted the girls' nails and only just remembered to do mine. I then had to dissuade Winnie from wearing her new biker boots. (Grace looked lovely in her first pair of kitten heels.) The flowers arrived: circlets of leaves for the girls' hair, baskets of petals and a bouquet of wild flowers for me, with buttonholes of rosemary for the male members of the wedding party. Phil has a much-loved linen jacket he had been planning to wear, but opted in the end for something unstructured and dark. As for the boys, there was much discussion around ties, Jack favouring a black shirt and Harry a white. And so we set off. Our appointment was for midday, eight years minus 24 hours since Phil and I first exchanged vows.

Hughenden Manor was built by Disraeli, but the church is much, much older and it sits in one of the most beautiful valleys in England surrounded by lush green meadows which, that morning, were yellow with buttercups.

Winnie runs to pick some to give me, her petal-filled basket joggling by her side, and Phil and I watch this tiny figure in a landscape like something out of Hardy. Later will come the throwing of petals but now – photographs done – we enter the cool peace of this ancient building and, arm-in-arm walk towards the altar.

Acknowledgements

My thanks are owed to many people.

Firstly the team at Michael Joseph: Louise Moore, Kate Adams, Natalie Higgins and Debbie Hatfield. I appreciate all that you did to bring this project to fruition. Thank you.

To John Rush, agent, friend and protector, and Luigi Bonomi, who persuaded me to do this by saying it would be easy. And to Pepsy Dening, for her expertise and fabulous scrambled eggs.

Thank you to Lyn Evans, David O'Brien, Anya Francis, Phillip Schofield and all the wonderful team and crew at *This Morning* who are simply the best in British television.

Without my mother, father and Cherry to fill in the gaps in my memory, this book would have been considerably thinner. I can't thank them enough for their help in pulling it all together.

I must also thank Jack, Harry, Grace and Winnie for allowing me the space and time to look back over my life. And Karen and Carole, who kept the home fires burning. As for Phil – without his support and encouragement, this book would simply not exist.

My thanks go finally to *This Morning* viewers, who provide so much evidence of the kindness of people.

Hard work brings good things. My love and thanks to you all.